Museum Basics

The International Council of Museums, supported by the Cultural Heritage division of UNESCO, answers, with *Museum Basics*, one of the most pressing training needs of the worldwide museum community. What are the basic principles that should underlie museum work everywhere? This clear, introductory text outlines ideas that can apply to all museums with few professional staff and limited financial resources worldwide.

Drawing on a wide range of experience, Timothy Ambrose and Crispin Paine propose the ideas which should underpin all professional museum training courses. Organised on a modular basis, *Museum Basics* provides a basic guide to best practice in every aspect of museum work, from museum organisation, through collections management and conservation, to marketing and security. The book is designed as a basis for training courses, to be supplemented by case studies, project work and group discussion.

Timothy Ambrose is Director of the Scottish Museums Council. Crispin Paine is an international museums consultant and Secretary to the Committee of Area Museum Councils in Britain.

The Heritage: Care–Preservation–Management programme has been designed to serve the needs of the museum and heritage community worldwide. It publishes books and information services for professional museum and heritage workers, and for all the organizations that service the museum community.

Editor-in-chief Andrew Wheatcroft

Architecture in Conservation:
Managing developments at historic sites
James Strike

The Development of Costume
Naomi Tarrant

Forward Planning: *A handbook of business, corporate and development planning for museums and galleries*
Edited by Timothy Ambrose and Sue Runyard

The Handbook for Museums
Gary Edson and David Dean

Heritage Gardens: *Care, conservation and management*
Sheena Mackellar Goulty

Heritage and Tourism: *in the global village*
Priscilla Boniface and Peter J. Fowler

The Industrial Heritage: *Managing resources and uses*
Judith Alfrey and Tim Putnam

Museum, Media, Message
Eilean Hooper-Greenhill

Museum Security and Protection: *A handbook for cultural heritage institutions*
ICOM and ICMS

Museums 2000: *Politics, people, professionals and profit*
Edited by Patrick Boylan

Museums and the Shaping of Knowledge
Eilean Hooper-Greenhill

Museums without Barriers: *A new deal for disabled people*
Fondation de France and ICOM

The Past in Contemporary Society: *Then/Now*
Peter J. Fowler

The Representation of the Past: *Museums and heritage in the post-modern world*
Kevin Walsh

Towards the Museum of the Future: *New European perspectives*
Edited by Roger Miles and Lauro Zavala

Museum Basics

Timothy Ambrose and Crispin Paine

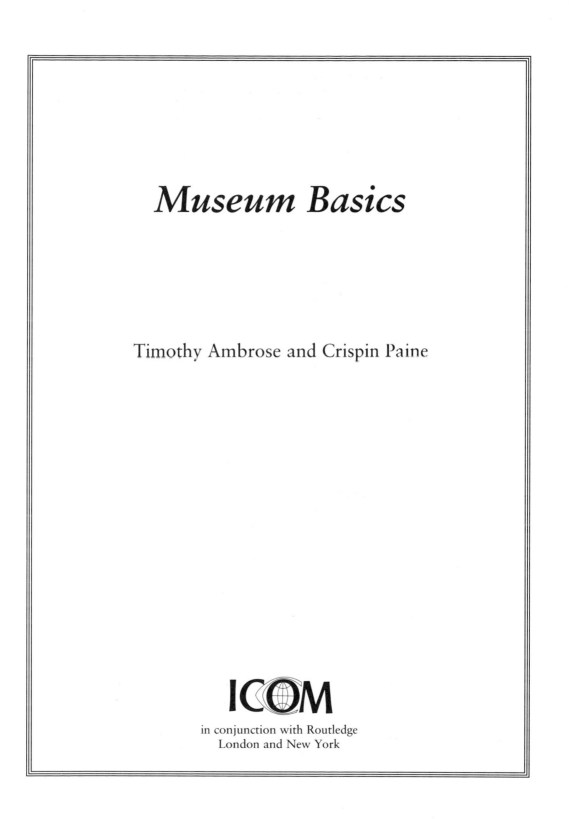

ICOM

in conjunction with Routledge
London and New York

First published in 1993
by Routledge
11 New Fetter Lane, London EC4P 4EE

Simultaneously published in the USA and Canada
by Routledge
29 West 35th Street, New York, NY 10001

Routledge is an imprint of the Taylor & Francis Group

© 1993 ICOM

Reprinted 1994, 1995, 1997, 1998, 2000

Typeset in 10/12pt Sabon Linotron 300 by
Florencetype Ltd, Weston-super-Mare
Printed and bound in Great Britain by
Butler & Tanner Ltd, Frome and London

♾ printed on permanent paper in accordance with American NISO Standards

British Library Cataloguing in Publication Data
A catalogue record for this book is available from the British Library.

Library of Congress Cataloging in Publication Data
applied for

ISBN 0-415-05769-8 (hbk)
ISBN 0-415-05770-1 (pbk)

Contents

Foreword
Alpha Oumar Konaré, President of ICOM   viii
Preface   ix
Acknowledgements   x

Section I   *Introductory*
Unit 1   About museums   2
Unit 2   About this book   3
Unit 3   Types of museums   6
Unit 4   The role of museums   9

Section II *The museum and its users*
Unit 5   Museums are for people   16
Unit 6   Understanding your market   18
Unit 7   Marketing your museum   26
Unit 8   Special audiences: museums and disabled people   30
Unit 9   The museum visit   34
Unit 10   Museum education services: within the museum   37
Unit 11   Museum education services: outside the museum   41
Unit 12   Events and activities: creating programmes   49
Unit 13   Facilities for visitors   56
Unit 14   Providing services: shops   58
Unit 15   Providing services: food and drink   61
Unit 16   Improving facilities for users   64
Unit 17   Introducing interpretation   67
Unit 18   Presentation techniques: graphics   71
Unit 19   Presentation techniques: three-dimensional   73
Unit 20   Presentation techniques: audio-visual/interactive   75
Unit 21   Presentation techniques: using people   77
Unit 22   Museum lighting   79
Unit 23   Museum showcases   82
Unit 24   Planning a new display   84
Unit 25   Research for displays   87
Unit 26   Writing text   88
Unit 27   Briefing a designer   95

Contents

Unit 28 Exhibition design and production 100
Unit 29 Evaluating exhibitions 106
Unit 30 Information services 111
Unit 31 Publications 114
Unit 32 Public relations and the media 118
Unit 33 Working with other organisations/supporters'
         groups 121
Unit 34 Types of collections 124
Unit 35 Policies for collecting 127
Unit 36 Policies for disposal 129
Unit 37 Donations, purchases and loans 132

**Section III   *The development and care of a museum's
            collections***
Unit 38 Collecting and field documentation 140
Unit 39 Fieldwork and record centres 142
Unit 40 Photography, film and video 144
Unit 41 Oral history and audio recording 147
Unit 42 Documentation systems 150
Unit 43 The role of collections in research 156
Unit 44 Conservation planning 158
Unit 45 Working with conservators 160
Unit 46 Preventive conservation: principles 162
Unit 47 Environmental monitoring and control: light 164
Unit 48 Environmental monitoring and control:
         temperature and humidity 167
Unit 49 Environmental monitoring and control: air
         pollution/insect and pest attack 171
Unit 50 Materials testing 173
Unit 51 Storage: large and heavy objects 176
Unit 52 Storage: small and light objects 178
Unit 53 Handling and packing 183
Unit 54 Remedial conservation: principles 185
Unit 55 Remedial conservation: practice 187
Unit 56 Disaster planning/insurance 189
Unit 57 Collections security: physical and electronic 193
Unit 58 Collections security: systems and procedures 195

Section IV   *The museum and its buildings*
Unit 59 Museum buildings: form and function 202
Unit 60 Planning new museum buildings 205
Unit 61 Working with architects 208
Unit 62 Preparing briefs for architects 209
Unit 63 Museum buildings security: management and
         maintenance 212

Contents

Unit 64   Access and accessibility   216
Unit 65   Atmosphere, pace and flow   220
Unit 66   Orientation   224

Section V   The museum and its management
Unit 67   Legal status and management structures   230
Unit 68   Management planning and policy development   232
Unit 69   Making a forward plan   235
Unit 70   Performance measurement for museums   239
Unit 71   Financial management   242
Unit 72   Fundraising   245
Unit 73   Internal communications and procedures   248
Unit 74   Staff structures   251
Unit 75   Volunteers in museums   252
Unit 76   Recruiting museum staff   256
Unit 77   Conditions of service   259
Unit 78   Performance standards for the individual   261
Unit 79   Job appraisal and performance measurement   264
Unit 80   Staff training   266
Unit 81   Health and safety   268
Unit 82   Administrative procedures   273

Section VI   Supporting resources and services
Unit 83   Glossary   278
Unit 84   Sources of information and support   281
Unit 85   Further reading   283

Appendix   *ICOM Code of Professional Ethics*   295
Note on illustrations   315
Index   316

Foreword

Professional training needs and the promotion of professional standards have been at the heart of our Organisation's concerns since its very foundation in 1946. ICOM's interest in the field of training is shared with UNESCO and this publication is the fruit of discussions held in 1989 between UNESCO's Division of the Physical Heritage and the late Herbert Ganslmayr, former Vice-President of ICOM, concerning a wide range of training-orientated activities.

The plurality of cultures and the divergence of social and economic situations in all parts of the world necessarily result in different museum concepts. However, certain basic principles can be identified and applied to the primary aim of preserving and making good use of our heritage.

I should like to express my thanks to UNESCO for its financial support towards the preparation of this work, as well as to all those colleagues who, working in cooperation with the ICOM International Committee for the Training of Personnel, have contributed to the production of this book. They have created a valuable tool which, used in conjunction with other materials, will provide constructive support for museum professionals all over the world.

Alpha Oumar Konaré
President of ICOM

Preface

On behalf of the International Committee for the Training of Personnel, I extend a warm welcome to this book. Not only have ICTOP members been closely involved with its development, but it advances ICTOP's fundamental purposes: to improve the standard of museum training throughout the world.

The authors and ICTOP recognize that training for museum work has to be adjusted to the needs of a particular museum, a region or a country. There are no universal prescriptions and this book sets out to provide advice about the 'best practice', drawn from the experience of many museums.

These are ideas that trainers everywhere could include in their training courses, and as the authors acknowledge, their work has benefited from the advice of ICTOP members and other ICOM members in many parts of the world.

Museum Basics marks a great step forward in the development of museum training internationally, and builds on the work undertaken by ICTOP over many years.

Dr Piet J.M. Pouw
Chairman, International Committee for the Training of Personnel
(ICTOP)

Acknowledgements

Museum Basics is the product of the international museums community. Jointly sponsored by the International Council of Museums and UNESCO, it has benefited from advice and encouragement from museum workers in all parts of the world. Their recognition of its value and importance as an everyday handbook for museums with few professional staff and limited financial resources has been a continuous source of encouragement throughout its production.

It is a pleasure to record here our thanks to the following individuals who have helped us to test sections of the book 'in the field', and advised us on its international applications:

Mr Martin Akanbiemu, Nigeria
Mr Luhfti Assiarto, Indonesia
Sra Lucia Astudillo de Parra, Ecuador
Dr Abdoulaye Camara, Senegal
Profesora Serafina Traub Borges do Amaral, Brazil
Dr Gary Edson, USA
Dr Saraj Ghose, India
Sra Cecilia Bákula, Peru
Dr Abi A. Derefaka, Nigeria
Professor Joe D.K. Nkrumah, Ghana
Dr Petr Suler, Czechoslovakia
Mr F. Karanja, Kenya
Dr Carol Stapp, USA
Mr Yui-tan Chang, Taiwan
Ms Alissandra Cummins, Barbados
M. Claude Daniel Ardouin, Senegal
Profesora Miriam Arroyo de Kerriou, Mexico
Mr Kit Neuman, USA
Ms Umebe N. Onyejekwu, Nigeria
Ms Verna Wheeler, USA
Sra Alejandra Pena, Paraguay
Mr Kenneth Perry, USA
Sr Sergio Duran-Pitarque

Acknowledgements

Dr Piet Pouw, The Netherlands
Ms Nicky Ladkin, USA
Dr Eilean Hooper-Greenhill, UK
Mr Andrew Hall, USA
Dr Susanne Peters, France
Dr Karyl Robb, USA

Our thanks are also due to Alexandra Bochi, Publications Coordinator at the International Council of Museums' headquarters in Paris for her friendly help and assistance in the production schedule, and to Hilary Moor at Routledge for her efficient administrative support.

In particular we would like to thank Dr Gary Edson, Ms Alissandra Cummins, Mr Andrew Wheatcroft and Dr Piet Pouw for participating in an editorial seminar in Rome which greatly helped in the finalisation of the draft text.

The production and publication of this book would not have been possible without the extensive support of Andrew Wheatcroft, the Editor in chief of 'The Heritage: Care–Preservation–Management' programme. His patience, forbearance, and encouragement in the face of innumerable questions and queries – and the occasional delay – were exemplary.

We must however take final responsibility for what is presented here. We cannot of course take the final credit. We have inevitably lent heavily on the work, published and unpublished, of colleagues worldwide. While it would not have been possible to acknowledge them all individually, it is a very real pleasure to record the value of their work in underpinning this publication. We trust the book will be of benefit to our international colleagues, and in a small way help to improve the quality of museum provision worldwide.

Timothy Ambrose and Crispin Paine
Edinburgh, Scotland/Cirencester, England
October 1991

Section I
Introductory

UNIT 1   ABOUT MUSEUMS

Related Units: 2, 3

Millions upon millions of people visit museums every year in countries throughout the world, and the number of museums increases day-by-day. Their popularity is assured. It is not the purpose of this book to discuss the advantages and disadvantages of the extraordinary upsurge of museum popularity in the last fifty years or so. This is nevertheless the context within which *Museum Basics* will be used, and it is appropriate that we comment briefly on museums and their position in the last decade of the twentieth century.

The arguments rage in professional circles as to whether there are too many museums chasing too limited resources, whether quantity and growth damage quality and viability or whether new forms of cooperation and partnership are needed to cater for a cost-effective scale of operation. The situation of course varies from country to country.

In Europe, for example, it is now estimated that for every museum which existed in 1950, there are four today. In other parts of the world, museum development is only just beginning. While the pattern of provision differs from one country to another, so too do standards – standards of collections management, standards of management and administration and standards of visitor service. *Museum Basics* has been written to assist in the improvement of standards.

Whatever the case for growth or containment, in every country museums need to operate in the context of a national policy for museums. Museum development and distribution, resources and quality of service, all need to be discussed on an informed basis. Professional and political resolution of these issues needs to be found.

Realistic support for museums in terms of adequate resources to allow for effective training programmes, proper standards of collections care and management, high-quality facilities of different sizes and a commitment to seeking new audiences through well considered marketing programmes, is essential if the museums service is to flourish to the benefit of the country and its people. A strong and vital museums service composed of museums operating in the public and/or private sectors provides a vast array of benefits – cultural, economic and political.

The status and standing of many countries today is in large part measured by the attention they pay to their cultural facilities.

International tourism, and the widespread economic gains it brings, now represents a major reason for investment in museums and their work throughout the world.

The increasing importance of resurgent national, regional and local identity, where museums can serve to reflect, objectively, change and continuity in traditional cultural values and development is of critical significance in museum development.

Museums have a key task to play in providing an understanding of identity and a sense of belonging to a place or community. In the face of immense and often painful cultural change in many countries, museums can provide a valuable sense of connection with the past and present, and serve as a springboard for the future.

Museums as a cultural phenomenon are of great antiquity. Their value has changed through time as political and cultural values have altered and developed. Today museums can play a major part in the cultural and economic life and well-being of a country. Taken as a whole, their collections represent a unique resource reflecting a country's achievements and progress, and its historical development.

Museums as part of the collective memory deserve to be supported for the range of benefits which they bring. Museum workers have a special responsibility in acting as guardians of that memory. Without our memory we cannot go forward.

UNIT 2   ABOUT THIS BOOK

Museums throughout the world have common needs and face common challenges. This book has been produced to help museums identify those needs and meet those challenges.

The book's key purpose is to provide a basic outline of good practice for museums with few professional staff and limited financial resources. The majority of museums internationally have inadequate staffing and resources to meet their large responsibilities. But despite this they still care for a unique resource, a significant part of the world's heritage.

Museum Basics has been written in consultation with a wide variety of museum workers in many different countries. Their ideas and comments on text and layout, topics and themes, have helped shape the book and increase its relevance to museums in countries which have different traditions of museum development.

Its organisation into six sections has been designed to allow the units within them to be read individually or in groups as a basic introduction to the topic(s) in question. Each of the book's sections moves from a general introduction to more specific issues.

Where a unit is being studied, information on related units is provided. Individual units may also be used as study texts within training programmes. Similar ideas and suggestions recur in different units. This is a deliberate approach designed to encourage readers to think about their application to different aspects of museum work.

Museum Basics is also supported by suggestions for further, in-depth reading in the different topic areas.

The book also includes a glossary of terms used in the text. There are variations in the use of terms in museum work internationally. While every effort has been made to make the text as widely applicable as possible, readers may wish to refer to the glossary where there is any doubt about the meaning or use of a word or phrase. We have included special *keyword boxes* throughout the text to explain particular terms in detail.

The book's coverage is wide-ranging. It is based on ideas which are already being used every day in many museums with limited budgets and few staff. It places a particular emphasis on marketing museums, an approach to museum work which may be unfamiliar in some countries; on caring for visitors and users; on managing collections, the unique resource of museums, effectively; and on managing staff. These are all aspects of museum work which have received particular attention in recent years, especially in the context of the massive growth in international tourism. Their emphasis is also a reflection of the significant increase in numbers of new museums being established worldwide.

Keeping up-to-date with new ideas and changing practice, learning from other museums about success and occasionally failure, is a considerable challenge to museum staff, especially in small museums, where time for reading and for training is often restricted. *Museum Basics* will therefore be regularly revised to help museum staff keep up-to-date with the changing museum world in which they are working.

The book forms part of a wider international publications programme – *The Heritage: Care–Preservation–Management* – and is therefore supported by a range of companion volumes which explore aspects of museum work in greater depth. The programme also includes *Museum Abstracts*, an abstracting journal which allows museum workers to keep up-to-date with new developments in museums worldwide.

The case study material in *Museum Abstracts* will help provide readers of *Museum Basics* with regular access to new examples for study and discussion.

Together, *Museum Basics* and *Museum Abstracts* provide museum staff with a basic resource to help them to improve the quality of their museums and to measure their achievements in a local, regional, national and international context.

No book about museums and their work can pretend to be comprehensive. While *Museum Basics* has been designed to address the main day-to-day concerns of museum managers, and has been written with the museum with limited resources firmly in mind, there will be other areas or topics which readers will want to explore. The publishers and the authors are concerned that later editions accurately reflect needs in the field. We would therefore welcome any suggestions for future editions which readers may wish to make. Please write to the authors, care of Routledge, 11 New Fetter Lane, London EC4P 4EE, United Kingdom.

One of the best characteristics of the international museum community is the willingness to share ideas and network information on good practice. This book has built on this commonwealth of experience and we trust that further editions will continue to do so in the future.

KEY WORD

MUSEUM MANAGER – the term 'museum manager' (in lower case letters) is used to describe any member of staff with responsibility for managing resources – people, collections, finance, buildings or equipment. The term has been used throughout *Museum Basics* to demonstrate that many people in a museum contribute to its effective working.

– the term 'MUSEUM MANAGER' (in upper case letters) is used to describe the senior member of staff (sometimes called the Director or Museum Curator) with overall responsibility for the museum's day-to-day operation who reports to the museum's governing body.

UNIT 3   TYPES OF MUSEUMS

Related Units: 1, 4

Museums are the treasure-houses of the human race. They store the memories of the world's peoples, their cultures, their dreams and their hopes.

Before modern museums developed, different societies found different ways of preserving objects and collections they held important. In ancient India, *chitrashalas* – painting galleries – were a means of education as well as a source of enjoyment, the paintings and sculpture providing lessons in history, religion and art. In Asia precious items were often deposited for safekeeping in temples, while in Europe churches sometimes preserved not only treasures, but curiosities too.

In many societies objects important to the group were appointed custodians. For example, in the Cross River region of West Africa certain masks were appointed an elder or other respected person to take responsibility for them. The fifteenth-century Scottish crosier shrine (bishop's staff) of St Fillan went to Canada with its hereditary keeper in 1818; today it is back in Scotland, in the Royal Museum of Scotland. In Imperial China collections of precious paintings were as important to members of the ruling class as they are in the West today.

Museums in the modern sense developed in Europe in the seventeenth century. The first use of the term 'museum' in English was in 1682; it described the collection of strange, rare and exotic things that the gentleman Elias Ashmole gave to the University of Oxford. From the private collections of courtiers and gentlemen, museums became the public educational institutions we know today.

Yet today museums vary enormously. They range in size from great international museums like Washington's Smithsonian Institution to the smallest one-room village museum. They vary enormously, too, in their purpose. Some are intended purely to amuse and entertain holiday-makers; others preserve the data on which scientific research is based. They vary in their collections: from insects to historic industrial machinery, from ancient statues to pathological specimens, from modern paintings to revolutionary flags. They vary in who runs them. They vary in the public they seek to serve.

Museums vary most controversially in the function they perform. Often the function that its managers ascribe to a museum is quite different to the function its critics accuse it of filling. Many national

BOX 1

Some types of museums

Classified by collections:

- general museums
- archaeology museums
- art museums
- history museums
- ethnography museums
- natural history museums

- geology museums
- science museums
- military museums
- industrial museums
- etc., etc.

Classified by who runs them:

- government museums
- municipal museums
- university museums

- army museums
- independent or private museums
- commercial company museums

Classified by the area they serve:

- national museums
- regional museums

- local museums

Classified by the audience they serve:

- educational museums
- specialist museums

- general public museums

Classified by the way they exhibit their collections:

- traditional museums
- open-air museums

- historic house museums

What other types of museum can you think of?

KEY WORD

HERITAGE CENTRE – a descriptive term widely used to describe a facility interpreting the natural and/or cultural heritage of a place or an area. In some cases heritage centres are collections-based and are thus functionally museums, even though they may use the term for marketing reasons.

BOX 2

Some definitions of 'museum'

The ICOM definition:

purpose and role in society (handwritten margin note)

> A non-profit making, permanent institution, in the service of society and its development, and open to the public, which acquires, conserves, researches, communicates and exhibits, for the purposes of study, education and enjoyment, material evidence of man and his environment.

The Museums Association (United Kingdom) definition:

> A museum is an institution which collects, documents, preserves, exhibits and interprets material evidence and associated information for the public benefit.

> 'Institution' implies a formalised establishment which has a long-term purpose. 'Collects' embraces all means of acquisition. 'Documents' emphasises the need to maintain records. 'Preserves' includes all aspects of conservation and security. 'Exhibits' confirms the expectation of visitors that they will be able to see at least a representative selection of the objects in the collections. 'Interprets' is taken to cover such diverse fields as display, education, research and publication. 'Material' indicates something that is tangible, while 'Evidence' guarantees its authenticity as the 'real thing'. 'Associated information' represents the knowledge which prevents a museum object being merely a curio, and also includes all records relating to its past history, acquisition and subsequent usage. 'For the public benefit' is deliberately open ended and is intended to reflect the current thinking, both within our profession and outside it, that museums are the servants of society.

The American Association of Museums definition:

object-oriented (handwritten margin note)

> A non-profit permanent, established institution, not existing primarily for the purpose of conducting temporary exhibitions, exempt from federal and state income taxes, open to the public and administered in the public interest, for the purpose of conserving and preserving, studying, interpreting, assembling, and exhibiting to the public for its instruction and enjoyment objects and specimens of educational and cultural value, including artistic, scientific (whether animate or inanimate), historical and technological material. Museums thus defined shall include botanical gardens, zoological parks, aquaria, planetaria, historical societies, and historic houses and sites which meet the requirements set forth in the preceding sentence.

museums, for example, claim to exist to promote national unity by fostering national culture. Their critics, though, claim that their hidden function is to encourage the public to accept the status quo, and thus to keep the present rulers in power. There has been much discussion in recent years of the need to analyse the underlying function of public institutions like museums.

The one thing that every museum has in common with every other museum is collections. Compare the definitions of 'museum' given in Box 2: do you know any museums that fit into none of these definitions? If you do, why do you think they are called 'museums'?

UNIT 4   THE ROLE OF MUSEUMS

Related Units: 1, 3

The function of museums has been described in Unit 3. Here we examine the wider role of museums in society and the benefits which they can confer to the communities within which they are located. It is perhaps convenient to explore this role under three broad headings – social and cultural benefits, economic benefits and corporate or political benefits.

Social and cultural benefits

Museums provide a significant range of social and cultural benefits to their areas, many of which are described in later sections. These benefits are well known. Museums ensure the preservation and conservation of the community's cultural and natural heritage. They serve as a cultural focus and a centre of expertise, providing opportunities for community involvement in their work through Friends' Groups, volunteers, project work and in other ways. Museums give support to educational organisations, and offer a facility for cultural events and activities. In a very real sense museums enhance the quality of peoples' lives and can play a key role in developing a sense of identity for the area in which they are located. In order to be successful, however, in providing social and cultural benefits, museums need to be effectively managed and well resourced.

Unit 4   The role of museums

Economic benefits

Museums can have an important role to play in economic regeneration in urban or rural areas. The economic role of museums is less well understood in many countries than their social and cultural role. In urban areas where, for example, the traditional manufacturing or industrial base has been destroyed, service industry development and tourism may represent an alternative economic strategy. Here museums can play a key role. In rural areas, where economic development needs to take place because of change, for example to traditional agricultural industries, museums may have a useful role in serving as a focus for explaining cultural change and continuity.

Museums can serve as part of an overall redevelopment programme where housing, service and manufacturing industries and cultural facilities provide a mix of use for the community living and working there. Museums can contribute to the development of a cultural infrastructure for an area alongside other facilities such as libraries, theatres, cinemas and concert halls. In many parts of the world such an infrastructure provides powerful support for attracting investment from companies and businesses, government organisations and others. Museums can thus help to regenerate or develop local economies at times of economic change.

Where tourism is part of the local economy, museums and other visitor attractions act as magnets for attracting tourist visitors. They will then spend money within the local area in shops, restaurants, garages, hotels and markets.

Another economic benefit which museums can bring to the local economy is the creation of jobs and increased levels of employment. The museum itself as an attraction and each new job in a museum will have an economic impact on the area within which the museum is located. The museum is therefore of help in developing and sustaining the economic strength of the area.

In many museums part-time or temporary jobs, perhaps as part of government training schemes, also have an important impact. Training programmes may be shared between the museum and other organisations. Museums can often attract financial support for managing training programmes directly for other museums or other organisations of similar type such as customer care, administrative or curatorial skills.

Museums attract financial investment from external agencies, such as government or international grants. This is of particular value in areas where local financial resources may be restricted. Arguments for investment can be supported by reference to the museum's broader economic role within the community.

Altogether it is worth considering and quantifying the range of economic benefits which your museum can or does provide to the local community. List the benefits which your museum provides such as providing jobs, attracting visitors to the area, or providing skills and training: then calculate how much they add to the economy. Quantifying the museum's value in these terms can help to support other arguments to the museum's governing body for increased resources and enhance political support for the museum's work.

Corporate or political benefits

For the organisation with responsibility for the museum, such as local government, a museum can help to foster a sense of local pride and belonging, and maintain traditional cultural values. It can serve to demonstrate change and continuity within the local area, and allow people to explore their community's roots. Museums can play a valuable role in public relations and publicity for their administering organisations where they are part of a range of services provided for local people and tourist visitors. Their work may also help to forge links with other external organisations of different type with consequent political or economic benefit.

All of these benefits, and more – economic, cultural and corporate or political – can be used to underpin arguments by museum managers for increased resources. Where such benefits are provided – and are seen to be provided – the reputation and standing of the museum is enhanced. It is a matter of judgement as to which benefits can be identified to help the MUSEUM MANAGER make his/her case for resources. The balance will vary from one museum to another. What benefits does your museum provide?

The role of museums is then much broader than a simple functional description. The successful manager will ensure that *all* the benefits his/her museum provides to the community are defined and used to advantage.

Unit 4   The role of museums

STUDY EXAMPLE

A museum wanting to attract funds from a local planning authority acquired a copy of the authority's policy statements on future development. The museum carefully analysed the policy objectives and forward planning proposals in these documents. It was then able to draw up a case for support which was based on the planning authority's own requirements. The museum identified the benefits it could provide and was successful in obtaining financial support.

Analysing what benefits the museum can provide through its services is a powerful way of arguing for additional resources and reinforcing the role of the museum in the eyes of its users.

Section II
The museum and its users

UNIT 5   MUSEUMS ARE FOR PEOPLE

Related Units: 6–9

Attitudes to museums and the expectations which people have of them are changing worldwide. There is a growing critical awareness of the 'political' nature of museums, and their role in maintaining the cultural values of elite or privileged groups in society.

With changing political structures, facilities run or supported by the state are coming under intense public scrutiny in terms of their role in cultural transmission. Questions about whose culture is being portrayed in museums and who is portraying it for whom are to be heard in countries throughout the world. This debate, with the growing consciousness of the powerful position which museums and similar facilities have in transmitting cultural values and information, is an exciting one. It presents many opportunities for museums to engage more directly with their users.

Museum users are increasingly expecting a greater degree of involvement and participation in museums. On the one hand this is true of the decision-making processes affecting museums where in multi-cultural societies people are becoming more interested in being appropriately represented through displays and exhibitions, collections and databases. This is especially true where museums have implicitly or explicitly denied opportunities for balanced representation in the past.

On the other hand it is also true of museum users who now expect a more active, participatory experience through their contacts with museums. The changing style of museums and the changes affecting presentation methods through the application of new technologies are generating greater interest in 'hands-on' experiences for users. It is not enough for museums to present collections and information in a passive way. Museums have to engage interest through active involvement with their users and build on it to achieve their objectives. Museum managers should encourage users to explore and discover the museum's collections and services for themselves. This is in contrast to the traditional approach still prevalent in many museums where expertise resides in the museum alone and users are viewed as passive recipients of what the museum determines should be on offer.

This rising public demand for involvement and participation in the 'process' of museum work means that museums have to understand the social and economic context within which they are working to a far greater degree than in the past. Everything that a museum does is ultimately for the public benefit. Understanding the public's interests and concerns, likes and dislikes, needs and wants, is of critical importance in providing successful museums and services. Museums are for people, and the successful museum recognises the opportunities which participation and involvement can bring to its work.

These changes in attitude and interest place a heavy responsibility on the shoulders of those managing museums, especially where public money is involved. Managing museums efficiently and effectively for the public benefit requires a detailed understanding of and sympathy with the various different interest groups within the museum's public. Developing such an insight requires detailed research on a continuous basis. It is only when the museum's public is thoroughly understood that the museum can effectively respond to the public's needs and requirements through its services.

Throughout *Museum Basics* there is a strong emphasis on the relationship of the museum with the people whom it serves. The concept of a 'market' where the museum along with other educational and entertainment facilities 'sells' or 'advertises' its 'wares' is developed in succeeding units. The idea of a museum operating in a 'market' may be unfamiliar to some readers, but it is of immense value in helping to analyse the relationships between people and museums, and in exploring how museums can respond to people's needs and interests.

The term 'market' signifies competition. Museums in all parts of the world are in competition, not simply with one another, but with all the other calls on people's leisure time. Operating within a market means being competitive, providing products and services which the public want and are prepared to pay for either directly, or through taxes. Successful museums are orientated towards the market and are outward-looking. They recognise that their future depends on people sympathetic to their objectives and on people who are prepared to be involved in what they have to offer. This involvement may go far beyond a casual visit to the museum, and may extend into fundraising programmes, voluntary work, patronage, membership of the Friends' group, donations, fieldwork and oral history and collecting programmes to name but a few. Building public interest and support is essential for long-term success.

As we enter the twenty-first century, the greatest challenge facing museums is to recognise that museums are for people, and that their future depends on developing and promoting themselves to meet the identified needs of the market.

UNIT 6   UNDERSTANDING YOUR MARKET

Related Units: 5, 7, 8

A *market* can be thought of as the social and economic context within which a museum operates. All museums operate within a market. The market will vary from place to place, country to country. Understanding the nature and composition of your market is of paramount importance for success. Researching your market will help you to determine whether your museum is offering the right type or mix of services to your users, at the right location, at the right time(s) and at the right level.

Market research is necessary whether you are starting up and developing a new museum, or managing an existing one. It should be a continuous exercise helping you to develop or change your services to your users in the light of their needs and responses to the museum. It will help you to address new *market segments*. Market research is not the preserve of specialist companies, although these can often be very helpful. It is essentially common-sense, and you can – as many museums do – work out your own research plan. It is about finding out information from all sources which will help your museum to be successful. It will also help in the drawing up of a forward plan for the museum (see Unit 69).

Market intelligence

You can find out much of this *market intelligence* using external information derived from published and unpublished information. You can also use internal information derived from your own observation, surveys and records, or specially commissioned research. By the time you have completed your research you should have some answers to the following questions:

– why will people visit my museum?
– who will visit my museum?
– when and how often will they come to the museum?
– how much time will they spend in the museum?
– who are my competitors?
– what are their strengths and weaknesses?
– what will my *market share* be?
– is the museum's market getting larger or smaller?

Researching your users

People use museums to meet all kinds of needs — some are straight-forward, such as information, somewhere to meet their friends, some-where to take visitors or children on holiday; some are more complex, such as to discover the spirit of place, to find a sense of identity, to spend time by oneself. Defining the services on offer and the range of benefits available will help you to understand your market more accurately.

Ask yourself the following questions:

— what business is my museum in?
— what overall '*product*' or 'service' is it providing?
— does it stand out in the market-place?
— is it accessible in terms of location and price?
— do people know about it? how do they know about it?
— do they speak well of it? are they satisfied?

Then identify the range and quality of services and experiences on offer to your users. Ask what benefits beyond its services the museum is providing its users in response to their needs and expectations.

It is unlikely that you will have the money or resources to provide for *all* the needs of *all* your possible users. You will have to decide what services it would be best to provide with the resources that you have. Market research will give you the information to make these decisions.

Remember that many people will use your museum but not visit it. They may require information by telephone or by letter, or request products from the museum shop to be sent by mail. They may meet their friends outside the museum because it is a landmark, or simply accept it as part of their 'landscape'. It may serve symbolically to give them a sense of cultural status. There are many ways in which people use museums.

Planning research

The next task in market research is to identify people who need the services and benefits which your museum is offering. In practice, there is not one huge uniform market of users, but a collection of many smaller groupings. Your market can thus be divided into *segments*, each of which represents a target market for the museum. There are many ways of dividing or segmenting your market. They include the following:

- AGE – people of different ages have different needs and the museum will need to cater for a range of age groups. How can your museum cater for different age groups successfully?

- SEX – many people visit museums in family or social groups. Is your museum able to cater equally for men and women?

- INCOME – different income groups have different spending power. Will your museum target specific groups or aim to appeal to all?

- EDUCATION – the level of education of your users may well determine the approach you take to exhibitions and displays, events and activities. How will your museum cater for different levels of educational attainment? Will your users have literacy and numeracy difficulties? How can these be overcome?

- LOCATION – museum users can be divided up by where they live, where they work and the places/facilities which they visit. Do you know where your users are coming from, and how they get to your museum?

- LEISURE PARTICIPATION – visiting museums is only one type of leisure/educational activity. Do you know what else they like to do?

- LIFESTYLE – different households have different lifestyles. Which lifestyles will your museum cater for? Will you have long opening hours, for example, to allow visitors to come after their work?

- PATTERNS OF USE – visitors to museums may go once, several times or regularly. Does your museum attract people on a regular or irregular basis and why? Very many people visit museums in family or social groups.

However you divide up your market into segments and whatever combination of characteristics you use, you need to ask the following questions:

- Can this market segment be measured? Can you estimate the number of users in each segment? How often will these users visit the museum? And at what times of the year? For example, census records may tell you how many children there are under ten years old in your area; your market research can tell you what proportion of that potential market segment is coming to your museum.

- Is the size of the market segment significant? Are there enough users in each segment to justify providing services for them? Can the museum attract more users by new developments or changes in marketing strategies?

■ If income is a consideration for your museum, is the market segment a profitable one? Will it support the costs of the service on offer? What income will it generate?

■ Can you reach and communicate with the market segment? Is it possible to inform the market segment of your services? And how? For example, you may have to make special efforts for those who cannot read or write.

Carrying out research

To find out more about your target markets and to allow you to answer these questions, you need to gather external information from published and unpublished sources, and internal information from surveys and observation methods. Published information can include:

- central and local government statistics on family/household expenditure on services/goods, lifestyle groups and trends in the marketplace;
- research publications and periodicals providing relevant case study material on museums;
- specialised publications on marketing, giving information about interests and attitudes of different groups;
- local trade organisations and business people holding information on local markets.

This 'desk research' can provide valuable information and is an important method of gathering information about your market. Not all of these sources may be available to you, but make use of what you can acquire and develop information over a period of time.

Remember: market research should be a continuous process! At a simple level observation of visitor behaviour, talking to visitors, noting visitor characteristics, can all be carried out on a day-to-day basis, and recorded. More complex research programmes such as market surveys (see below) may be undertaken, perhaps seasonally or annually. Much will depend on the museum's resources.

Market surveys

To complement this external information, an important and useful method of gathering information is the *market survey*. Market surveys can help to provide a range of specific information about users and non-users.

On the one hand market surveys can be very specialised and detailed. They may be carried out for your museum by specialist companies experienced in gathering information on statistically reliable lines and carrying out computer analysis of the results. On the other hand, they can be relatively simple and carried out by the museum itself. They do nevertheless need to be well designed and to provide information which will allow you to build up a detailed picture of your market.

Regular use of market survey questionnaires can also help to identify changing trends in your museum audience, and identify why people do *not* come to the museum!

A simple market survey questionnaire might, for example, gather the following information about a sample of your visitors:

– age range – up to 12, 12–18, 18–25, 26–35, 36–45, 46–55, 56–65, 66–75, 75 and over
– sex – male/female
– transport to museum – foot, bicycle, bus/coach, train, car, other
– group numbers – adults/children
– occupation/occupation of head of household
– distance travelled from home
– location of home
– reason(s) for visit
– frequency of visits
– enjoyment of visit
– suggestions for improvements

Market surveys on people who do NOT use the museum as well as users can also help to pinpoint the reasons why people do not visit your museum. Some of these will be beyond your control or influence. But finding out about why people do not visit your museum is another way of developing or improving services for the future to attract new audiences. The museum may wish to hold discussions with groups or representatives of different communities to discover people's attitudes to the museum and its services.

Researching your competitors

Observation and research in other museums can provide very valuable data. Try to find out who visits other museums and similar facilities, and analyse the services/benefits which they provide. Look at their pricing policies and opening times. Look at how their organisation's identity is promoted in the market-place through their advertising or print matter. Ask why they are successful or unsuccessful. Test for yourself the quality of service on offer.

Don't simply look at museums. Analyse what is happening in other service organisations and environments. Assess shops, hotels, restaurants, offices – what quality and standard of environment and service are people in these facilities expecting? Won't they expect your museum to offer at least the same level and quality of services?

Market analysis

Compare your market share, anticipated or actual, with other museums. Are there trends in the market-place apparent over 3, or 5, or 10 years? Are visitor numbers or numbers of museums on the increase or decrease? Why is there this pattern? Is the museum business successful or unsuccessful at the moment? How will it fare in the future? Discuss these figures with colleagues and advisers to get a better understanding of where your museum fits into the overall market.

All of this market research and analysis should be designed to make you examine the quality, range and delivery of your museum's services.

The successful museum provides services to meet the needs of its users.

The successful museum understands who its users are and what they need.

It has researched its market.

Factors influencing museum visiting

These are some of the headings which you might find helpful in analysing your market. The more one knows about what factors influence museum visiting, the more one is able to understand the composition of the market.

- Location
- Cost of transport
- Distance to be travelled
- Availability of transport
- Type of transport
- Knowledge of museum
- Time spent travelling
- Pricing policy
- Appeal of subject
- Facilities/services available
- Accessibility
- Previous visits
- Previous experience
- Peer group recommendations
- Weather
- Time of year
- Available time
- Interest level/range
- Family/partner/social group agreement

People in households

It is useful to know what sort of social groups visit the museum. Here are some household types for reference purposes.

- Living alone
- Married couple, no children
- Married couple, with dependent children
- Married couple, with non-dependent children
- Single parent with dependent children
- Multiple occupation
- Extended family

Gathering information

Here are some sources of information for museum marketing research.

- Publications
- Unpublished reports
- Visitor counts

- Observations
- Market surveys
- Questionnaires
- Interviews
- Analysis of bookings
- Analysis of comments in visitor books
- Talking to visitors

KEY WORD

MARKET – The overall social and economic context within which a museum operates. The term implies an exchange between the museum in terms of its services and products and the 'market place' which consists of people using or purchasing the museum's services and products.

The notion of competition within the 'market place' also encompasses other services and products which are competing with museums for people's time and money.

STUDY EXAMPLE A

An industrial museum wanted to find out about its visitors. Everyone visiting the museum was offered a free cup of tea in the museum café if they completed a simple visitor questionnaire first. By the end of the year the museum had collected over 10,000 questionnaires at a cost of just £500.

The museum gained new insights into the sources of its visitors, but the survey information also led to three key improvements – in the organisation of the museum shop, the siting of the museum's donations boxes and a different seating arrangement in the café. These improvements in turn provided a net increase in income of 400 per cent, and improved customer satisfaction.

This was a simple example of good market research providing a range of benefits both to the museum and its users.

STUDY EXAMPLE B

A museums service in a medium-sized industrial city was concerned to discover why people living on the peripheral housing estates did not visit its four museums in the city centre. A small team of researchers interviewed a range of people in their homes, chosen to be representative of the various types and lifestyles of people living on the estates. Each interviewee was given a voucher to purchase food in local shops in payment and spent between one and two hours discussing their cultural interests and attitudes to museums with the interviewers. The interviews were transcribed and a report on the findings presented to the museums. The museums were able to develop new marketing plans to encourage new visitation from these areas of the city.

Market research had helped the museums service identify and reach new audiences.

UNIT 7   MARKETING YOUR MUSEUM

Related Units: 5, 6, 8, 9

Market research (see Units 5–6) has shown who your users are or might be, why they visit the museum and use your services, and what their needs are. Marketing the museum successfully depends on a combination of factors, sometimes known as *the marketing mix*, and conveniently described as product, price, place and promotion.

Within the marketing mix, the museum has to strike a balance between these four factors. It has to develop a product or services to meet the needs and interests of the market. It has to ensure that the way in which that product is made available or priced will generate demand. Where possible, for example with a new museum building, it has to ensure that its physical position or outlets are effectively sited. And it has to promote and publicise its services in the market-place.

It has to develop a good working relationship or good public relations with its users and patrons in order to maintain and develop interest in the museum's services and to fulfil its mission.

PRODUCT

What is the *museum product*? Understanding the museum product and developing it in line with your users' needs is the task of museum management and a key component in the marketing mix. It is an amalgam of services, people, buildings, facilities, atmosphere, customer care, access and accessibility, corporate presentation, collections, events and activities and many other quantifiable and non-quantifiable factors. It is what differentiates your museum from any other museum, or market competitor. It is essentially what makes the museum's identity and personality.

PRICE

Managing any museum carries with it costs – costs of staffing, displays, exhibitions, conservation, documentation, promotion and all the other responsibilities of a museum. How those costs are met will vary from museum to museum. Some museums will have their costs met wholly or in part by public authorities, others will have only minimal public funding and rely heavily on admission charges and retail sales for their income. How the museum will meet its costs is a task of management, but the price charged is a key component in the marketing mix. The successful museum ensures that its pricing policy does not damage its markets, and allows it to meet the full range of its responsibilities.

PLACE

What is the best location for a museum? Museums are established in many different types of location in town and country, in specially built or reused buildings, in rich or poor communities. Their location is one of the key factors in their accessibility, and a determining factor behind who visits them. There are no optimum locations other than ones which ensure the widest possible audiences, however large or small, for their services (see Units 59–60).

PROMOTION

How can museums effectively promote themselves in the market-place? One of the most important points to bear in mind in setting up a marketing or promotional strategy for your museum is how you can test its impact. If there is only a limited amount of money available for promotion through posters, advertising, mail-outs, leaflets and the broadcasting media, you will need to know whether your marketing budget is being spent to the best effect.

In advertising your museum ensure that the benefits to the user are stated clearly, and wherever possible seek creative advice. Much money is wasted on poorly conceived marketing materials, poorly distributed and poorly received by potential users. Promoting the museum may cost nothing other than enthusiasm, hard work and using existing information providers like the press and radio creatively. Bear in mind that word-of-mouth publicity from satisfied users is a very powerful means of developing support for the museum.

Developing a good working relationship with your users is important in marketing the museum. But developing and maintaining a good working relationship with the museum's patrons is also important. Managing effectively the relationships between the museum, the museum's users and the museum's patrons is a central task of the museum management.

The museum's patrons might include central and local government agencies, corporate sponsors, charitable trusts, individual donors, international funding bodies and local businesses. The museum's success will depend in large part on how well your achievements and successes, as well as needs, are understood by these supporters or potential supporters. Significant amounts of time need to be spent on maximising their assistance.

Promoting success, and encouraging your users to demonstrate their satisfaction with the museum to patrons will help secure the investment needed by the museum to carry out its work successfully. If insufficient attention is paid to one of these three areas of responsibility, and too much emphasis is placed on one area to the exclusion of another, the museum will suffer. It follows that effective *public relations* for all your constituencies of interest are of importance. Good relations with your public form an essential complement to marketing.

There are various means of promoting the museum in the marketplace. The communications and promotional strategy you employ whether it be through the broadcasting media, print and/or audio-visual materials will help to attract audiences to your museum and keep your museum in public focus. What methods are available? The following checklists give an indication of the wide range of methods available to you. In practice, some will be unsuitable, but all are worth serious consideration.

Some advertising and publicity media

■ *Newspapers*
  – daily
  – weekly
  – weekend
  – colour magazines
  – domestic
  – foreign
  – international
  – news stories
  – features
  – photographs/captions
  – editorials
  – letters
  – advertising
  – advertising features

- *Magazines*
  - weekly
  - monthly
  - quarterly
  - annual
  - occasional
  - domestic
  - foreign
  - international
  - general readership
  - special readership groups
  - trade/commercial

- *Television*
  - features
  - news stories
  - interviews
  - documentaries
  - talk-shows
  - quizzes
  - advertising

- *Radio*
  - features
  - news stories
  - interviews
  - documentaries
  - talk-shows
  - quizzes
  - advertising

- *Printed material*
  - posters
  - leaflets
  - direct mail
  - brochures
  - letters
  - information fliers
  - banners/flags
  - advertising fliers

- *Displays*
  - shops
  - travel centres
  - cultural facilities
  - fairs
  - promotional events

Advertising your museum

Advertising and promoting your museum and its services to the public requires careful consideration. Your market research will have identified a variety of audiences for the museum, and you will have developed services to meet the needs of the different market segments. How do you reach them, and reach them efficiently without wasting money? Paid advertising, whatever media you use, means that the museum is in charge of what it wants to say and how it wants to say it. Free editorial copy in a newspaper or news coverage on the radio or television can be helpful but it is also selective and others are in control of editing and presentation.

Targeting your advertising effectively at your market segments is the key to obtaining value for money; some media are better than others in this respect. Do not be afraid to take professional advice and do not be afraid to experiment. Whatever form of advertising is used, the museum should ensure that it is of good quality and well presented, whatever the target audience at which it is aimed. Your advertising should be designed to create an identity or personality for your museum in the public mind, and should consistently reinforce this. If you are using a variety of advertising media to promote your museum in the market-place, this is of particular importance.

Remember that there is enormous competition with other organisations seeking to gain attention, and your advertisement needs to attract attention, identify the key benefit on offer and be memorable. Successful museums target their advertising on the basis of good market research. They use creative ideas. They maintain consistency of identity. They build up constituencies of support by providing the benefits to the user which have been promised.

'Successful marketing is about marketing success.'

UNIT 8   SPECIAL AUDIENCES: MUSEUMS AND DISABLED PEOPLE

Related Units: 5, 7, 9

Disability does not discriminate. People of all ages and in all walks of life can suffer from various forms of disability. We are all likely to suffer from some form of disability as old age approaches. A substantial proportion of people in any community will suffer from some form of disability. People may have difficulty in walking, people may be blind or partially sighted, people may be deaf or hard of hearing, or people may have a mental handicap or suffer from fear of heights, open spaces or closed spaces.

If your museum is to be accessible and hospitable to all, then you will need to take account of disability and develop policies and programmes of practical action to provide for disabled people. Legislation on disability varies from country to country, and the museum will have to take account of the legislative framework within which it is working and any necessary legal requirements.

The checklist below provides an indication of the sort of questions museum managers should be asking of the external and internal features of museum buildings:

OUTSIDE THE MUSEUM

☐ *Orientation for disabled visitors* – Are there appropriate signs/ landmarks for blind/partially sighted visitors?

☐ *Access routes/paths* – Are access routes clearly marked and free of obstructions? Are kerbs and edges defined and surfaces slip-free? Are signs, gratings, litter bins a hazard? Do windows/doors open out into paths?

☐ *Ramps and steps* – Are entrances accessible for wheelchairs? Are ramps at the correct gradient? Are there handrails alongside ramps and steps? Is there adequate lighting?

☐ *Entrance doors and halls* – Are doors wide enough for wheelchair users? Is the door too heavy to open? Are there steps associated with the door? Can people see through the doors? Are glazed doors clearly marked? Can automatic doors be used instead of swing doors? Do halls and lobbies allow for wheelchair manoeuvre?

INSIDE THE MUSEUM

☐ *Orientation* – Is there sufficient, legible signing for partially sighted visitors? Are there aural or tactile landmarks to assist blind/partially sighted visitors? Do the surface colours of walls/floors aid orientation?

☐ *Levels* – Are there warnings about changes in floor levels? Are stairs well lit and signposted? Are information desks/hooks/washbasins/ shop displays/telephones at a suitable level for wheelchair users?

☐ *Lifts* – Are control buttons easily seen and located? Is there a

31

handrail inside the lift? Are signs and directions clearly marked and lighted?

☐ *Seating* – Is there sufficient seating available for visitors? Is it stable and at varied heights?

☐ *Materials and surface finishes* – Are surface finishes chosen with a view to avoiding discomfort or injury? Are there sharp angles on walls or junctions? Is sound or light reflection an aid or a hindrance? Can colours be used to provide guidance? Are displays presented without distracting surfaces behind them so that objects stand out effectively?

☐ *Lighting* – Are windows designed to minimise glare? Can they be opened and locked easily? Is display lighting effective for partially sighted visitors?

☐ *Heating* – Are heating systems such as radiators dangerous to touch?

☐ *Disaster management* – Are disabled people able to get out of a museum building easily in the case of fire or other disaster? Are there procedures laid down for staff to follow? Do staff know what to do in case of emergency?

☐ *Induction loops* – Is the museum/gallery/lecture room/education centre fitted with an induction loop to help people using hearing aids?

☐ *Signs* – Are signs legible and consistent? Are they positioned well? Are braille letters within hand reach and at an appropriate level and angle?

☐ *Touch exhibitions/displays/tours/workshops* – Does the museum provide touch exhibits/handling opportunities for blind or partially sighted visitors?

☐ *Toilets* – Are there specially designed toilets for disabled visitors?

These are only some of the questions which museum managers should be addressing in the design of new museums, the adaptation and development of existing buildings and the provision of visitor facilities and services, whether these be displays/exhibitions, education services, guided tours, publications or demonstrations and workshops. Understanding the needs of disabled people in order to put improvement programmes into action or to ensure new facilities/activities meet their needs effectively requires proper communication and consultation with disabled people.

A museum manager should take every step to liaise with disabled individuals or liaison groups to identify needs. There is a wide range of organisations available to provide general and specific advice on needs. The museum may wish to establish an advisory panel to help inform its policies in this area. Consideration should also be given to the museum's own policy of employing disabled people.

Working with disabled people can be a rewarding experience for museum staff. There is a need however for all staff to be trained in such work, and in assisting disabled visitors in appropriate and sensitive ways. It is worth remembering that many disabled people do not appear disabled. The museum should make every effort to publicise how it is able to assist disabled visitors. Disabled people need to know in advance whether it is worth their effort to visit a museum, and publicity material should provide information on access and accessibility. Every museum should aim to create a universally accessible environment, and equal opportunities for all to use the museum's services.

STUDY EXAMPLE

Recognising that many blind people find visiting places outside their homes difficult, especially for the first time, a museum established a special gallery for visitors with visual impairment. The gallery had a series of changing tactile exhibitions with items selected for their tactile interest and the museum provided a number of workshops in which individuals and groups discussed touch items and handling collections.

The museum developed this service for its users by working with blind associations, and sending invitations on audio-tape to all registered blind people in their area. Museum staff were trained in receiving blind people into the museum, and in appropriate methods of guiding them.

Exhibition staff also visited a number of blind people in their homes in conjunction with helpers from the blind association to encourage them to use the new facility. The museum later established a blind users' group which allowed for members to act as advocates for the museum's services and helped to develop a new and important audience for the museum.

By working in this way museum staff gained new understanding of groups with special needs and a section of the community was better served.

UNIT 9   THE MUSEUM VISIT

Related Units: 5, 8

A visit to a museum is a complete experience, to which every aspect contributes. Dirty toilets or offhand staff or poor publications will spoil the visit just as much as poor displays. The museum staff should consider how to improve every aspect of the visitor's visit.

Here is a checklist of the things that go to make up the visit experience. How well does your museum measure up?

☐ *Transport* – How do visitors get to the museum? Can access be made easier? Could public transport be improved, or could the museum provide transport of its own? Is the car-park large enough and well-designed?

☐ *Arrival at the museum* – Is the walk from the bus-stop or car-park pleasant and easy, not only for fully fit people, but also for elderly people, small children or people in wheelchairs? (See Unit 8.) Can the way be made more pleasant, and can tourists be protected from harassment by touts selling souvenirs, taxi-drivers, etc.?

☐ *Appearance* – Is the museum easy to recognise? It should be announced with a large well-designed sign. Does the museum look attractive? Even an old building can be improved with well-designed signs and perhaps flags. Is there a well-designed notice giving opening hours and price of admission? Are the warders and museum staff at the entrance smart, efficient and welcoming? (See Units 7, 16, 65, 66.)

☐ *Buying a ticket* – If there is a charge to visit the museum, is it obvious where to buy a ticket? Is the ticket-office itself well-designed? Does the ticket-seller have plenty of change? The ticket itself should be attractive and well-printed. Does the price of the ticket represent good value for money? Can one buy a season ticket, to allow repeat visits? The ticket-seller is probably, for the visitor, the most important person in the museum. The museum will be very largely judged on the friendliness and efficiency of the ticket-seller. He or she should be carefully trained to give every visitor a smile and a word of welcome, and to be able to answer the most common questions visitors ask – or to direct them to an Information Desk (see Unit 66).

☐ *Opening hours* – Is the museum open at times convenient to most potential visitors? Too many museums are open at times to suit their staff, forgetting that many people work every day, and can visit museums only in the evening or on public holidays.

☐ *Cloakroom* – Is there a cloakroom where visitors can safely leave bags, coats, umbrellas, etc.? If visitors leave bags and coats they will feel more comfortable and at home, and the museum's security will be improved.

☐ *Psychological orientation* – As the visitor leaves the busy street, he or she needs to relax and adopt a calm, receptive mood before he or she enters the displays. It is instructive to look at how temples are designed in many parts of the world: they very often have an entrance court, garden or hall where the worshipper can get into the right mood before entering the temple itself (see Unit 66). The design and 'mood' of the museum's entrance hall will greatly affect the mood in which the visitor enters the displays (see Unit 64).

☐ *Physical orientation* – Before entering the displays, the visitor needs to know what there is in the museum, and how to find it. It is also important to know roughly how long the visit will take. If possible, every visitor should be given, when buying the ticket, a leaflet with a plan of the museum and a brief description (with photographs) of the displays, listing the most important items. There should be a clear plan of the museum at the entrance, and in a large museum signposting throughout the museum (see Unit 66).

☐ *Intellectual orientation* – Before entering the displays the visitor also needs to know what he or she is going to see and what he or she might learn. The leaflet given with the ticket is one way of telling the visitor this; another is by an Orientation Gallery. An Orientation Gallery tries to tell the visitor what he or she is going to see, and also to suggest how to see it – what aspects to look at and what questions to ask. For example, an exhibition of Coptic icons could be looked at from different points of view: how were they made? Who are the saints depicted? How were they used by worshippers? How did the artistic style change over the centuries? An Orientation Gallery could encourage the visitor to look at the exhibition from one or other points of view. By changing the Orientation Gallery it is possible, to some extent, to change the visitor's experience of the exhibits (see Unit 66).

☐ *The museum staff* – The museum staff are the most important element of all in the visit experience. According to how efficient, smart, helpful and friendly they seem, the museum will be judged (see Units 73, 76, 78, 80).

☐ *Sequence and flow* – If the displays are designed to be seen in one particular order, it must be obvious to the visitor which way to go. The designer can use various techniques to encourage the visitor to follow the proper sequence: physical barriers, pools of light which attract, arrows, numbered panels. Generally, visitors should circulate in the direction in which they read: left to right or right to left (see Unit 64).

☐ *Pace* – 'Pace' refers to the variety of stimuli the visitor receives and the changes in his or her environment as he or she walks around the museum. Visitors quickly get bored if all parts of the museum look and feel much the same. By changing the floor surface, light levels, colours, display style, ceiling height, etc., the display designer can help keep the visitor alert and interested (see Unit 64).

☐ *Food and drink area* – The quality of the museum's food and drink area, its appearance, comfort, service and food is of enormous importance to the visitor's experience of his or her visit (see Unit 15).

☐ *Toilets* – The toilets are important, especially in a large museum. There must be enough to meet visitors' needs, conveniently located. They must be kept spotlessly clean.

☐ *Seating* – There should be plenty of places throughout the museum where visitors can sit down.

☐ *Visitors with special needs* – Not all museum visitors are fit adults. Consider how your own museum provides for:
– elderly and infirm visitors
– visitors in wheelchairs
– blind or visually impaired visitors
– nursing mothers
– small children
Everyone should be welcome in a museum, and everyone should be able to use and enjoy its facilities (see Units 8, 13, 16).

☐ *Photography* – Some museums still forbid visitors from taking photographs. There seems no good reason for this. The ability to take a few photographs to remember the visit by often adds greatly to the visitor's enjoyment of the museum. The introductory leaflet should say that photography (without tripod or flash, which may annoy other visitors) is permitted for personal use only; photographs for publication or commercial use require a permit.

☐ *The museum shop* – The museum shop, even if it is very small indeed, is an important part of the visit experience, and its quality will – like that of the food and drink area – reflect on the museum (see Unit 15).

☐ *Publications* – All except the smallest museums need five different kinds of publication. But they do not have to be elaborately or expensively produced:
– a simple leaflet – free or very cheap – which describes briefly what is

to be found in the different parts of the museum, and which
contains a plan
— a booklet, if possible in colour, which describes the contents of the
museum in more detail. It should be as attractive as possible, with
many photographs, so that visitors will buy it as a souvenir of their
visit. It should be priced so that almost all visitors buy one
— a guide-booklet for children. This should be specially written for
children, and will probably contain drawings to colour, puzzles to
solve and quizzes to answer. It should be very cheap, so that
children can buy it
— a full guide-book and catalogue which describes most of the objects
or groups of objects in the museum
— scholarly publications: books, monographs and journals (see Unit 31).

UNIT 10   MUSEUM EDUCATION SERVICES: WITHIN THE MUSEUM

Related Units: 11, 12

Museums have an important role in providing education services to
users, whether these are children or adults. Some education services
will provide a range of formal teaching opportunities in the
museum; others will work closely with teachers to allow teachers to
make better use of the educational resources available through displays and exhibitions, databases, handling collections and museum
staff.

The look of wonder on a child's face can be the reward for a
lifetime's work in museums. It is the aim of museum education to
foster contact between people — whether children or adults — and
objects: not to teach facts, but to sow a seed of interest, a spark of
inspiration.

In an ideal world, every museum would have at least one education
specialist who would be a trained teacher who also had an under
standing of museums and museum collections, and a vocation to help
people — and especially children — use and learn from them.

For most museums the establishment of such a post should be high
priority. A museum education specialist can be of enormous value to a
museum. He or she may be the only member of staff with training in
the psychology of learning, and may have considerable experience of
analysing complex concepts and presenting them in a simple way to a

non-specialist audience. The education specialist may be, indeed, the only professional communicator or interpreter in the museum.

It is clearly sensible, therefore, for the museum to make full use of his or her skills, and to involve him or her in all aspects of interpretation and the planning of new displays. Museum education is not just about teaching children, though children may be its principal audience.

Many small museums may not be able to employ an education specialist of their own. For them, there are other possibilities. One is that the Local Schools Service may be able to coopt a teacher to the museum, perhaps for two or three years, who could be trained to apply teaching skills to the museum context. Another is that suitable volunteers may be available in the community – perhaps retired teachers, or teachers not presently working – who may be willing to give some of their time to the museum. Another possibility is sponsorship: a large company might be willing to finance the appointment of an education specialist for a few years.

CONTACTS WITH SCHOOLS

Whether or not the museum is able to provide an education specialist, it is an important part of the work of every museum to establish strong links with its local schools. Someone on the museum staff – perhaps the MUSEUM MANAGER – should have responsibility for maintaining contact with the teachers at local schools, making sure that the schools know what is going on at the museum and how they can make use of it, and making sure that the museum staff know about developments in the schools.

Unfortunately few teachers learn, as part of their training, about how to use museums in their teaching. Teachers of art or of history may be familiar with museums, but teachers of (for example) mathematics or craft and design or languages may need to have the possibilities museums offer presented to them.

Every museum should try to organise – perhaps once a year – a training day for teachers. Ideally this would be arranged through the Local Schools Service, and the teachers be given time off to attend. It should be held at the museum, and might be led by a museum education specialist brought in for the day. However, all the museum staff should be involved, because museum staff and teachers getting to know each other will be a major benefit of the day. The day must be carefully planned, especially if it involves some real teaching of real children!

EDUCATION MATERIALS

Museums should help teachers make use of museums by providing education materials. What these should be will depend very much on the character of the museum, and the needs of the local schools. The first step will be to ask local teachers what they need. They may find simplified catalogues of the collections most useful, or booklets describing projects based on the displays, or filmstrips or worksheets.

Many museums provide worksheets for visiting schoolchildren. Some teachers value these; others hate them. The sign of a good worksheet is that it encourages the user to *look*. If the user can answer the questions without really looking, it has been badly constructed. Questions that ask children to count things, for example, are less useful than ones that ask how something was made or how it was used – that require deduction from observation.

Museums hoping to attract visits from more than one or two schools should publish a booklet describing the services they can provide to schools. It should include:

– a description of the displays
– the name of the education specialist
– how to book a class visit
– what services are available, e.g. talks, school visits, etc.
– the facilities available to visiting groups:
    education room
    shop
    clipboards, pencils, etc.
   information about access: is it suitable for disabled children?

PLANNING A MUSEUM VISIT

Teacher and curator or museum education specialist should together plan every school visit to a museum. It is essential that teachers visit the museum before they bring any children, and essential that every visit be booked in advance.

The visit should be part of the work the children are doing at school, *not* just an 'end of term treat'. The preparation for the visit will therefore take place in the classroom. When the children get to the museum they will already have a good idea of what they are going to see and what work they are going to do. It will lead on naturally from the schoolwork they have been doing in the classroom. The skilful teacher is one who can ensure that the children's work is guided and purposeful, but can use the special stimulus which museums can provide.

THE MUSEUM EDUCATION ROOM

If possible every museum should have an Education Room. It should be big enough to accommodate a normal-size school party, and at least should have seats. It might also contain:

— a clean water supply
— a blackboard or whiteboard
— a slide-projector and/or overhead projector
— paints and paper

Many museums will not be able to provide these things, or even a separate Education Room. They might, however, consider providing basic equipment such as clipboards and pencils.

THE SCHOOL VISIT

Schoolchildren arriving at the museum deserve a warm, relaxed and friendly welcome. They need:

— to be welcomed by a member of staff
— to be shown where to put their things
— to be given an opportunity to use the toilets
— to have an introduction to what they will be seeing and doing
— to be given any necessary materials

The introductory talk should be very short. Museums still sometimes get asked by unimaginative teachers to provide 'a general tour'. Such requests should be discouraged, since the children will learn little. Instead the museum staff should discuss with the teacher more effective ways of using the children's precious time in the museum.

Even if the museum's education specialist is leading the particular class visit, the children's teacher must be present throughout and fully involved in the programme. It is he or she who will be leading the follow-up work back at school.

FOLLOW-UP WORK

Just as the museum visit should continue naturally from the work the children were doing in the school classroom, so the museum visit should be followed by further work at school.

Ideas for follow-up work include:

- Written work, perhaps an imaginative account of the lives of the people who made or used some of the objects seen, or of the 'lives' of the objects themselves.
- A display of classwork deriving from the visit or a classroom 'museum' or exhibition.
- Drama, dance and music. Could the class create a play based on their museum work, or learn songs and dance of the period or people being studied?
- Models, using measured drawings, or costume-figures or imaginative historical reconstructions.
- Crafts; many craft activities, that relate to the museum's collections, can be carried out by children.
- Art work might include making a frieze or collage, creating life-size models or printing fabric or paper using designs copied from museum objects.

UNIT 11   MUSEUM EDUCATION SERVICES: OUTSIDE THE MUSEUM

Related Units: 10, 12

The liveliest museums are not content to wait for people to come and visit them: they take their services out into the community. Similarly, Museum Education Services are not limited to helping visiting school-children – they include many different ways of taking the museum out into the schools and into other parts of the community. Some of these ways are noted in this unit.

SCHOOL LOAN SERVICES

The lending to schools of objects from the museum collections or from special loan collections is commonly called a 'School Loan Service'. The choice of material to be used in this way must take into consideration conservation and security requirements.

The principle of a School Loan Service is that real museum objects are lent for short periods to schools, so that teachers can integrate learning from objects into their normal classwork.

School Loan Services vary greatly in size. The smallest simply mean that teachers are encouraged to borrow objects from the museum collections. The largest services have big collections, specially built up for the purpose and quite distinct from the main museum collections. The objects are provided in specially-designed boxes, and accompanied by notes for teachers. Objects can be ordered from a published catalogue, sent every term to every school in the area, and are delivered by the Loan Service's own van. Such large services employ many staff: education specialists, technicians, drivers and clerical staff.

The benefits a Loan Service can bring are very great. Objects which might otherwise simply remain in store are serving a real educational purpose in the hands of teachers and children, while using objects in school encourages teachers and children alike to visit the museum itself.

However, any museum considering setting up a School Loan Service should also weigh seriously the drawbacks.

- If objects are borrowed from the museum collections they will inevitably decay or be damaged quite quickly.
- If a special loan collection is set up, might it be competing for objects with the museum itself?
- Administering even a simple service is very time-consuming if things are not to get lost, while a large service is very expensive indeed.

MOBILE SERVICES

A few museums have set up 'mobile museums', large vans containing museum objects and displays, which can take a small taste of the mother museum out to local schools, or – for example – to rural villages. They have been found particularly beneficial in large countries like India and Canada, though on a smaller scale they have been successful in England, both in big cities like Liverpool and in rural areas. In both Australia and Sweden, museum trains have been used to bring museum collections and displays to more remote communities. In Sweden indeed the *Rikstutstallningar* (Swedish State Exhibitions) has pioneered ways of reaching a wider public.

TALKS IN SCHOOLS

Children always appreciate someone other than their teacher talking to them, so even curators who feel shy of talking to children are often made to feel very welcome!

CHILDREN'S CLUBS AND HOLIDAY ACTIVITIES

Nothing gives such an impression of liveliness in a museum as a rich programme of holiday activities for children. Many children who have been involved in them have been inspired to an appreciation of their environment and a love of art which has benefited them throughout life.

Before rushing ahead and announcing such activities, the museum would be well advised to consider what resources they would require. Is the effort required cost-effective in terms of the number of children who will benefit? How can the children the museum most wants to reach be encouraged to come? Sometimes much of the museum's educational effort seems to go into amusing children who are already privileged.

However, if the educational benefit has been well thought through, and the marketing of the programme well targeted, museum activities for children can be hugely beneficial.

Holiday activities are usually open to any child who wants to come, and they take place on various days during the school holidays. Children's clubs usually meet at weekends or after school and they are limited to members, though any child can join if there is a place.

A museum without an education specialist could very possibly attract one or more local teachers – or possibly retired teachers – to undertake holiday activities, while a children's club for older children could be run by a curator, and could do really useful work for the museum.

The range of possible activities involving children and museums is limited only by the imagination of the organisers.

SPECIAL EVENTS

One of the most effective ways of providing a museum education service is by organising special events (see Unit 12). These can last half a day, a weekend or two weeks. They can take all sorts of forms. A common approach is to choose one theme – which might be an activity like 'cooking', or a class of object like 'wheels' or a historical period. If intended for schools it should relate to the schoolwork the children who take part are doing, though if it takes place in the holidays a seasonal theme might be appropriate. A whole programme of events and activities is then planned around the theme, and school parties or individual children book places to take part.

BOX 1

Learning from objects

One of the aims of museum education must be to help people learn to look at objects, and, by asking questions, to learn directly from the objects themselves. Here is a sample worksheet, taken from Gail Durbin, Susan Morris and Sue Wilkinson, *A Teacher's Guide to Learning from Objects* (English Heritage, 1990).

Initially you may want to give children a worksheet like this to help them analyse an object. Ultimately they should be able to frame their own questions and set about answering them.

Looking at an object

The main things to think about	Some further questions to ask	Things found out through looking	Things to be researched
PHYSICAL FEATURES What does it look and feel like?	What colour is it? What does it smell like? What does it sound like? What is it made of? Is it a natural or manufactured substance? Is the object complete? Has it been altered, adapted, mended? Is it worn?		
CONSTRUCTION How was it made?	Is it handmade or machine-made? Was it made in a mould or in pieces? How has it been fixed together?		
FUNCTION What was it made for?	How has the object been used? Has the use changed?		
DESIGN Is it well designed?	Does it do the job it was intended to do well? Were the best materials used? Is it decorated? How is it decorated? Do you like the way it looks? Would other people like it?		
VALUE What is it worth?	To the people who made it? To the people who used it? To the people who keep it? To you? To a bank? To a museum?		

BOX 2

Museums Education Policies

Some museums are finding it useful to write a formal Museums Education Policy; it helps them to define their priorities, and to present their ideas to others.

The following example of a Museums Education Policy is adapted from Eilean Hooper-Greenhill, *How to Write a Museum Education Policy* (Dept of Museum Studies, University of Leicester, 1991).

THE EDUCATION POLICY

■ **Aims**

1. To enhance the education of children and adults through the imaginative use of the museum and its collections.
   - Excitement and motivation are the foundations of successful learning; museum visits should be challenging, memorable experiences resulting in personal enrichment for all.
   - The study of evidence in museums should promote enquiry and interest and be concerned mainly with the process of learning and the acquisition of skills. Knowledge, although important, should be part of a broader learning process that has interest and understanding as its principal objective.

2. To assist the museum to maximise the educational potential of its collection, buildings and other resources.
   - The experience and expertise of the museum education service should be used to assist the museum to realise its commitment to education in accordance with the Collections Management Policy, and to promote the status of education within the museum generally.
   - The educational effectiveness of the museum is affected by the public's perception of the museum as a whole, and is not restricted to the displays. All aspects of the museum's interface with the public should therefore be 'user friendly' and create a positive and harmonious atmosphere conducive to effective learning.

■ **Audience**

   To provide a service for the following groups, in order of priority:
   - Teachers and pupils from schools and colleges funded by the Local Schools Service.
   - Educational institutions/organisations funded by the Local Schools Service

or by any other county council source, such as pre-school playgroups, social and welfare groups.
- Adult education groups.
- Museum staff.

■ Type of provision

1. To provide direct teaching to schools, colleges, educational institutions and organisations and to adult education groups.
   - Teaching will generally take place in the museum's schoolroom and the relevant galleries, although extra-mural teaching may be undertaken at the discretion of the education specialist.
   - Teaching styles will take cognisance of the principles of good practice.
   - Wherever possible teaching styles will be used which focus students' attention on the artefacts. These might involve handling real artefacts, using replicas and creating situations that promote students' interest and inquisitiveness in the artefacts. This could be achieved through the use of project or topic work, active learning and drama, across the curriculum.
   - Visits by schools and adult education groups should promote understanding of museums and their role in contemporary society.

2. To provide learning resources which support the educational use of the museum.
   - Resources to include ideas for worksheets, teachers' notes and information on related sites/visits in the county.

3. To assist with enquiries of an educational nature.
   - The museum is an invaluable database for local studies. As far as is practicable and in keeping with museum guidelines regarding conservation and security, access to the reference collections by interested parties should be facilitated.

■ Staffing

- Although it is anticipated that the education specialist will do most of the work outlined above, specialist advice and assistance from curatorial staff will be necessary on occasions, as well as additional assistance from volunteers and freelance workers.
- The production of teachers' packs may involve a working party comprising local teachers.

■ Resources/budget

- To increase and diversify the range of items available for handling and study purposes.

- To increase the involvement of curatorial staff and volunteers in the implementation of the education programme.
- To explore alternative methods for funding freelance workers such as writers and artists in residence.
- To upgrade existing administrative provision with particular reference to the use of information technology.
- To allocate approximately 75 per cent of education staff time and funds to the provision of schools-based activities and resources.

■ Roles and functions within the museum

- To ensure that educational considerations are included in managerial decisions and the formulation of museum policies.
- To establish and maintain an entitlement to key resources such as funding and the allocation of space, in line with the museum's other core activities.
- To take an active role in the planning and evaluation of temporary exhibitions and permanent displays.
- To monitor goods on sale in the museum shop in terms of educational value, and advise on possible new lines.
  To encourage a balanced programme of publications of general as well as specialist interest.
- To improve the provision of facilities for visitors, particularly for disabled and handicapped people.
- To ensure that the layout of the museum is readily comprehensible through clear and accurate signposting.

■ Networks outside the museum

1. In order to keep abreast of developments in museums and education and to provide an effective and worthwhile service capable of responding to the needs of its clientele, close links should be maintained with the Local Schools Service and museum professionals.

2. Contact should also be maintained with the following:
   - Specialist teachers groups, e.g. local history teachers
   - Professional education centres
   - Field study and outdoor education centres
   - Professional groups
   - Local archaeological team
   - Societies with local involvement

■ Training

1. The museum education specialist should:
   - Have professional educational and museum qualifications, or be prepared to undergo the necessary training.

- Be an effective classroom practitioner.
- Comply with the relative Code of conduct for museum professionals (see Appendix).
- Develop managerial skills through participation in management training courses in order to become more effective in senior management.

2. To provide in-service training for teachers and museum staff:
   - In order to promote the educational role of the museum, teachers and museum staff should have some understanding of the principles of good practice underlying both professions. In-service training should therefore facilitate opportunities for discussion and the interchange of ideas between both parties, and provide opportunities for working together.
   - In-service training should assist teachers to use the museum's resources to respond to local and national initiatives, where appropriate. Museum staff and volunteers should be kept informed of recent educational developments, and of the implications for the museum.

■ **Marketing**

In order to keep people informed about the nature of the services provided, and to attract new audiences within the county, the education specialist will continue to use the following channels:
- participation in Local Schools Service courses and meetings with advisory teachers and probationary teachers
- meetings of local teachers
- entry in Local Schools Service handbook listing local educational resources
- publicity for special events in Schools Circular and fly posting to schools.

■ **Evaluation**

- Wherever feasible evaluation should be carried out in order to ensure the continuing effectiveness and credibility of the museum's education service.

Another approach is the Living History day, when children come to the museum and act out a story from history, often dressing in reproduction period clothes, and trying out some of the crafts and activities associated with the chosen time and country. These days need very careful planning if they are to be successful.

Special events are perhaps particularly appropriate in a small museum because limited resources can be concentrated on a short period of time. Staff or volunteers can be hired specially, the event can be marketed effectively and disruption is limited to just a few days.

UNIT 12   EVENTS AND ACTIVITIES: CREATING PROGRAMMES

Related Units: 7, 10, 11

Museums which organise lively programmes of events and activities will find that such programmes are a powerful means of building support for the museum. Events and activities can significantly affect the ways in which the public perceives your museum and help develop market interest.

Programmes of events and activities can be developed to enhance the core services which the museum provides and to meet the needs of specific target groups or market sectors (see Units 5, 6). Arranging events and activities programmes within the museum is one approach; another is for the museum to organise activities in other locations to interest visitors and to develop new audiences for the museum.

Approaches and opportunities

The list below gives an indication of the range of opportunities available to museums:

- Temporary exhibitions of objects/specimens of the month/week/day exploring items from the collections, loans or new acquisitions;
- Film/video programmes;
- Touring exhibitions from the museum;
- Workshops for children/families on theme/objects in the museum;
- Print/picture loans;
- Family workshops in art or science;

- Hospitality mornings/evenings organised by museum support groups;
- Museum stands/exhibitions/demonstrations at local fairs/shows;
- Lectures and illustrated talks programmes;
- Special interest/special needs group meetings;
- Recorded music clubs;
- Meetings;
- Guided walks programmes;
- Fieldwork programmes with volunteers;
- Training events for the public such as photographic recording, map reading, oral history recording or caring for collections;
- Training events for museum professionals;
- Arts festivals;
- Foreign visitor days;
- Oral history recording workshops;
- Demonstrations of museum skills, e.g. conservation;
- Competitions and quizzes for children/families/special interest groups;
- Craft exhibitions;
- Publication launches;
- Exhibition previews;
- Dance performances;
- Hospital visiting programmes;
- Dramatic performances;
- Informal education programmes;
- Transport rallies;
- Historical re-enactments;
- Pageants.

Not all of these suggestions of course will be relevant to every museum. Some museums will include a number of these approaches in their core services, some will only be able to develop a few ideas because they have limited money or staff. Together they provide a menu of opportunities from which museums can pick and choose to suit their own needs. There are of course many more ideas which can be added to this list.

By organising regular activities programmes of this type, active museums can develop general interest in their work, and build political as well as public support for their services. By experimenting with different approaches for different market segments, the museum can develop a body of valuable marketing experience.

Considerable opportunities will always exist in developing events and activities programmes in collaboration with other museums or other organisations. Sharing experience, costs and resources can often help make a programme possible where otherwise a museum might not be able to undertake the programme by itself. Raising financial support for joint programmes can also be easier as the constituency of support for the programme can often be broadened and more people involved in the activities. Forging new working relationships with other bodies by undertaking events and activities programmes is another valuable benefit for the museum.

Policies

Organising events and activities programmes is time-consuming. A careful balance has to be struck between allocating resources for events and activities and allocating resources for other areas of the museum's work.

In policy terms, the museum's management also has to decide where the emphasis of its work is going to be put within a spectrum of formal education through leisure learning to entertainment. Some museums will wish to focus resources on their formal education responsibilities, others will wish to see these balanced by developing informal educational activities or leisure learning programmes.

Using the museum's facilities for entertainment purposes related to the collections such as music recitals or performances is another area for consideration. Using the museum for entertainment purposes unrelated to the collections such as corporate entertainment, where there are no specific educational objectives, is a further area for consideration (see Unit 16). You may wish to consider a differential pricing policy for different types of activity.

Planning programmes

What steps does the museum need to take in developing events and activities programmes? We examine here the middle of the spectrum described above – leisure learning or informal education. Formal museum education provision is discussed in Units 10 and 11, facilities use and entertainment is discussed in Unit 16.

In planning activities, it is helpful to draw up a 'menu' or list of suggestions. This list should include an outline of:

– how the activity could be organised,

— the audiences which it might attract or be targeted at,
— the names and addresses of speakers, artists and performers,
— any opportunities for collaboration with other organisations,
— the resources required,
— and the anticipated staff time and costs involved.

The museum can then make a choice from the planning list and run the programme(s) over whatever timescale is chosen.

Ideas for activities can be obtained from a wide variety of sources — museum staff, other museums or educational centres running similar programmes, published case studies, visitors, schools, libraries, etc. — the list is a long one. Activity leaders can be found within the museum's staff, or can be artists or craft workers, teachers, performers in dance, music, drama, mime, puppetry, community workers or volunteers with special skills.

The museum should establish an archive of ideas for events and activities to which it can continuously add as information becomes available. It should also develop a list of available and possible activity leaders for the future.

Audience groups

People of all ages learn more effectively through participation. While the museum may be able ultimately to offer events and activities or leisure learning programmes to all of its visitors, it is better to target specific groups and develop experience progressively. Some of the groups which events and activities programmes can be targeted at are:

■ Families — families cut across age and special interest groups, and are represented in every socio-economic group. Museum visiting is for many people a social activity, and families form an important social grouping for the museum to target.

■ Pre-school children and their carers — pre-school children and their carers are also present across the socio-economic spectrum, and this group has special needs often disregarded by museums.

■ Children — children represent the museum-visiting audiences of the future. Children's events and activities programmes not only help the museum but will always be of interest to other members of the family.

■ Young people — young people respond readily to events and activities specifically related to their needs and interests. Programmes developed with young people tend to attract other young people.

■ Adults – adults are often interested in leisure learning activities which are related to their occupation or leisure activities. The museum may find it worthwhile to approach adults through organised groups such as clubs or societies or workplace groups.

■ Disabled people – provided that physical access to the museum is suitable, disabled people will respond to events and activities programmes as enthusiastically as any other group. Museums should be prepared to take suitable activities programmes to disabled groups or people in hospitals or other venues where access to the museum is not possible.

Care must be taken in publicising your events and activities to ensure effective targeting and distribution of publicity materials. These must be appropriately designed for the intended target groups.

The museum should as a matter of course evaluate the success of a particular activity in a written report or case study, and where possible or relevant record the activity visually.

These reports will also ensure continuity of understanding and expertise within the museum. The body of information thus built up can be a powerful method of demonstrating success to others such as governing bodies, funding organisations, press and media contacts. It can serve as an important component in a case-for-support to develop your programmes further.

STUDY EXAMPLE

A museum organised six temporary exhibitions each year. For each of these exhibitions, it targeted a special user group and developed a programme of events and activities for the group. The programme was carried out in conjunction with a variety of different organisations and individuals. In particular, a balance between sciences and arts activities was sought. Each of the programmes was recorded with a mixture of colour slide and audio-recording to produce tape-slide programmes, and video-tape.

For each, the museum drew up a detailed report to a standard format analysing the resources which had been required, staff-time, costs and practical successes and difficulties encountered. The reports and the visual records were developed over a five-year period to demonstrate to the museum's governing committee and funding bodies the work that the museum was carrying out to attract new audiences.

In this way, additional resources were made available to the museum to further the museum's marketing programme and to sustain the events and activities programme. Later the reports were published as a text book helping other museums learn from this museum's experience.

KEY WORD

CARER – children are looked after by many different people – parents, relatives, child-minders, friends. In many cases children are looked after by 'carers' when their parents are at work. The term 'carer' is used here to encompass all these.

Temporary exhibitions

The value of temporary exhibitions for a museum is that they provide change and variety, and can focus on collections or topics not otherwise presented in the museum's displays. They may on the other hand allow the museum to extend coverage of a topic or subject which has only limited coverage in displays.

The value of a touring exhibition hired in to the museum is that it provides a ready-made temporary exhibition and thus can save time on the part of curatorial and design staff. It may be designed to a higher standard than is possible in-house and help to influence standards for the future. It may be based on collections/information which the receiving museum may not otherwise be able to provide for its users. A touring exhibition may complement existing collections or provide new material to extend the museum's services. Touring exhibitions may however be expensive and every care should be taken to ensure an accurate understanding of the full cost implications.

If museums are to develop programmes of temporary exhibitions, there are a number of issues of policy and practice which should be borne in mind (see Units 24–9). The following checklist provides some points to note:

☐ *Policy*
– how do temporary exhibitions relate to the museum's overall policy objectives?
– how do temporary exhibitions relate to the museum's policies for communications, and education?
– what type of temporary exhibitions will the museum make available? will they include a percentage of touring exhibitions hired in? will they include some exhibitions designed to tour to other museums?

- will external organisations such as community groups be allowed to develop temporary exhibitions within the museum?
- what controls over standards or quality will the museum wish to exercise?
- what sort of temporary exhibition policy should be established?

☐ *Ideas and planning*
- what themes or topics should be explored?
- how are these determined? through market research?
- what curatorial objectives does the museum have in developing temporary exhibition programmes?
- what resources will need to be made available – time, money, space, equipment?

☐ *Development*
- are collections available for the chosen theme of the exhibition? Is additional collecting/borrowing required?
- is additional research needed?
- what is the timetabling requirement?
- who will prepare the storyline or select objects?
- what additional information/graphics are needed?
- who will draw up the brief?
- who will design the exhibition?

☐ *Collections care*
- what are the conservation constraints on the material to be exhibited?
- what are the security constraints?
- what type of display equipment should be used?
- what are the packing and transport requirements of a touring exhibition hired into the museum or an exhibition to be toured by the museum?

☐ *Administration*
- what are the administrative requirements for exhibitions which the museum has developed for touring or which are hired in to the museum?
- what hire fees will the museum charge for touring exhibitions?
- will there be an admission charge for special temporary exhibitions?
- what are the conditions imposed by the museum on exhibitions originated for touring – security, preventive conservation, promotion, acknowledgements?
- what are the delivery/collection arrangements for touring exhibitions?
- whose responsibility is it to erect/dismantle a temporary or touring exhibition?

— are there possibilities for collaboration in the production, administration and marketing of exhibitions?

These questions are not designed to be comprehensive but they do give
an indication of the sort of questions which the museum will need to
be aware of in developing temporary exhibition programmes.

KEY WORD

OUTREACH – the method by which a museum can take services out into the
community which it serves through, for example, touring exhibitions, schools
loan services, events and activities programmes. It reflects the opportunities
for museums to reach wider audiences outside the walls of the museum
building(s).

UNIT 13   FACILITIES FOR VISITORS

Related Units: 14–16

The overall package of facilities and services which you provide for
visitors to your museum will in large part determine the success of the
museum. Visitors should be made to feel welcome and comfortable,
and encouraged throughout a visit to return again or recommend the
museum to others.

The MUSEUM MANAGER and the museum's staff should ensure
that the success of a visit is not damaged by poor support facilities or
services. Even the smallest museum with very limited resources can
make visitors feel very welcome and provide basic visitor facilities. At
the very least museum staff can give guidance to visitors as to where
car-parks, bus stops, refreshments, toilets are located if the museum
itself has none of its own.

The checklist and questions below give an indication of basic facilities
which museums should consider providing.

☐ *Seating* – Is there somewhere for your visitors to sit down? Are they
able to sit down in the display/exhibition areas? Is there a special rest
area? Is it furnished appropriately with comfortable chairs, tables for
reading matter, etc.? How can it support the museum's educational
objectives through information provision? Is it kept tidy and clean? Is
it clearly marked a no-smoking area?

☐ *Coats/hats/umbrellas* – Is there somewhere for visitors to leave their coats, hats or umbrellas? Is the area safe and secure? Can it be effectively staffed? Is it an appropriate size?

☐ *Toilets* – Does the museum have visitors' toilets? Are they kept appropriately supplied, and clean and tidy on a regular basis? Are they equipped effectively for disabled visitors? Are they properly sign-posted?

☐ *Information points* – Does the museum provide an information point or desk where visitors can obtain information about the museum, its collections and services? Are staff trained to handle enquiries? Are they able to use languages familiar to the main groups of the museum's users? (See Unit 30.)

☐ *Shops/sales areas* – Is there a shop or a sales area in the museum selling souvenirs, education material, publications, etc? (See Unit 14.)

☐ *Food/drink* – Does the museum provide refreshments for visitors? Is the area kept clean and tidy on a regular basis? Are visitors allowed to smoke in the area or not? (See Unit 15.)

☐ *Special needs* – Does the museum make sufficient provision for visitors with special needs, such as visitors with disabilities (see Unit 7), children, family groups with young babies, school groups, etc.

☐ *Voluntary support* – Can visitors who are interested in the work of the museum offer to support its work through volunteer help? Are they encouraged to do so in the museum?

☐ *Admission charges and times* – Are the opening hours of the museum convenient for visitors? Are the admission charges sensitively set to different groups of visitors? Does the museum provide special discounts?

☐ *Other facilities* – Depending on the size of your museum you may wish to develop further facilities. In particular, there may be opportunities for special study facilities available to particular groups. A number of museums make their library available to the public, and others include special study rooms for students incorporating a range of equipment such as micro-fiche readers, interactive video disc and study collections. Special education centres with classrooms or lecture theatres may be used for a wide range of audiences.

External areas of the museum, such as gardens or parks, can also be used for a wide range of events and activities, and special facilities such as tents or marquees, or demonstration units, can be erected to cater for visitors. Special provision may need to be made for volunteers or Friends' groups, or corporate supporters.

All of these topics and questions are not meant to be exhaustive. They are cited to act as triggers for museum managers to analyse the range of visitor facilities and services supplied at present, and to question whether these can be extended or improved. In a number of cases we explore them in greater depth in other units in this book.

However, museum managers should put themselves in the place of their visitors, and ask themselves (as well as their visitors!) whether the museum visit *as a whole* can be made more enjoyable. Try visiting your own museum perhaps with some friends or members of your family to experience what the visitor experiences. A first-class experience for the visitor will encourage repeat visits, and good word-of-mouth publicity encouraging others to visit – a poor experience can damage the museum's reputation and standing.

Finding out about your visitor's needs is an important part of market research (see Unit 6). Caring for visitors, looking after their needs and wants through the provision of good quality visitor facilities and services, is one of the principal responsibilities all museums have.

STUDY EXAMPLE

Over a period of two years, a museum carried out a detailed survey of its visitors to examine visitor facility needs. The survey showed visitors wanted better facilities, above all for disabled and infirm people. As a result, it was able to implement a development programme which included the building of a new visitor reception centre providing a range of facilities designed to accommodate visitors of all types, including those with special needs. A new reception centre was constructed because it would have been too expensive to adapt existing facilities effectively to serve disabled people.

Funding for the centre was derived in part from a number of organisations with special responsibility for disabled groups. The centre allowed the museum to market itself more widely and as a consequence, the museum saw its visitor numbers increase substantially.

It had put the care of its visitors first and reaped the benefits.

UNIT 14   PROVIDING SERVICES: SHOPS

Related Units: 13, 15, 16

Shops and sales areas play an important role in museums of all sizes (although in some countries there are still, surprisingly, legal restrictions on selling in museums). They provide opportunities for visitors to take home a souvenir of their visit, help to provide more information about the collections, serve as a point of personal contact with staff and of course generate income for the museum. They therefore have an important public relations and educational role to play for the museum.

Location and layout

The location of the shop or sales area also needs to be carefully considered. Most museums site their shops at the exit/entrance, for the simple reason that most people tend to buy goods at the end of their visit. For small museums, the advantage of siting the shop at the museum's entrance/exit, where these are at the same point, is that staff can service both incoming and outgoing visitors.

The design and layout of a shop or sales point need careful consideration. Is the approach to be self-service or over the counter? Self-service, where customers can pick up and handle goods in advance of purchase normally generates more sales than traditional over-the-counter shopping. Whatever method is chosen, the sales area needs to present its goods in an attractive and organised way, clearly labelled and priced. The layout and presentation needs to encourage people to buy, but also needs to ensure security against theft. High value items need special protection, perhaps behind glass or beyond reach.

Stock

Decisions on what stock to obtain for resale should be taken in the context of a clearly defined purchasing policy. The museum manager should determine what the purpose of the shop is, and what range of stock can best serve that purpose. Museum shops should stock material which is well-designed and of good quality. They should provide value for money, and relate in a general or a specific way to the collections. Historic artefacts of course should never be sold! Material can be bought in ready-made from wholesalers or specially produced for the museum. It can be customised with the name of the museum, or it can be accompanied with information about the item/collection it reflects. It is well worth having packaging printed with the museum's name. In public relations terms, items bought from a museum shop should continue to promote the museum long after the purchase.

In selecting items for resale, it is also important to identify and guard against possible competition from other sales outlets. A museum is well placed to develop items for resale which are not available in other shops.

Income and expenditure

The museum shop must make profits, and therefore pricing policy is important. So too is the buying policy – the shop's investment in stock for resale, although the unit cost of items for resale can be reduced through bulk ordering such as postcards. The museum must be sure that it is not tying up hard-earned capital in stock which is slow to sell and which can progressively go out of date or fashion. It is worthwhile looking at the prices of goods in other shops with which to compare your museum's prices.

Museums may wish to license other organisations to produce sales items based on their collections. In this way the museum itself may not have any production or purchase costs to meet, but can simply earn a percentage of the profits made by the licensee. The museum may itself take some of the licensed items for sale through its shop. This approach can mean that an item based on the museum's collections such as a print or a replica is sold far more widely, perhaps internationally, than would otherwise be the case through the museum's own shop. Merchandising collections in this way can be a powerful way of generating income. Care needs to be taken in the contractual arrangements between the museum and licensee and professional legal advice should be sought. Reference should be made to the ICOM Code of Ethics (paragraph 2.10) on the issue of licensing.

Stock should be considered as an asset, and looked after appropriately. Storage of items for resale should be clean, tidy and secure.

The MUSEUM MANAGER should ensure that a regular audit is carried out. Cash receipts from the shop should be scrupulously recorded and banked on a regular basis.

Careful attention should be paid to each 'line' or category of item stocked to find out the pattern of sale. The person responsible for managing the shop, and purchasing stock, should provide regular reports on its sales performance to the museum manager.

Customer care

Museum shops are an important point of personal contact with visitors. Friendly and courteous service is essential, and staff working in the shop should be effectively trained in their duties. The museum may also wish to consider training shop staff in the languages of their main visitors. Customers should be made to feel welcome, encouraged to buy items and thanked for their patronage. Wherever possible, museum shops should be accessible independently of a visit to the museum, and customers encouraged to shop on a regular basis rather than only on a visit to the museum.

STUDY EXAMPLE

Bulk purchase of items for resale in a consortium of museum shops was developed by a museums cooperative forum. Unit costs on a range of items were reduced, and the museum shops were able to stock a wider range of items than they would have been able to do individually. One museum took a lead role in coordinating the administration of the project for a small handling fee. The forum later entered into a range of merchandising projects, and established a joint trading company to run and develop a purchasing programme. Later still, the company began a mail order catalogue and distributed the museums' shop goods very widely.

By working together museums were able to extend the range of services available to users and to generate profits from cooperative activity.

UNIT 15   PROVIDING SERVICES: FOOD AND DRINK

The type and scale of provision for selling food and drink to visitors varies widely in museums. At one end of the spectrum is a refreshing drink with tables and chairs provided. At the other end of the spectrum is a meal in a restaurant with waiter service. The spectrum is a wide one. Whatever your resources allow, visitors are likely to find some provision for food and drink in a museum welcome. A hot or cold drink can often encourage a longer, and more relaxed and pleasurable, visit.

Apart from improving the quality and extent of customer service, food and drink in the museum, as with shops, can generate useful additional income. Catering services should therefore be designed to make a profit. As with shops, visitors should be encouraged to use catering facilities through good quality design and layout, and sensible location. Food and drink areas should be well serviced and regularly cleaned.

Theming

Significant opportunities exist for making food and drink areas interesting places to visit by theming. There are all kinds of ways to create a special feel or theme for the catering facility, which relates to the museum's collections and services. Examples include 'period theming', where a particular historical period is evoked by decoration, layout and design of menus, foodstuffs or even staff dress; theming through special decor and fittings, for instance transport or natural history; or theming by reference to particular collections or items in the collections.

Such an approach helps to create a distinctive image for your food and drink area and a talking point for customers. If, like your museum shop, there is an opportunity for the facility to be independently accessed by visitors this can be an additional, competitive advantage over other catering facilities.

Customer care

However simple or elaborate, catering facilities should be well designed throughout, emphasise cleanliness and hygiene and provide good value-for-money in the food and drink provided. Service should be courteous and users should feel valued. A good experience in a museum café or restaurant can make a great deal of difference to a visitor's enjoyment of their overall visit. A bad experience can ruin enjoyment, and can create poor word-of-mouth publicity.

In most countries there are legal and licensing restrictions and requirements on catering. Compliance with statutory and religious requirements is essential. The MUSEUM MANAGER must ensure that the museum is operating within the law at all times. In particular, laws relating to health and hygiene must be scrupulously observed.

Food and drink can be provided by the museum's own staff or through franchise, licensing or perhaps through a trading partnership. It is essential that legal advice is sought if a franchise, or licensing arrangement or trading partnership is entered into.

Careful records need to be kept of income and expenditure, and supplies need to be kept in clean, secure and appropriate storage, such as refrigeration. Supplies should be subject to regular inspection and stocktaking by museum management.

Food and drink in the museum may be required for special occasions like receptions, exhibition previews, evening entertainment or corporate hospitality events. A catering service may be well placed to provide for such special occasions.

Cafés, restaurants or coffee points all present good opportunities for providing information about the museum, its collections, services, events and activities programmes to visitors. Tables can carry information cards about events programmes in the coming weeks. Slide projectors can provide illustrations of items in the collections with checklists supplied on tables. Information about the museum can be provided on place mats or on the reverse side of a menu card. Copies of exhibition posters for sale in the museum shop may be displayed on the walls of the food and drink area. It may be possible to display appropriate collections in this area too, provided that conservation and security standards can be met effectively.

A little imagination and a flair for providing an enjoyable and different experience can provide added value to the museum visit.

STUDY EXAMPLE

A museum in a capital city with extensive social history collections piloted a series of themed dinners in the museum restaurant for tourist visitors, linked to special tours with a member of the curatorial staff. Costings were carefully evaluated, and the programme was monitored and assessed in detail.

The dinners were organised in conjunction with a local hotel who used the programme as a training exercise for kitchen staff under supervision of the hotel's head chef. The dinners and tours programmes were so successful that the museum established the programme as a regular event during the tourist season.

The immediate benefits were substantially increased profits for the museum's café/ restaurant, additional training for the museum's own catering staff and increased donations from visitors attending the events. The museum developed a range of new expertise. Visitors were able to experience a range of regional recipes and foods, relating to the collections on view.

The series of dinners provided a different experience for visitors and it was reported on in a number of travel trade publications which resulted in increased attendances from overseas visitors.

UNIT 16   IMPROVING FACILITIES FOR USERS

Related Units: 13–15

Many museums are able to make their facilities available to outside organisations in order to generate additional income, and to attract potential new audiences. Much depends on what range of facilities your museum can provide. Display areas or lecture theatres/rooms may be booked for a variety of events ranging from education to entertainment – awards ceremonies, dance performances, conferences and seminars, lectures, meetings and gatherings, theatrical presentations, musical performances, craft fairs, corporate entertainment and many others. There are however a number of ethical and practical issues to be borne in mind, which we discuss below.

Areas outside the museum in the ownership or control of the museum – gardens, parks, archaeological sites, car-parks – might also be used by external groups for historical re-enactments, fairs, craft demonstrations, transport rallies and the like.

There is a wide range of opportunity to use museum facilities in accordance with a clearly defined policy to the museum's advantage. Such activities however should be relevant to the museum's mission and its educational objectives, and also be relevant to the museum's collections.

Every care should be taken to ensure that the museum's facilities are not hired by inappropriate or unacceptable organisations and that the museum's integrity is not in any way discredited. It is helpful to define the type of organisations deemed to be appropriate and acceptable in your policy and why, how and when they may use the museum's facilities so that staff can take effective executive decisions.

Policy and planning

You should consider the following points:

■ The museum may be competing with other organisations in providing facilities for hire, and there may be implications for external relations which have to be taken into account.

■ The purpose for which the facilities are to be used should be acceptable to the museum's management and not put the museum's collections at any risk. Conservation, fire prevention and internal and external security requirements should be observed at all times – no smoking, no food and drink in display/exhibition spaces and adequate ventilation. Security staff should be fully briefed on the security implications of facilities use and the nature and size of each group using the facilities.

■ The organisation(s) to which the facilities are being provided should be trustworthy and their bona fides established.

■ The full cost implications should be understood. These cover additional security or staffing requirements and costs, insurance cover, depreciation costs or general wear and tear and energy costs. Unless the museum's policy allows for certain organisations to be subsidised, museum managers should ensure that the museum does not suffer any financial loss.

■ The museum should have adequate support facilities such as cloakrooms, lavatories, car-parking, to cater for groups using the museum's facilities.

■ A clearly written contract or conditions agreement encompassing the museum's requirements should be drawn up and signed by all relevant parties; a deposit should be required.

■ An acceptable form of acknowledgement to the museum should be agreed for publicity material/invitations.

■ Any special legal requirements should be fully met such as licensing laws, health and hygiene laws for catering or laws relating to the reproduction of recorded music.

■ An internal booking system for those organisations hiring the museum's facilities should be established with staff designated to be responsible for agreed procedures.

The museum's staff should be aware of all the implications of facilities use by external organisations, and understand their practical needs. For example, if an organisation has booked a display area for an evening of musical performance and illustrated talks related to the museum's collections, how much time before the audience arrives will caterers require to organise their catering arrangements, or musicians require to arrange audio systems? Will this mean additional security arrangements or the display space being out of public use for the afternoon? In drawing up a contract form, a checklist of questions like these will help to ensure that arrangements work smoothly for all concerned.

☐ *Conditions* – Here are some conditions of hiring facilities to outside organisations which need to be considered in drawing up a contract form or conditions of hire:

- Provisional bookings – how long will you allow a provisional booking to be kept open before the facility is relet for that date?
- Deposit – if you charge a deposit when the booking is confirmed, what percentage of the booking fee will the deposit represent?
- Cancellations – a sliding scale of charges for cancellations may be appropriate. If cancellation is made less than two weeks before the agreed date, then the full booking fee is charged. If you are providing additional sub-contractors such as caterers, tent erectors, extra security staff, there may need to be additional charges to cover their costs too.
- Damage to museum property – what level of charge will be made to the organisation hiring the facility if damage occurs?
- Liability – will the museum be able to disclaim liability if personal possessions are lost or damaged?
- Responsibilities – who will be responsible for insurance, meeting legal requirements, clean-up and removal procedures, health and safety requirements, security arrangements, catering?
- Final details/numbers – when is the last date by which the hirer must provide final details of arrangements and numbers of those attending the event?

☐ *Standards* – Where the museum is hiring facilities for use by outside organisations, it is important to ensure that the standard of care for these organisations is of the highest. Their audiences or members will be visiting your museum, and while they may be coming to the museum to take part in another organisation's event, the quality of customer care and the standard of facilities which you provide is important for the museum's reputation and the future successful marketing of your facilities.

Having organised groups visit the museum for whatever reason always provides opportunities to promote the museum and its services, and encourage people to return to the museum on other occasions. Working with the organisation hiring your facilities to ensure a successful event is important. After all both parties have much to gain from success. Ensuring that each other's responsibilities are clearly defined, agreed and understood is the key to that success.

STUDY EXAMPLE

A museum had regularly hired its small lecture room to a local archaeological society for its meetings for a number of years at nominal hire charge.

The museum management wished to increase income from the use of its facilities and began a marketing campaign designed to promote its facilities to a wide range of organisations in the not-for-profit and for-profit sectors. In consequence the archaeological society found that the hire charge for the lecture room had increased considerably and that the availability of the room was reduced.

The society therefore decided to hold its meetings at another venue, and the relationship with the museum – important in terms of its mission – was weakened.

The museum might have established a sliding scale of charges to allow for priority relationships with external organisations to be maintained, rather than impose a single charge.

UNIT 17   INTRODUCING INTERPRETATION

Related Units: 18–29

What is 'interpretation'?

'Interpretation' usually means translating from one language to another. In the museum world, though, it has a special meaning: *explaining* an object and its significance. Almost everyone in the world, if shown a knife, will know roughly what it is meant to do; it is meant to cut. But if shown – say – a Tibetan prayer wheel, probably most people will not have any idea what it is, and fewer still outside Tibet will know *why* it is used or *how* it is used. To be fully understood and appreciated it needs to be *interpreted* or explained.

Museums interpret things all the time. Almost every time you put an object on display, or simply take it out of its storage box and show it to a visitor, you are interpreting it. However, interpretation can be done in a huge number of different ways, some more complicated or more sophisticated than others. It is worth spending a little time thinking about the different ways museums interpret the objects in their collections, and considering which are the best techniques for interpreting different things to different people.

Interpretation, too, is not limited to museums. Indeed, the use of the term in this sense originated in North America among people responsible for the care of the National Parks and of historic sites. Many museum managers, of course, are responsible for caring for ancient sites and buildings, and for interpreting landscapes. The approach is the same, whether one is interpreting a plough, or the landscape the plough created. Interpretation may not only explain an object and its significance, it may also provide a conservation message about the object and its context.

Identifying the audience

To interpret something, you have to have someone to interpret it *to*. That person will of course come with his or her own interests, assumptions, beliefs, knowledge and curiosity. Every individual is distinct, and good interpreters, like good schoolteachers, adapt their technique to the people they are talking to.

The audience for museums comes with particular goals. These may include:

− filling up time
− sheltering from bad weather
− seeking inspiration
− idle curiosity
− eager desire to acquire knowledge
− to educate children
− to be in the fashion
− to spend time with family or friends

It has been suggested that interpretation can fail because the interpreter's goals do not match the audience's goals; when, for example, the audience's curiosity and commitment to learning are either seriously over-estimated or seriously under-estimated.

The museum needs, therefore, to tailor its technique to the audience's

− education level,
− goals and
− intelligence.

In reality it is impossible to please everyone at once, so before planning a piece of interpretation, the museum needs to decide who its *target audience* is to be. For example, the target audience for a lecture on Greek statues could be:

− young children
− specialist art historians
− sculptors
− visitors from a foreign country

The lecture would in each case be very different. So it is with other types of interpretation: the interpreter (in our case the museum) must be clear who is being addressed.

Deciding the aims

The next step for the museum must be to decide what the interpretation is aiming to achieve. Is it, for example, to introduce foreign visitors to Greek statuary, with enough information to enable them to enjoy it? Is it to summarise the latest research? Is it to awaken the sense of wonder, or to point out historic carving techniques?

The more precisely the museum can define the aim of the interpretation, the more successful it will be.

How to choose the right technique

Having decided *what* to say, and *whom* to address, the museum must decide what *techniques* to use. If you want to tell the story of farming in your particular region, is it better to create a display, publish a book, make a film or arrange lectures? If you decide a display is best, what sort of display should it be? There is a huge number and variety of techniques available, some of them more suited to some audiences, some more suited to some subjects (see Units 18 21). New techniques are being invented all the time: video-discs, for example, are still very new, but are proving an invaluable additional technique within traditional museum displays.

There is no magic way of choosing techniques. Factors to be considered include:

■ Cost. In some countries electronic equipment will be formidably expensive, in others it may be cheaper than employing people.

■ Climate. Techniques suitable for interpreting an archaeological site in the Tropics are very likely not going to be suitable in the Arctic!

■ Conservation. It is vital to consider the impact that any technique might have on the objects or site being interpreted. Sound and Light, for example, might require dangerously high levels of light (see Unit 47).

■ Custom. People learn most easily when they are relaxed. To use techniques that make people feel uncomfortable is clearly foolish. For example, computer-based techniques might not be suitable where computers are not familiar; live interpreters might be unsuitable where it is not customary to speak to strangers.

■ Participation. Does the technique involve the audience? Does it encourage them to participate? We all learn more readily when we are

BOX 1

The 'Communication Policy'

Some museums find it helpful to adopt and publish a formal policy document, which outlines their approach to interpretation. This is often called a 'Communication Policy' because it covers all the ways in which the museum communicates with its visitors. The best-known example is probably *Communicating with the Museum Visitor: Guidelines for Planning* of the Royal Ontario Museum. This is a big book, intended to make sure that the departments of the museum achieve a consistently high standard in their communication with the visitor. It sets out the principles behind interpretation in the museum, but also goes into great detail, for example in prescribing styles of lettering, setting out procedures for commissioning audio-visual productions or laying down rules for light levels in displays.

BOX 2

Interpretation techniques

What techniques does your museum use?

Underline the interpretation techniques (*media*, they are sometimes called) used in your museum. Would your visitors enjoy the displays more, or learn more, if you used a wider variety of techniques, or do you think that these are the most appropriate ones for your visitors?

Interpretation techniques

static	*dynamic*
objects	sound-guides
models	lectures
drawings	film/video/slide-tape
photographs	working models
dioramas	live interpreters
tableaux	computer-based displays
information	interactive video-discs
sheets	objects for handling
guidebooks	drama

actively involved in *doing* something than when we are simply looking or listening. Good teachers do not just lecture: they encourage their students to participate in learning projects. The good museum tries to do the same.

KEY WORD

DISPLAY – the term 'display' is used throughout this book to cover all forms of presentation in museums. We have used the term 'exhibition' or 'temporary exhibition' to cover short-term presentations.

UNIT 18   PRESENTATION TECHNIQUES: GRAPHICS

Related Units: 17, 19–23

Graphics can be simply defined as words and pictures. Every museum uses such presentation methods perhaps in temporary exhibitions or together with displays of objects. The more carefully their design is planned, the more effective they will be.

One person (probably the curator) should be responsible for coordinating the content of the display/exhibition, and one person (ideally a qualified designer) should be responsible for its design. It is essential for them to work very closely together.

A temporary exhibition, for example based solely on graphics might consist of a series of display panels, either fixed to the wall or fixed to screens standing on the floor. The first thing to decide, therefore, must be how many display panels will be needed.

Each panel may well be devoted to one section of the exhibition, and will consist of a sub-heading, some written text and one or more pictures (photographs or drawings).

The screens

Museums often need to use screens standing on the floor to increase their wall-space – sometimes they can be used together with showcases to create flexible display systems. Such screens can be bought commercially, or they can be made out of plywood or blockboard. They can be painted, or covered with cloth. Choose a cloth or colour appropriate to the exhibition; for example, an exhibition of local history might use a cloth of traditional local design to cover the screens. The screens will need some sort of feet to make them stand up, or they can be joined together and so support each other. To join them together you can buy special clamps, or a local blacksmith can make hooks and rings.

The panels

The designer needs to have all the pictures and text that the curator wants to have included. He or she can then design the layout of each panel in the form of a simple scale drawing, showing where the headings, text, photographs, drawings, diagrams and captions will go, and how large each will need to be. Screw or glue the panels, which can be made out of cardboard or softboard, onto the screens. It is important to choose an appropriate colour.

In the following pages we discuss some of the techniques for making panels, and some of the things – headings, pictures and text – that can go on them.

Photographs are used in museum displays for a variety of different purposes. These include creating a mood, illustrating the present appearance of an archaeological site, illustrating comparable objects, bringing into the story buildings or big objects which could not themselves fit into a gallery, enlarging very small objects, illustrating the artist who painted pictures and so on. Museums should avoid the temptation to use too many photos, and they should only be included if they serve a real purpose in the interpretation.

Sign painting is another technique for making effective panels. Some countries still have highly-skilled traditional *sign-painters*. Using painted signs in the museum gives it a special character and helps preserve a traditional craft. It is also often the cheapest way!

Enlarged photographs are one of the commonest and best ways of preparing information panels in museums. In this case the panels consist of one large photograph, incorporating heading, text and pictures, which can then be dry-mounted onto a plywood panel.

Silkscreening is one of the best ways of preparing information panels. It is attractive and long-lasting, and can be used for both text and pictures and for a wide variety of designs. It is usually expensive if done commercially, and time-consuming if done in the museum. Sometimes it is possible to get silkscreening carried out by a local school or college.

Dry-transfer lettering ('Letraset' or a similar product) is often used in small museums for short labels; it allows even beginners to achieve professional-looking results. But it is quite expensive.

Alternative approaches include *stencilling* or *cut-out letters* which can be obtained through commercial suppliers. Cut-out letters are made from cork or plastic, and can be glued or pinned to display boards.

If you can really not afford any of these methods of preparing text for display, then write or type your information as clearly as possible on the best paper you can find, and fix it neatly to the display panel.

UNIT 19   PRESENTATION TECHNIQUES: THREE-DIMENSIONAL

Related Units: 17, 18, 20–3

Museums use many different techniques to present their collections to visitors and to tell their stories, some of them simple, some of them very sophisticated. The next units show a few of the techniques used in museums today. Here we examine some of the three-dimensional techniques.

Everyone likes to be able to touch as well as look at objects. Touching is an important way in which we experience things. For those with poor or no eyesight it is of course essential. Wherever possible, therefore, museums should try to allow visitors to touch exhibits, though in very many cases this will for conservation reasons not be possible. The museum may however wish to consider creating good quality replicas for such purposes. Replicas, if used, should be well made, but be marked clearly to show that they are replicas.

Room settings may – in an historic building – be genuine original arrangements, or they may be modern reconstructions based on the best available evidence. The room setting is an effective way not only of presenting furniture or pictures in the settings for which they were originally created, but of making historical points. For example the living-space of poor people may be contrasted with that of rich people. Visitors can be allowed into the room, into part of it, or allowed only to look in.

A *tableau* is like a reconstructed room, but includes life-size models of people arranged in a scene from history. Tableaux include figures in costume and often furniture, decorations and even whole buildings.

Tableaux are used to show visitors how an historic building was used, to give a glimpse of life in past times or distant lands and to portray famous historic events. In museums they can be used very effectively together with more conventional displays; one or two figures, carefully chosen to make an important point, can help greatly in a museum's interpretation scheme. Outside museums, tableaux have been used for centuries in 'waxworks' shows and are now being used, together with 'people-movers' (see below) and audio-visual effects, in so-called 'heritage centres'.

People-movers are small cars or other vehicles in which visitors ride through displays – usually through or past a series of tableaux. They enable the museum closely to control the number of visitors and what they see. People-movers are derived from fairground rides, and have been used in exhibitions for at least a hundred years. Recently, with improved technology, they have been used increasingly in 'heritage centres'. The idea of people-movers can of course be adapted to local situations. A ride in a horse and cart through the streets of an open-air museum is also a people-mover!

A *diorama* is partly a picture and partly a model. Usually there are model people or animals or landscape in the foreground, while the background is a painting; the skill of the diorama-maker comes in merging the two together in a lifelike way. Like tableaux, the diorama, too, is a technique used in museums for well over a century. Dioramas are especially effective in natural history and geology museums, used to show the habitat in which animals live or the conditions under which different rocks were created. Full-sized dioramas are also used to portray domestic life in the past or in other societies, while small-scale ones portray famous battles or archaeological sites.

Models are very widely used in museums and can be invaluable aids to interpretation. Everyone finds models fascinating, and they are much easier to understand than maps. They are especially useful in showing the development of archaeological sites or historic buildings, but they are also used to interpret historic boats, modern machinery, dinosaurs, railway engines and cars, military uniforms – in fact almost anything!

Dioramas and models need to be well made and on an appropriate scale relative to the visitor, to be successful. Museums should explain the basis of evidence on which they are presented.

UNIT 20   PRESENTATION TECHNIQUES: AUDIO-VISUAL/INTERACTIVE

Related Units: 17–19, 21–3

Audio-visual techniques are very common in museums. Too often, though, museums install them without thinking hard enough about why they are using them. Even in highly-developed countries audio-visual techniques are often expensive to install and time-consuming to run. They can help the visitor to understand the museum, but the museum must be clear why it is using them and be sure that it can maintain them. Some of the most popular techniques are described here.

Also described are some of the simpler *interactive* techniques that can be used in museums. People learn best when they are *involved* in some way, not just passively looking or listening.

Slide-tape programmes have been used in museums for many years to help interpret the displays. Often they are used as an introduction, to orient the visitor before seeing the displays themselves. The simplest arrangement uses just one projector, a tape-player and a speaker, but big displays have used hundreds of projectors coordinated by highly sophisticated programmes. For a small museum, the rule must be to use equipment that can be easily maintained by the staff. There is nothing more depressing for visitors than a blank screen with a notice 'out of order'. Ensure that one member of staff is responsible for maintenance or maintenance contracts.

Video is rapidly replacing slide-tape in museums. It is much more reliable, and tapes relevant to the museum are becoming more widely available. However, programme production *must* be done well to be acceptable, and normally that means employing a professional, which is always very expensive. You may wish to consider working in collaboration with local tourist organisations or television companies to produce videos.

There is a variety of *audio systems* available which give a spoken commentary on the displays through headphones borrowed by the visitor at the museum entrance. This is a very effective method of interpretation, incorporating many of the advantages of a live guide, but is both cheaper and can be switched off! Small museums should, however, look carefully at the costs involved, which include the rent or purchase of the equipment, the cost of making a programme and the

75

administration. These must be weighed against the number of people likely to use the system.

Tape recordings can be used in all sorts of ways in the museum. There are three main techniques: a loudspeaker which is switched on by the visitor, a loudspeaker which repeats a continuous-loop tape endlessly and a set of telephones through which the visitor can listen to the tape. The tape can include sound effects and 'oral history' material as well as a spoken commentary. Potential problems include technical difficulties (a non-working telephone gives a very bad impression), and sound spilling into neighbouring galleries.

'Pepper's Ghost' is a simple technique which, by setting two pictures or models at right angles divided by a glass screen, allows the visitor to see one merge into the other simply by switching the light from one to the other. It is an excellent technique for comparing (for example) a model of an ancient site as it is with one as it was, or comparing an archaeological object with a reproduction of its original form.

The development of *computer systems* that can also involve sound and video is creating a whole new medium of interactive displays in museums. So far these systems have been mostly used to provide information about the exhibits – information that increasingly includes moving pictures and sound as well as still pictures and text. The most exciting developments are those that give the visitor choices. For example those that apply computer game techniques to historical situations. The opportunities for museum use of these new techniques are enormous – though at present they are still very expensive.

A *'talking head'* is a costume-model onto the blank face of which a video film of someone talking is projected. The aim is to make it look as much as possible like a real person talking. The technique is often used to enable a historic person to introduce a museum or exhibition or historic site to the public. Costume-figure, sound and video all have to be designed extremely well if it is not to seem absurd!

'Animatronics' is the name given to techniques which make models actually move. Used for years in toys and fun fairs, these techniques are becoming more sophisticated and are being used in museums. An example is a recent exhibition of full-size model dinosaurs which move their heads and necks in a life-like way and roar at the visitor! In this example a great deal of careful research went into the design of their movements and sound.

Simple interactive techniques are often the best. In everyday life we are interacting all the time with other people, and the more natural the museum can be the more effective it will be. Teachers know that asking questions is one of the most useful ways of arousing interest. It is possible to design very simple displays that ask the visitor questions. One method is to show objects in a showcase, and invite the visitor to answer questions about them. The visitor has to lift a little flap to uncover the correct answer. Many science centres have developed very effective and inexpensive interactive techniques. The only limit to the number of simple interactive devices possible in a museum is the imagination of curator or designer.

UNIT 21   PRESENTATION TECHNIQUES: USING PEOPLE

Related Units: 17–20, 22, 23

A person talking is the oldest, most natural and most common presentation technique of all. It can also be the best, but only when the person involved is really well-informed, skilled at the technique he or she is using and in sympathy with the audience. Using people needs as careful planning as using any other technique.

The *guided tour* is the oldest of all interpretation techniques, and – except in the hands of a very skilful guide – probably the least successful. The guide requires a natural flair and enthusiasm for the job, considerable experience of talking to parties of people of different ages, backgrounds and interests, and a really good knowledge of the subjects being studied. A good guide can be inspiring: a poor one can quickly extinguish any spark of interest! North American museums are particularly good at training volunteers to become 'docents': museum guides. Training guides effectively is a key responsibility of the museum.

The most interesting people are those who not only talk well, but who really know what they are talking about. Some museums – especially those concerned with recent history – encourage *local people* to come to the museum and talk about their own experiences. For example a gallery devoted to local agriculture will come alive in a new way if the visitor can meet a retired farm worker who will tell about his or her own experience. The museum should ensure that the material provided by the guide is historically accurate.

Talking to a group sitting down is very different to talking to a group walking around; usually it is much more successful. Arranging '*gallery talks*' on different subjects, perhaps at lunchtime so that local workers can attend, is an excellent way of serving people with a special interest, and of making use of curators' knowledge.

The formal *lecture* is still one of the principal ways in which a museum can present its collections and its knowledge. All but the smallest museums should have a room that can be used for lectures. A lecture programme can be an effective way of communicating with visitors (see Unit 12).

Many museums use *demonstrators* to bring their collections to life, sometimes in the museum gallery itself and sometimes outside or in a separate room. There is almost no limit to what can be demonstrated. How something was made and how it was used can very often be explained best by a demonstration. Craftspeople are often happy to work in a museum if they can then sell what they make to visitors. It is important, though, that they have the time and skill to talk to visitors and explain what they are doing.

The use of *actors* playing the part of historical characters has revolutionised visitors' perception of some museum galleries in recent years. Sometimes the actors involve visitors in acting out little scenes relevant to the displays around them, sometimes they merely greet the visitors and – speaking 'in character' as a historical person – explain the displays. The use of actors needs to be very carefully managed.

'Living History' or '*re-enactment*' is an increasingly popular hobby, especially in North America. People spend a great deal of their spare time dressing up in historic costume and re-enacting scenes from the past. American Civil War battles are very popular, but so are seventeenth-century settler life, pioneer farming or early fur-trading. Living History is an exciting and imaginative way for museums to bring history to life.

A more formal use of theatrical techniques in museums is when theatre companies put on small plays in the museum. This technique is (like Living History) increasingly used with school parties (see Unit 11).

UNIT 22   MUSEUM LIGHTING

Related Units: 17–19, 46, 47

Good lighting makes all the difference to a museum. How we see – and perceive and understand – an object is crucially affected by the character of the light falling on it.

Ideally every display would have lighting designed by a specialist lighting consultant. In practice this is rarely possible. But good lighting can transform an otherwise dull display, and to redesign the lighting and the labelling is often all that is needed to make an old-fashioned gallery seem renewed.

DAYLIGHT

Daylight, as a source of light for exhibits, has great advantages: it is free, it is natural and its changing qualities give the visitor a variety of impressions of the exhibits and a link with the outside world. On the other hand, daylight is difficult to control, and contains a high level of ultra violet radiation, again difficult to eliminate. It may therefore prove an expensive form of lighting. Further, its variability and its contrasts of light and shade may be a disadvantage in the museum, and may not correspond to the light for which the exhibits were originally designed. Greek marble for instance looks cold and flat in north European light.

Compromise is possible. For example, parts of a gallery can be lit by daylight, while the light falling on the exhibits themselves can be artificial.

The danger that daylight offers to the conservation of objects, however, requires that we control it carefully (see Unit 65).

TUNGSTEN LIGHT

The commonest form of lighting in many countries is the ordinary round tungsten light bulb or 'globe'. In addition there is a variety of different lamps designed specially for display purposes. Tungsten lighting has many advantages: it gives a warm light which can easily be adjusted, it emits little ultra-violet radiation, and it is very adaptable. Its chief disadvantages are that it gives out a lot of heat, and that its colour temperature (see Box) is difficult to control.

The first disadvantage has been met by the recent development of low-voltage lighting, which is also very cheap to run. This is a form of lighting which seems ideal for museums; unfortunately it is expensive to buy, and in many countries still difficult to obtain.

FLUORESCENT LIGHTING

Fluorescent lighting is cheap to run and efficient, readily obtainable everywhere, can give varied colour temperatures and gives out little heat. However, it cannot be dimmed, is available in very few lamps suitable for use in displays, may give poor colour rendering (see Box) and emits a high proportion of ultra-violet radiation. It is essential to exclude the ultra-violet element from fluorescent light (see Unit 65).

LIGHTING IN SHOWCASES

Too many showcases have bad lighting. Lighting should *never* be in the showcase itself, but always in a separate lightbox, which must be well-ventilated to prevent heat building up.

A new possibility, especially useful inside showcases, is the use of fibre optics. These give a precise beam of light without any heat.

IS IT EASY TO USE?

How easy will it be to maintain and use? This is the crucial question to ask when considering a museum lighting scheme. It may be beautiful, but if it requires fifty switches to be turned every morning and evening and no-one can reach the lamps to replace them, it is no good. Where will the switches be? Can the display lighting be turned off and the security and cleaning lighting be left on? Can all the lamps be reached so they can be replaced? Are replacements easily available, and can the museum afford to buy them? Do any showcases need to be opened in order to change lamps or adjust lighting? This should *never* be necessary.

CLEANING AND EMERGENCY LIGHTING

In many galleries it will be necessary to have two quite separate systems of lighting from the normal display lighting. The first is the cleaning lighting, needed to ensure that the cleaners can see what they are doing: often this is sets of fluorescent lights on the ceilings, not used when the museum is open to visitors. The second system is the battery-powered emergency lighting which comes on in the event of power-failure.

BOX

Colour temperature and colour rendering

Both the colour temperature of a light source (whether it looks cool or warm) and its colour rendering (whether it correctly reflects the true colours of an object) can be measured. Its colour temperature is measured in °K; one can say quite objectively that this lamp will distort colours, while that lamp will give no appreciable distortion.

With daylight and tungsten light there is no problem, since both give perfect colour rendering and the colour temperature cannot be altered. With fluorescent lamps, however, there are two choices to be made: fluorescent tubes are manufactured in a range of colour temperatures from cool (6500°K) through intermediate (4000°K) to warm (3000°K).

In the end the choice of colour temperature is a matter of taste. But remember that the eye adapts to its surroundings, so that in a gallery lit with a warm light a showcase lit with a cool light will look blue; the other way round and the showcase will look yellow. Objects should be presented in their true colours.

Having decided whether you want a warmer or a cooler light, you need to choose a fluorescent tube that both meets your needs *and* gives good colour rendering. The trouble is that manufacturers do not normally supply such information, so that it is necessary to seek advice from a specialist.

UNIT 23   MUSEUM SHOWCASES

Related Units: 17–19, 46–50, 57, 58

In most museums, showcases are the most important pieces of equipment, both in protecting objects and in presenting them to visitors. They have four functions:

— to protect the objects inside from theft and damage,
— to provide a micro-climate in which constant levels of relative humidity, temperature and controlled light can be maintained,
— to protect the objects inside from pollution, dust and insects,
— to provide a 'theatre stage' on which to exhibit and interpret objects.

The perfect showcase has still not been designed; museum designers say that designing showcases is often the most difficult job they are called on to do. Whether they are built by museum technicians or bought 'off the shelf', museum showcases are too often unsatisfactory. Often they are very expensive too!

The following is a checklist of standards that every museum showcase should meet.

Showcases must:

☐ keep out pollutants and dust with well-sealed joints and tightfitting doors.
Too often one sees dust inside museum showcases. The only way in which to be certain that the showcase is free of pollution and dust is to pressurise it slightly by pumping in filtered air so that any pollution or dust is pushed *out*. This technique is too expensive, though, for most small museums who must simply ensure that there are no gaps between the sides or at the top and that the door fits as tightly as possible.

☐ be stable, to prevent vibration.
Showcases often have very thin legs, for cheapness or lightness or looks. The heavier the showcase, and the more solid its base or legs, normally the better protected the objects inside will be from damage by vibration.

☐ be secure, with good locks.
The showcase is the museum's last line of defence against the thief. But most museum locks are either very easily picked, or very easily forced. See how quickly you can break into one of your showcases; a thief will be able to do it very much faster.

☐ be easily opened by curators.
If the showcase is difficult to open it will be vibrated in the process, and the curator may be tempted to leave it open 'just for a minute'.

☐ be made of materials which cannot damage objects.
Many of the materials which might be used in the construction of showcases give off gases which can harm objects. Some examples are given below.

− Polyvinyl chloride (PVC) is a risk to copper.
− Felt, wool, viscose, rubber-based adhesives and certain fabric dyes should not be used with silver.
− Lead, copper, paper, parchment and leather are all affected by materials releasing acetic acid, such as paints, lacquers and some woods and wood composites, for example cardboard, plywood, chipboard and blockboard.
− One-component silicone sealants, cellulose acetate and some poly-vinyl acetate adhesive may also present a similar risk.
− Formaldehyde is emitted by the wood and resin binders in many wood composites and some adhesives.

Not all museums will be able to avoid − or even to have tested − all these materials, but all should do their best to protect their objects from these risks (see Unit 50).

☐ help maintain constant relative humidity inside.
The showcase should help to protect the objects inside from fluctu-ations in relative humidity. The more solidly it is constructed the better it will do so. Sometimes it is worthwhile designing a showcase that incorporates pre-conditioned silica gel, but only if the museum is able regularly to recondition the silica gel.

☐ help maintain correct light levels.
Light levels inside showcases are often far too high for the safety of the objects. It is very important that both the light level and heat given out should be carefully controlled. Where the showcase has its own light-ing, the light source and all electrical equipment *must* be outside the showcase itself, and must be well ventilated.

☐ raise objects to a height to enable them to be seen clearly.
Remember that your audience consists of people of different heights, and includes people who are in pushchairs and wheelchairs.

☐ bridge the scale differences between small objects, people and the building.
Tiny objects in a great big room can look insignificant and lost. One important function of the showcase is to give them scale and importance.

☐ be constructed of appropriate materials which respect environmental concerns.

For example, it would be inappropriate to use wood from an endangered primary forest in a display case providing a display on ecology and conservation!

☐ relate to the design of the galleries.

Display cases should be attractive to look at and complement the design of the gallery.

UNIT 24   PLANNING A NEW DISPLAY

Related Units: 25–9, 31, 32, 44–50, 57, 58

The advantages of display

The public is quite right to identify museums with displays. Although museums do many other things as well, and use many other techniques to communicate with the public, their unique and special method is display. Displays have three great advantages over every other form of interpretation:

- Displays can reach a large number of different people at one time. They thus tend to be very cost-effective.
- Displays contain real objects.
  Visitors respond to 'the real thing' with a special respect that they do not give to the printed word, to photographs or to reproductions.
- Visitors can use displays at their own level of interest and speed.

Deciding on the target audience

The museum should already know a lot about its visitors (see Unit 6). They will be very varied: adults and children, townspeople and country people, wealthy people and poor people, educated people and uneducated people. It will scarcely be possible to design a display that suits everyone.

The museum must start, therefore, by deciding who the new display is aimed at. It could be intended chiefly for children, or for foreign tourists, or for specialists, or for any other group of visitors.

The display will be aimed at this 'target audience', and designed to meet their needs and interests, though we very much hope it will also please and interest other visitors as well. The interpreter targets the display at a particular audience or group of visitors because if he or she tries to please everyone he may end up pleasing no-one (see Unit 17).

As planning the new display goes on we shall learn a lot about this target audience, through the process known as 'front-end evaluation' (see Unit 29).

Deciding on the theme

The number of possible themes for a new display may seem at first sight almost limitless. In fact, though, your choice will be limited by a number of things:

■ The *mission of the museum* (see Unit 86). Clearly any new display must serve the overall purpose of the museum. There is little point in defining the mission of the museum as 'to present the history of the Nile Valley' if you are then going to arrange displays on Buddhist art from Thailand!

■ The *target audience*. Theme and audience must match; you are giving yourself unnecessary problems if you insist on presenting a display on a theme in which you know that your target audience has no interest! That said, you may feel that you want to try, and if your techniques are good enough you may succeed in giving a lot of people an inspiring new interest. If so, you are a very good interpreter.

■ The *museum collections*. Probably you will want to base your display on part of your existing collection, on the results of field collecting, on a new acquisition or on a borrowed collection.

■ *Money*. A small and poor museum is unlikely to be able to arrange a display of Van Gogh paintings, or a display demonstrating the latest techniques of space research.

■ *Knowledge*. It is important to choose a display theme that the museum staff (or visiting experts) have sufficient expertise to treat adequately (see Unit 25). The public looks on the museum as a source of knowledge and scholarship, and the museum therefore has a moral responsibility to ensure that what it presents in its displays is based on the most accurate and up-to-date information possible.

What kind of display?

Having decided on the theme of the display, the curator and his or her colleagues need to decide what kind of display it is to be. Museum displays can be divided into six types:

■ *Contemplative display.* Here beautiful or inspiring things are put on display for the visitor to contemplate. This is the theme adopted by most art galleries, though even they often try to tell a story as well, if only by grouping paintings or statues by similar artists together.

■ *Didactic display.* Here the display tries to tell a story, to teach something. The story may, for example, be the prehistory of the country, or the biology of lizards, or the folk art of the region; objects help to tell the story.

■ *Reconstruction display.* Here a genuine or imaginary scene is reconstructed. Open-air museums like Skansen in Sweden, where whole streets of historic buildings are rebuilt and refurnished, fall into this theme, as do small tableaux in museum galleries.

■ *Grouped display.* Here groups of objects are displayed together with very little interpretation. Archaeological museums, for example, often have a room labelled 'Bronze Age', with many small objects but very little to tell the visitor why they are important or what happened in the Bronze Age. This type of display is probably the most common type of all, and is found in museums all over the world because it is so easy to do: it requires very little thought. But it is also the least useful or interesting, except to specialists.

■ *Visible storage.* Early museums used to put everything they owned on display. Then curators learned that people could enjoy a few things well displayed and interpreted more than hundreds of things crowded together. Many museums put only their best things on display, and the rest in store. But now visitors are asking 'why can't we see the thousands of things you've got hidden in your stores?' One answer is to keep the fine displays, but to open the stores to interested visitors, making only those improvements needed to protect the collections.

■ *Discovery displays.* This is almost the opposite of the didactic display. There is no overall order, but visitors are encouraged to make their own discoveries. The museum can of course help visitors to follow their own interests and to make their own discoveries. In one recently-opened ethnographic museum all the objects were arranged in alphabetical order, but booklets and soundguides were available covering a wide variety of visitors' interests, from 'power in the community' to objects made from wood.

Can you think of any other classes into which displays could be divided?

Which classes do the displays in your own museum fall into?

UNIT 25   RESEARCH FOR DISPLAYS

Related Units: 24, 26–9, 35, 38–41, 43

No-one would consider writing a book without allowing time to do the necessary research, yet museums quite often plan new displays without planning who is going to do the necessary research, and how much time they will need to do it, and where they will find the necessary information.

There is an important distinction between research on the collections, which is a responsibility every museum carries, and research specifically for a new display. Research on the collections should be a continuous process, carried out according to a research policy and closely tied to the museum's collecting policy (see Units 35 and 43). Research for displays is tied to the particular display the museum is planning.

It is important, first, to ensure that the museum has the *expertise* to research and put on a display. If the museum is thinking, for example, of arranging a new display of its collection of netsuke (Japanese carvings), does anyone at the museum know about them? Or can an expert be brought in from outside to do the research and to supervise the arranging of the display?

Second, it is important to make sure that enough *time* is available to carry out the research. A major exhibition in a large museum may involve two or three people researching for two or three years: a major exhibition or permanent display should be thought of like a scholarly book. Even a small gallery in a small museum requires some weeks' or months' research. Every new display or temporary exhibition should be based on the most accurate and up-to-date information possible, even if it is aimed at schoolchildren or other non-specialists.

There is never any excuse for inaccuracy in museum displays any more than in a published book.

Third, the museum should ensure that the researchers have access to adequate *sources of information*: libraries and other experts. Of course, this will be more difficult for a small and poor museum in a remote place than for a large well-staffed museum with a big library and perhaps near a university. But the small museum can concentrate on displays on topics it can research: for example local ethnography or local wildlife.

Finally, the people who do the research, if they are not also writing the brief for the designer (see Unit 27) and writing the labels (see Unit 26), must work very closely with those who do. The display must be based on well-researched, accurate and up-to-date information.

UNIT 26   WRITING TEXT

Related Units: 24, 25, 27, 29

Most museum visitors get their information from museum text. Yet most museum visitors read only perhaps one tenth of the text. Even if they are very interested, it is difficult to read standing up and walking around. And while some visitors are very interested, and want a lot of information, others may be put off by a lot of text or complicated labels, and may be made to feel inadequate.

So writing, designing and positioning museum texts and object labels is one of the most difficult but most important tasks a museum manager has to do.

The aim and audience of the exhibition

Whether one is planning a new display or temporary exhibition or improving an old gallery, the first question to answer is, 'what is the aim of the exhibition?' The aim could be to tell a story, to explain a concept or simply to display fine objects.

The aim of the exhibition depends on the audience. A clear idea of whom the exhibition is *for* is essential to exhibition planning.

The overall scheme

The simplest and most common text scheme in a conventional exhibition has three parts.

- An *introductory panel* explaining the purpose of the exhibition and giving its title.
- *Section panels* which – like chapter headings in a book – give background information on the objects in that showcase or that section of the exhibition.
- *Object labels* giving more detailed information about the individual objects on exhibition.

The introductory panel gives the title of the exhibition, and explains its purpose. It should encourage visitors by telling them why the objects are worth exhibiting, why visitors should be interested in the exhibition and what they can learn from it. In a larger exhibition it should also explain briefly how the exhibition is organised, so that the visitor knows in general what he or she is going to see, and how long the visit will take.

The section panels give background information about the objects in that section of the exhibition, and should explain why they are grouped together. Each section panel should have clear headings.

The object labels explain what each object is, and why it is significant.

How to write text

Most museum texts and labels are much too complicated. They are written by specialists who know a great deal about their subject and about the objects, and forget that most of their visitors will know very little about either.

When many of the visitors are foreign tourists, the problem is even worse. There will be much that the curator has known and understood since childhood that to the visitor is mysterious and strange.

Some museum labels are much too simple. A label reading 'old plough given by Hilda Beckenham' is quite useless. Most visitors can recognise a plough, but very few have ever heard of Hilda Beckenham!

WHO IS IT FOR?

As with every aspect of planning an exhibition, always keep in mind who the target audience is. Labels written for schoolchildren will be different to labels written for university professors! Find out what level of education and what knowledge of the subject your visitors are likely to have.

Consider what languages the labels should be written in. In some countries it may be necessary to have labels written in two or three local languages and in one or two foreign languages. It depends entirely on who your visitors are likely to be. If you are getting labels translated into other languages, do try to get the translation done by a native speaker of that language; a bad translation may make your visitors laugh, but it will not help them to understand your exhibition!

KEEP IT SHORT

Text on an introductory panel should have no more than 150 words; 50 words would be better.

Text on section panels should have no more than 200 words; 50 words would be better.

Object labels should have no more than 40 words. If you feel it is essential to say more than this, then put the extra information in a guidebook, or in a give-away leaflet. This is also the best solution if some visitors want detailed information.

KEEP IT CLEAR

Write simply, avoiding jargon and technical terms. Put the main point of what you want to say at the beginning. Use the language that most visitors would use.

When the panel text or the label is written, show it to three or four randomly selected visitors, and then ask them to tell you what it says in their own words. It will soon be clear whether they have understood it!

Then subject what you have written to the Fry and Cloze tests (see Box 1).

It is often best to ask someone completely unconnected with the museum, ideally a writer or journalist, to write the labels based on your information.

BOX 1

Readability and comprehension

These two tests will tell you whether your text is intelligible to English-speaking visitors.

THE FRY TEST

This test shows how much education a reader needs to have had in order to read text easily.

— Randomly select two or more passages, which combined contain about 300 words. Count the words. (A hyphenated word counts as two words.)
— Count the number of sentences.
— How many sentences per 100 words?
— How many syllables per 100 words?
— Plot the intersection of these two values on the graph to estimate the reading level.

Aim at an education age of 14–15 years for labels and texts on panels and 12–13 for text on introductory panels.

The Fry Test graph

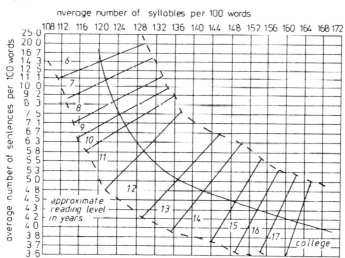

The dotted lines indicate the boundary of the region of the test's maximum reliability. As can be seen, the test establishes reading level through sentence and word lengths. Although time-consuming to calculate, it gives an objective assessment of your prose style and reveals whether you are likely to communicate successfully with your audience.

THE CLOZE TEST

This test shows how easy or difficult your label is to understand.

— Take several examples of your text. Type or write them out again, deleting every fifth word and replacing it with a standard-sized blank. Count the number of blanks.
— Give copies of the retyped versions to a broad sample of visitors and ask them to fill in the blanks.
— Score a word as correct only if it is exactly the same as the one deleted from the original (except misspellings).
— For each response the Cloze score = number of correctly filled-in words x 100 divided by the number of blanks (deleted words).

— Add together the total number of Cloze scores and divide by the number of responses to get the mean.
— Mean Cloze scores above 55 are good. 57–61 means that almost everyone understood it. The text is too difficult if the score is 35 or less.

(Source: E. Kentley and D. Negus, *Writing on the Wall*, National Maritime Museum, 1989)

Designing text

The following rules are useful to remember when designing section panels and object labels:

In a good light, and using conventional lettering, words can be read at a distance of the 'cap height' multiplied by 200. ('Cap height' means the height of the capital letters.)

Black lettering on a white background is easiest to read.

BOX 2

What to say and how to say it?

LABELLING OBJECTS

Writing labels is an art. The label should include all relevant details, but not be too long; it should avoid vague or inexact statements, but give some indication why the object is worthy of being displayed in the museum. Information should be verified before it is included on a label.

Examples of what *not* to include:

Sewing Machine
Believed to be a hundred years old.

A hundred years old – when? It is possible to date many historical items accurately; reference books including trade catalogues can be used.

Sewing Machine
Belonged to donor's grandmother. She came to W.A. in 1890 and spent several years in the district. Donated by Mrs Jane Smith.

Is the display about the sewing machine, or the donor's grandmother? A label generally shouldn't try to cover both aspects.

Sewing Machine
Such machines were widely used in the early days.

The 'explanation' really adds nothing to our knowledge of the object.

Sewing Machine
This machine is unusual because it was made in America.

This label would be inadequate unless it described the only American-made machine in a collection of English-made machines. Even then information about the nature of the difference would be required.

Sewing Machine
Donated by the late Mrs Jane Smith.

In fifty years time, most of your donors will be 'late'!

A better label might be:

Standard Sewing Machine, about 1884
   Built by Standard Sewing Machine Company, Cleveland, Ohio. Purchased in Ireland and brought to Augusta in 1890 by Mrs Margaret Murphy. Donated by her granddaughter Mrs Jane Smith.

A 79. 31

Or, in a display primarily about Sewing Machines

Standard Sewing Machine, about 1884
   Built by Standard Sewing Machine Company, Cleveland, Ohio, 1884–1931.
   The Standard Company was later acquired by Singer, and the marque disap-
   peared in about 1931.

A 79. 31

(Source: Elizabeth Willis and Sarah Bennington, *Handbook for Small Museums*,
Western Australian Museum, Perth, 1985)

BOX 3

Producing simple texts and labels

Handwritten labels can be the best of all: but only when they are written by a real expert in traditional handwriting.

Modern typewriters with carbon ribbons produce excellent results. Even the smallest museum can probably borrow a modern typewriter.

Modern photocopiers will enlarge your texts and labels to the size you need.

Some countries still have highly-skilled traditional sign-painters. Using painted signs in the museum both gives it a special character and helps preserve a traditional craft.

A personal computer with a word processing or, better still, a Desk-Top Publishing program and a good printer will enable you to produce high-quality labels and other text.

Lower case text (a combination of large and small letters) is easier to read THAN ALL UPPER CASE TEXT, simply because it is more familiar.

Text is easiest to read when placed at a height of between 1.0m and 1.5m, though for some visitors (for example children or people in wheelchairs) panels will, of course, have to be placed lower.

Producing text

Museums which employ designers directly or on a contract basis will have a large variety of methods of producing text and labels to choose from. These will include type-setting, silkscreening, 'Desk-Top Publishing' and photographic processes.

Other museums can use more simple techniques (see Box 3).

The rule to obey is that all the text in one gallery should be produced in the same way, and all should be neat and clean. There is nothing worse than a museum where some text is (badly) handwritten, some is written on one typewriter, some on another and everything is untidy and faded. Text and labels should be crisp and smart. It is therefore a good rule to use a technique for producing them that will be available to produce replacements when necessary.

UNIT 27   BRIEFING A DESIGNER

Related Units: 24–6, 28, 29, 44–50, 57, 58, 64, 65

More and more museums are using their limited resources to buy the skills of professional designers. It is not always a happy relationship. When new displays prove disappointing, curators blame the designer. When new displays result in damage to objects, conservators blame the designer. When objects go missing from new displays, security officers blame the designer. When children cannot enjoy a new display, the education specialist blames the designer.

In fact, it is very probably *their* fault: they failed to make their needs clear. The Design Brief is the chief way in which the designer is told what to try to achieve. It is the most important part of the whole process of creating a new display.

Different designers ask their clients to provide information in different forms. This unit, however, lists the information that every Design Brief should contain.

Design Brief: Part 1

The first part of the Design Brief should be prepared before the designer is chosen, if an outside designer is to be employed. It describes the nature and purpose of the proposed new display.

WHY: THE PURPOSE OF THE NEW DISPLAY

What are the aims of the project – intellectual, philosophical and educational? If you can write these down in fewer than 250 words, it will demonstrate that you have thought hard about what you want to achieve.

WHAT: THE NATURE OF THE DISPLAY

Is it to be a permanent gallery or a temporary exhibition? How long is it expected to last? What sort of display is it to be: mostly graphic, mostly objects or some of each? Are the objects large or small? Will they need to be in showcases? Will they need special environmental conditions or security?

WHERE: WHERE IS THE DISPLAY LOCATED?

Where is the new display to be? Describe and give details of the space into which it must fit. Does the space have any special restrictions such as floor loadings, ceiling heights, power supply or access?

WHEN: THE TIMETABLE

When must the display be completed? Are there any special time constraints, such as a building programme, major events, availability of funds, etc.?

WHO: THE TARGET AUDIENCE

Who is the target audience? It is crucial that you define your target audience at the very beginning of the project. See Units 5–6.

HOW MUCH: THE BUDGET AVAILABLE

If you are able to state a budget for the project at this stage, the designer will be able to assess whether it is enough to achieve your aims, the standard of finish that can be achieved and how much his or her fees and expenses are likely to be. If you are unable or unwilling to state a budget at this stage, the designer will be able to assess how much he or she would expect the project to cost.

Design Brief: Part 2

The second part of the Design Brief is given to the designer when he or she is appointed. Its purpose is to describe in detail every single thing that is to be included in the new display.

Every single item is given a unique number, and for every item a form is completed with the details described below.

OBJECTS

– The title of the display.
– The title of the section.
– Description of the object, with a photograph or sketch.
– Viewing details: how the object is to be displayed.
– Conservation required before display and special environmental conditions required whilst on display.
– Any special security requirements.
– Overall dimensions of the object when on display. Always use the same conventions, e.g. length x width x height (mm).
– Does the object require any special stands or supports? Who will supply them?
– Weight of object.
– Where is the object now kept? Can the designer see it?
– The object's accession number.
– A unique number, used just for this project.

GRAPHIC IMAGES

– The title of the display.
– The title of the section.
– A description of the graphic image and a photocopy or photograph of any reference material to be used in preparing it. A sketch, however rough, will help to explain what is required.
– A list of any appropriate reference material.
– A unique number.
– The unique number of the caption which must accompany the graphic image.
– The unique number of any objects or main text with which this graphic should be associated.

MAIN TEXT

- The title of the display.
- The title of the section.
- The actual text, including any title and sub-titles. The text must be *perfect*: it is not the designer's job to correct mistakes, unless you pay extra! Any corrections later will be *very* expensive. If possible the text should be typewritten, double-spaced.
- A unique number.

CAPTIONS FOR PHOTOGRAPHS AND OTHER IMAGES

- The title of the display.
- The title of the section.
- The requirements for captions are the same as for main text. But ensure you make clear that these are *captions* – to accompany pictures, drawings, diagrams, maps or other graphic illustrations – not main text or labels.
- The unique number of the graphic to which the caption relates.
- A unique number.

LABELS FOR OBJECTS

- The title of the display.
- The title of the section.
- The requirements for labels are the same as for main text and captions. But ensure you make clear that these are *labels* – to accompany original objects, specimens and works of art – not main text or captions.
- The unique number of the object to which the label refers.
- A unique number.

AUDIO-VISUAL SLIDE SHOWS AND VIDEO

These need to be treated almost as separate displays, with mini-briefs of their own. Each producer will have their own way of working; however, the main information required will be:

- The title of the display.
- The title of the section.
- Frame, shot or slide number.
- Visual description of shot or slide.

BOX

Choosing a designer

If the museum does not have its own designer, it will be necessary to use one from outside, probably a commercial designer.

The best way to start finding a suitable designer is to ask colleagues in other museums, and to look at as many recent exhibitions and museum displays as possible.

Discuss with other museum managers how well their designers managed the design project as a whole – quality of design, cost control, understanding of conservation needs, time management, quality of ideas and so on.

Make a short list of designers whose work you like, and either interview them at their offices, or invite them to give a presentation at your museum. If you want them to give their initial ideas on your project you will need to give them the first part of your Design Brief (but don't expect them to prepare any designs without being paid!). Make sure that all the members of your Display Team are there, and that the designers send the people who will actually be working on your project.

– Voice-over script.
– Special instructions to photographer or cameraperson.

COMPUTER-DRIVEN INTERACTIVES

Like audio-visuals, these need their own mini-briefs, though the Design Brief must refer to them so that the designer understands their role in the display. The programmer will need:

– To know what the program is aiming to achieve. For example, is it just for fun, or is it intended to teach specific things?
– The text, set out in the same format as the exhibition text.
– Illustrations of the graphic images.
– If appropriate, a network diagram of how each page of information relates to all others.

Conclusion

This unit is based closely on notes prepared by an experienced museum designer. He concludes

Almost every curator I have ever worked with has balked at the thought of filling out the many different forms which are required at the detail design stage, with claims of lack of time, lack of resources, lack of patience. However at the end of the job every one has agreed that it has made the process of achieving a good conclusion a great deal easier.

UNIT 28   EXHIBITION DESIGN AND PRODUCTION

Related Units: 17–27, 29, 44–50, 57, 58, 64, 65

The organisation, design and production of a new display or temporary exhibition is very complicated. All that can be done in this unit is to draw attention to the different stages that must be gone through, and the different skills that will be employed.

The process is made more complicated by the bewildering variety of technical terms that different writers use, and the fact that most writers are thinking about very large projects in very large museums in Western Europe or North America.

But even the smallest project has to go through the same process. In a small project only one or two people may be needed where in a large project hundreds may be required. It is still essential to plan the process logically and carefully.

What follows is an attempt to set out the stages that any new exhibition must go through. For more information see the books listed in 'Further reading' (see Unit 85).

1   Planning

1.1 The original idea. Everyone can have good ideas: the difficulty is in persuading the museum authorities to agree and to pay for them!

1.2 Set up the Exhibition Team. This should ideally include Curator, Conservator, Education Specialist, Security Officer, perhaps Administrator and (when appointed) Designer. If the exhibition is to be built by the museum's own production staff, the Head of Production will be a member, too. The Team will continue to meet until after the exhibition is opened, and will be responsible for all aspects of it. In small museums many of these tasks will have to be done by one or two people.

1.3 Development of idea:

— what is the target audience?
— what is the aim of the exhibition?
— what collections would be exhibited?
— what collecting/conservation work would be needed?
— what staff would be involved?
— when will the exhibition open?
— how much, roughly, would it cost?

1.4 Permission given to go ahead, at least to next stage.

1.5 Feasibility Study. For a small exhibition this stage may be combined with 1.3, but for a larger one it will be a substantial stage on its own. The Feasibility Study will involve significant study of:

— the target audience, including front-end evaluation (see Unit 6)
— the theme
— the collections
— the research required
— the timetable/Work Plan
— the cost

1.6 Permission given to go ahead!

1.7 Research. Even the smallest new exhibition, if it is to be worthwhile, involves new research. All museum work depends ultimately on the quality of the scholarship that underlies it. But research is the aspect that most often gets cut short; it is vital that sufficient time is allotted to the necessary research in the exhibition planning process (see Unit 25).

1.8 Design Brief drawn up. The Design Brief, which will be based very closely on the feasibility study, will probably be the most important stage of the whole process (see Unit 27).

1.9 Fundraising, if necessary.

2   Preliminary design

2.1 Appointment of designer (see Unit 27).

2.2 Presentation of Design Brief.

2.3 Discussion of Design Brief. There is no substitute for detailed discussions between designer(s) and the members of the Exhibition Team. Even in the best Design Brief some important things will have been forgotten, and – even if he or she is very experienced in working with museums – the designer will need to learn a great deal about the subject of the new display if he or she is to do it justice. If (as often happens) the designer is *not* used to working in museums, the museum staff will have to do a lot of educating!

2.4 Site survey. The designer will obtain all necessary technical details of the site.

2.5 Preliminary designs. The designer prepares drawings, sketches and diagrams to show his or her initial ideas.

2.6 More detailed discussions between designer and Display Team.

2.7 Formative evaluation: the testing on real visitors of mock-ups of displays (see Unit 29).

2.8 Costings. Ideas are now sufficiently developed for much more accurate estimates of cost to be made.

2.9 Work Plan approved (see Box).

2.10 Approval. All concerned agree on the general character of the display.

3   Final design

3.1 Designer prepares final designs.

3.2 Conservation programme underway on objects to be displayed.

3.3 Script writer drafts all text for panels, labels, catalogues, etc.

3.4 Audio-visual specialists create programmes.

3.5 Exhibition Team meets regularly during this phase to monitor progress and to iron out difficulties. As designs develop in their final form, Conservator, Security Officer, Fire Officer, Education Officer and Curators all ensure that their own concerns and requirements will be met by the finished design. The Administrator keeps a close watch on the budget.

3.6 Final designs presented and agreed by the Exhibition Team and – if necessary – by the museum authorities. This is the second most important stage of the whole process, and is very demanding for the members of the Exhibition Team. They will each have to check very carefully every aspect of the design and specifications. The Education Officer must check, for example, that the text is understandable by children and adults and the objects viewable from a wheelchair. The Fire Officer must check that the materials specified are fire-resistant and the electrics designed to minimise fire risk. The Security Officer must check that there are no places for a thief to hide, and that the showcases are secure. The Conservator must check that Relative Humidity will be controlled. The Curator must check that the exhibition will do what he or she originally wanted it to do.

3.7 Final text approved.

3.8 Final choice of objects agreed.

3.9 Timetable for production and opening date agreed.

4   Contracts

4.1 Contracts drawn up, for work not being done by museum staff, and put out to tender:

- exhibition construction
- production of text and graphics
- production of audio-visual installations and programmes
- installation of lighting scheme
- carpeting and other furniture

4.2 Designs modified, if necessary, to meet budget.

4.3 Contracts awarded.

5   Construction and installation of exhibition

5.1 Construction and installation of:

- painting
- exhibition carcase and showcases
- carpeting/floor covering
- lighting
- text panels and graphics
- showcase linings and fittings
- environmental control equipment
- security installations

5.2 Catalogues and other print such as posters, invitations to opening ceremony, information sheets, education packs, go for publication.

6   Case-dressing

6.1 Case-dressing. This phase, the installation of the objects themselves, is the third most important phase of the whole process. It is extremely important that enough time is allowed for this phase, and that – if the construction phase is delayed – it does not get shortened or hurried. It is a time of great danger for the objects, when breakages and thefts can occur. The Curator, Conservator and Security Officer will be chiefly involved.

6.2 Testing of conservation conditions.

6.3 Adjustment of lighting and other minor adjustments.

7   Opening to public and publicity

7.1 Publicity. The publicity for the new display will have been planned from an early stage, and will have been building up in parallel with the development of the display.

7.2 Appointment and training of any extra warding, interpretation or sales staff required for the new exhibition.

7.3 Press previews and private views arranged.

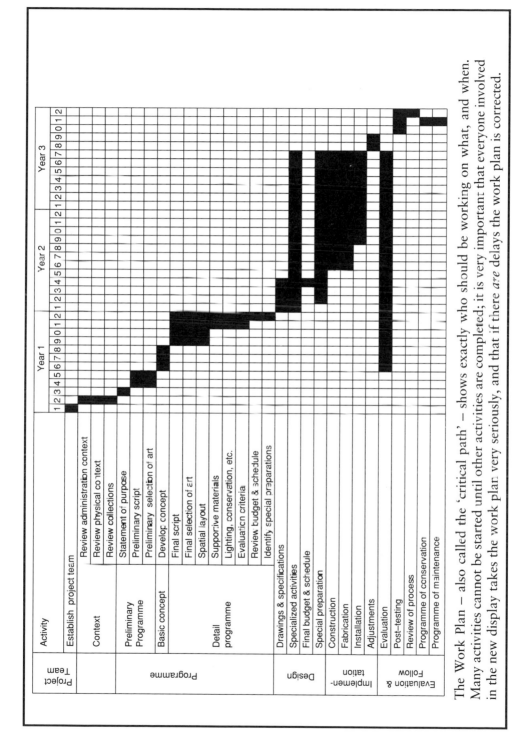

The Work Plan – also called the 'critical path' – shows exactly who should be working on what, and when. Many activities cannot be started until other activities are completed; it is very important that everyone involved in the new display takes the work plan very seriously, and that if there *are* delays the work plan is corrected.

7.4 Opening ceremony!

7.5 Exhibition open to the public.

8   After the opening

8.1 Maintenance begins, and the maintenance programme is adjusted in the light of experience.

8.2 Summative Evaluation begins (see Unit 27).

8.3 All administrative matters completed, bills paid, etc.

8.4 Exhibition Team carries out review of success and failure leading to:

8.5 Redesign and adjustments. There will inevitably be things which have gone wrong: mistakes shown up by the Summative Evaluation, maintenance difficulties, conservation problems, etc. It is important that – from the very beginning of the process – this is expected, and money and time are set aside to make the necessary corrections.

UNIT 29   EVALUATING EXHIBITIONS

Related Units: 17–28, 44–50, 57, 58, 64, 65

'Evaluation' in museums is the technique of measuring the success of museum exhibitions and displays. Museums spend a great deal of time and money creating and maintaining exhibitions to inform and inspire visitors: how successful are they? Do visitors go away understanding more than when they came? Can we learn to create more successful exhibitions?

There are three principal types of evaluation, to which specialists have given the terms

– 'front end' evaluation (at the beginning)
– 'formative' evaluation (in the middle)
– 'summative' evaluation (at the end)

These clumsy jargon terms have been taken from the literature of educational research. Formal evaluation in museums is still in its infancy, and the techniques we use now will in years to come no doubt seem very crude.

Beginning ('Front End') evaluation

Front End evaluation is done before any exhibitions have been produced, or even designed. It is the testing of ideas and proposals for exhibitions, and its purpose is to avoid mistakes by collecting relevant information before the exhibition is designed.

The first step, as always, must be to decide the *purpose* of the exhibition, including who it is chiefly intended for. For example, a temporary exhibition on painting may be intended chiefly for people who themselves paint as a hobby, or a museum may arrange an exhibition chiefly to appeal to a local minority group. This is the 'target audience'.

The second step is to find twenty or so representatives of that target audience, and to discuss in detail with them your ideas for the display. The aim is to find out the needs and interests of the target audience. Their comments will probably change your ideas considerably!

At the same time, discussions can be held with two other groups. The first is the experts. Thus if you are preparing an exhibition on seventeenth-century Chinese ceramics, it is very sensible to listen to the views of *other* specialists before your ideas for the exhibition become too firm. If you are planning an exhibition on the history of a town, it is essential to hold detailed talks with a wide variety of groups in that town before ideas for the exhibition become fixed.

Another group with which to discuss your ideas is your fellow professionals. Museum curators, designers, journalists, teachers and advertisers are all specialists in conveying information and ideas to the public. Their suggestions and comments on your ideas may prove very valuable.

Middle ('Formative') evaluation

Formative evaluation is the name given to techniques of testing the effectiveness of exhibitions as they are being produced. The purpose is to try out design ideas and, if they do not work, to modify them.

The usual way of doing this is to build a mock-up of the exhibition (or part of it), using cheap materials, hand-written text and so on. The mock-up display is then shown to a small sample of visitors (about twenty or thirty), and their reactions are obtained by observing them, by interviewing them in detail and by questionnaires. As comments and criticisms are received, weaknesses discovered and improvements suggested, the mock-up exhibition is changed bit by bit until it seems to be successful.

End ('Summative') evaluation

Summative evaluation is the type of evaluation study that is carried out on the completed exhibition once it has been built and opened. The aim is to discover whether the exhibition works: whether it actually achieves the aims its designers intended. Every curator likes to think that his or her new exhibition is a success. But the only way to get answers to the questions 'does it work?', 'can it be improved?', 'do people like it?', is to carry out a summative evaluation. At present there are three main techniques.

The first technique is systematically to *watch or track* visitors, and to note both the direction they take, and how long they spend in front of each display or showcase. You can then draw a map showing the routes taken by visitors, and a chart of how long individual displays are looked at. These will help show whether the layout of the exhibition is successful and which parts are most popular.

The disadvantages of this technique are obvious. First, it may be difficult to watch visitors without their noticing and becoming nervous: some museums have used hidden watchers or even cameras for this reason. Second, you learn nothing of *why* visitors are attracted to one section rather than another.

The second technique is to *interview* a fairly large random sample of visitors. The questions will have to be carefully devised to make sure that they do find out the information you need. A number of different approaches are possible:

- to find out what the visitors learned by asking them questions about the exhibitions they have been looking at;
- to ask the visitors which sections they found most interesting or stimulating, and if they can explain why;
- to ask the visitors what improvements and changes they would suggest.

Summative evaluation techniques are limited in what they can achieve. If the aim of the exhibition was to give the visitor certain pieces of information – for example, to explain the history of a region – then it is comparatively simple to design an evaluation technique which will discover what the visitor has learned.

But it is important to remember that a museum is not a school. Visitors to museums may be seeking inspiration and understanding rather than information.

> A small but crucial amount of learning takes place, with visitors getting excited about perhaps one thing out of 150 presented. That small piece of knowledge can, however, produce a . . . change in the visitor. Museums can awaken a desire for education through this small piece of learning or interest. (Friedman 1987)

The techniques must be used sensitively. You can learn from them whether the visitor has acquired extra knowledge, which are the most popular exhibits, whether the display could be better arranged, how much of the text is read and so on.

What you cannot learn is whether the exhibition has lit that spark of imagination in one visitor's mind, or started a new enthusiasm or opened the door to a new understanding.

> The child who is fascinated by shadows on a wall of the Exploratorium [a Science Centre in San Francisco] as they shift and merge in every colour of the rainbow cannot tell you what he or she has learned. But years later the teacher who explains how colours combine to make white light will find it a little easier, and the student will find it a little less intimidating. (Tressel 1984)

The third summative evaluation technique is *critical appraisal*. This means simply inviting an outside expert to prepare a detailed critique of the completed exhibition.

> The value of critical appraisal lies in having a sensitive expert, one who can identify problems applying skills which the museum professional does not have. This approach can be particularly useful when an exhibition which has been in existence for a number of years is due to be modernised. The aim is to learn about the strengths and weaknesses of the exhibition as it stands now so that strengths can be built on and weaknesses overcome when the exhibition is redeveloped. (Griggs 1985)

Unit 29   Evaluating exhibitions

STUDY EXAMPLE A

A natural history museum was planning an exhibition aimed chiefly at amateur naturalists. Front End evaluation was intended to find out what the target audience wanted from the exhibition.

At first the museum curators thought a taxonomic display of specimens would be best. But perhaps, since amateur naturalists normally concentrate on fieldwork, a habitat approach would be more acceptable?

It was decided that a small number of qualitative interviews would be better than a large number of short questionnaires. Fourteen visitors who met the criteria of 'amateur naturalist' were given interviews of between 30 and 45 minutes each.

None of the visitors interviewed thought that the exhibition should just present specimens in a taxonomic display. Several stressed that they did not want to see butterflies pinned up in rows. So the curators accepted that there was a convincing consensus in favour of a habitat approach, and that is how the exhibition was done.

Front End evaluation was used here to ensure that the exhibition met the needs of the target market and that resources were effectively used.

STUDY EXAMPLE B

A city museums service was planning a new museum. Called 'The People's Story', it was to be a museum devoted to the lives and work and struggles of the ordinary working people of the city. The question was: how to ensure that the displays really did reflect the lives of the city's people, not just in the distant past, but up to the present day?

The museum staff linked up with the organisation that already ran adult education pro-grammes in the city. Together they set up a project – called *Memories and Things* – which brought together local history and reminiscence groups from different parts of the city to handle and talk about everyday objects from the past.

The groups met weekly, and members brought in family photographs and objects, which helped stimulate discussion on themes like budgeting, days out, unemployment, customs, food, living conditions, shopping and so on. The sessions were all tape-recorded, and the group members were given transcripts of the tapes.

Out of these discussions grew the new museum's displays. Group members agreed on the main themes that should be presented and helped find appropriate objects. The displays used many quotations from group members.

As a result 'The People's Story' reflects the life of the people of the city in a way few museums achieve.

Formative evaluation was used to test the effectiveness of the displays as they were produced.

UNIT 30   INFORMATION SERVICES

Related Units: 31, 32

Museums provide information to their users in a wide variety of ways – through exhibitions; publications; telephone enquiry services; posters and leaflets; reception desks; identification services; lectures and talk programmes; correspondence and many more.

Information about your museum is also provided by other people outside the museum – tourist information officers, Trustees or Governors, volunteers and Friends, corporate supporters and visitors. It follows that however information is provided by the museum it is important that it is accurate, clearly presented and communicated, and is in accordance with your organisation's communications policy.

Remember that significant numbers of visitors may not be able to read because of factors such as poor education or visual impairment, or because they are unfamiliar with the language in which information is given. We outline below a number of ways in which information is provided by the museum, and how this can most effectively be done.

RECEPTION DESKS

For the visitor, the museum reception or enquiry desk is often the first point of contact with the museum. Information provided normally covers the following areas:

– admission charges and discounts;
– times of opening and closing;
– general information about the museum and its collections;
– the range of facilities and their location in the museum;
– the range of services and their availability;
– events and activities programme(s);
– identification of items.

It is essential that staff at reception desks are fully trained to welcome visitors and respond accurately and courteously to their enquiries, in the languages of the principal user groups. First impressions are important. It helps staff and visitors if basic information, for example about admission charges, times of opening or closing, regulations about smoking, animals, prams and children's push-chairs and so on, is clearly and logically displayed using signs and symbols to reduce the number of times the same question is asked.

While basic information about the museum and its collections is best provided in leaflet or publication form, visitors may nevertheless welcome the opportunity to talk about the museum and its collections with staff in more detail.

User services staff should be trained in the principal languages of their users to provide basic information about the museum and its collections, but refer more detailed enquiries to curatorial staff.

Information about the museum's facilities provided at reception desks needs to be clearly related to the signposting system used in the museum, and can also be carried on leaflets/publications about the museum. It is important to guard against printing in an expensive format information which is liable to go out of date. Much better to carry such information on well-designed, but cheaper forms of publicity/information material.

Information about events and activities programmes needs to be provided in a variety of ways in order to encourage take-up: leaflets, posters, advertising in newspapers or broadcasting media all help to create a sense of immediacy and vitality for the museum. The reception desk should be conceived of as a key 'point of sale' for the museum.

It is important that user services staff on the reception desk are aware of the range of information being provided and are made fully aware of any changes to published information or details. It is also important that they are trained to be consistent and proactive – recognising opportunities to provide information to visitors of different types – rather than simply passive. The reception desk can be used to promote services and facilities, events and activities effectively, and staff should be aware of the important role they have in promoting the museum and its work.

IDENTIFICATION OF OBJECTS

Reception desks are often the first point of contact for visitors bringing items into the museum for identification. Items brought to be seen later by curatorial staff should be recorded on a standard entry form, assigned an entry number, passed to a secure area and processed according to written guidelines developed for curatorial staff (see Unit 42).

Where material cannot be left in the museum for identification/ enquiry, a simple enquiry form should be completed for any later follow-up needed. Visitors with items for identification should be provided with a written report, but not a valuation. It is possible that items which are first brought in as enquiries for identification may later be acquired for the collections. Courteous, prompt and friendly service can often help to secure items for collections at a later date.

TELEPHONE ENQUIRIES/CORRESPONDENCE

Museums will receive numerous enquiries by telephone or by letter. Staff should be trained to respond effectively in both forms of response. The wider availability of word processors/computers is now making it easier to develop standard replies which can be tailored to meet the specific needs of the enquirer. Standardising forms, letters and information sheets can help to reduce staff time. Be aware, however, that a personalised response to an enquirer can help to develop a long-term relationship between the museum and the enquirer.

MARKETING MATERIALS

Perhaps the commonest forms of information vehicle used by museums are the leaflet and the poster. There is every reason to ensure that these are well-designed, and well-printed, and carry the museum's logo or corporate identity. Good design is not necessarily expensive, and it is often possible to obtain help in kind or advice on leaflet and poster design and layout from art colleges, schools or design companies at no cost.

It is critical however not to waste hard-earned resources on marketing materials carrying information about the museum which are not clearly targeted and effectively distributed. Information, as part of the museum's overall communications policy, is only useful if it is successfully and appropriately communicated to the museum's various market sectors. Distribution patterns and evaluation of impact of marketing materials need to be carefully monitored by the museum.

RESEARCH ENQUIRIES

All museums have to provide information for researchers, whether these be schoolchildren carrying out classroom projects or academics undertaking postgraduate research. It is important to ensure that answers are given promptly, and at an appropriate level. Regular enquiries can often be answered through specially prepared information sheets, but enquiries can often be time-consuming on the part of museum staff. Well-organised filing systems, museum libraries, databases and information retrieval systems can save valuable staff time. Care also needs to be taken to ensure that the museum is properly acknowledged for any research input staff make in this way. Museums should be credited for their contributions to publications and research programmes.

Museum managers should be aware that the ways in which information is provided to visitors and users is a key part of the way in which the museum's corporate identity is promoted and reinforced. Your museum needs to develop a clear communications policy within which the museum's information services have a defined role.

STUDY EXAMPLE

One method of tracking the impact of a marketing leaflet which a number of museums use is the discount voucher. The leaflet carries a tear-off voucher providing the visitor with a discount on admission or for purchases in the shop or café.

If the print-run of leaflets – say 10,000 – has been numbered sequentially on the discount voucher, and the museum keeps track of where numbered sequences of leaflets have been distributed to, it is then possible to monitor the impact of the promotion when visitors hand in their vouchers.

For example if the first 1000 leaflets have been distributed through tourist information offices, and 250 discount vouchers are returned, then a minimum of one in four visitors received their information through the tourist information offices. If 5000 leaflets were distributed to schools, and only 100 vouchers are returned then the impact of the leaflet here – translating information into visitation – is much less successful.

Building up knowledge in this way helps to ensure appropriate and cost-effective methods of marketing and promotion are used for the future.

UNIT 31   PUBLICATIONS

Related Units: 30, 32

Publications based on the museum's collections and produced by the museum form an important resource for visitors/users. They reflect the role of the museum in contributing to knowledge and play an important part in placing the museum's collections in a wider context. Publications may be produced and published by the museum itself, produced by the museum and published by a publishing house for the museum or produced and published by an independent author and publishing house.

They can take a wide variety of forms ranging from scholarly catalogues of collections to popular guidebooks, to articles in specialist journals to children's activity books. They can also include interactive video-discs, audio-tapes and computer software. The various approaches which are taken will depend on a number of factors including the following:

– finances
– expertise
– time
– market potential
– marketing and distribution systems
– existing policy and practice

FINANCES

Developing a range of in-house publications – at whatever level(s) – can be expensive. The museum has to decide whether the necessary investment in research and author time/costs, and design and publication costs, is worthwhile in terms of the rate of return through sales on the capital invested. The museum may decide that a subsidy can be justified. It may seek sponsorship or grants to help reduce the unit cost or to keep the retail price at a lower level. Whatever the case, it is important to:

– analyse the full costs of publications in advance of commitment.
– ensure that firm cost quotations for design, typesetting, printing are obtained from relevant individuals/organisations.
– consider additional costs of marketing, distribution, discounts for bulk sales and storage (see below).

EXPERTISE

Writing for publication carries with it substantial responsibility on the part of the author to ensure accuracy. All publication carries with it the need for research. In some cases this may be extremely time-consuming and complex, in other cases it is more straightforward.

Commitment to publication carries with it commitment to dedicating

115

sufficient time for research. Whatever the publication – promotional leaflet, guidebook, article, information sheet, catalogue – it is important that museum managers ensure that authors with sufficient and appropriate expertise are used for research and writing. Editors (who may be the same people as the authors) should be capable of seeing a publication through the publication process.

Marketing and selling also requires expertise. It is of no value to the museum to produce large quantities of publications at great expense if they then languish in store because their market has been poorly researched or too few retail outlets are available to stock them.

TIME

It is easy to underestimate the amount of time needed to produce publications. Research, writing, typescript/word processing, editing, proof-reading, picture research and selection, liaising with designers, type-setters and printers; marketing; publicity; publication launches; stock control and audit; all of these stages and activities represent time, and therefore costs to the museum. It follows that in determining a publications strategy for the museum, the scheduling of publications (as well as their costs) needs careful consideration.

MARKET POTENTIAL

The value of publications is related to their markets. As we noted in Units 5–6, the services which a museum provides must be related to its various market segments. Publications are no different in this respect, and publications should be produced on the basis of the museum's understanding of its markets. The museum's publications policy should seek to service as much of its market as possible. It is important to investigate the marketability of different types of publication by comparing what other museum shops produce and sell, and their prices.

MARKETING AND DISTRIBUTION SYSTEMS

The development of a publications programme for the museum must take into consideration the marketing and distribution systems needed for publications. Do not assume that everyone will beat a path to your door to buy your publications! There is plenty of competition, and the success of the museum's publications will depend on good publicity and promotion within and outside the museum.

Museum publications can be sold through many outlets – not just the museum shop, and mail order is only one method of extending the museum's sales reach. For example, use your existing mailing lists to your supporters' groups as a basis for marketing publications. If the museum is in partnership with a publishing house, the strengths of a marketing team and existing distribution network will be able to support the museum's publications programme.

EXISTING POLICY AND PRACTICE

Publications should reflect the purpose and objectives of the museum. They should conform with museum policy, and seek to provide information relating to the museum's collections. Museum managers should be careful to ensure that time is not spent by staff on the production of publications which have limited or marginal relevance to the museum and its mission.

Museum managers should be aware that copyright is now a vital consideration with new international legislation in force.

OTHER PUBLICATIONS

The museum may wish to stock publications produced by other authors/organisations in its shop or through its mail order catalogue. The principles outlined above should apply to material bought in for resale.

STUDY EXAMPLE

A museums service composed of four museums under one management developed a series of attractive information sheets exploring aspects of the area's cultural and natural history. Topics chosen were based on a questionnaire to museum visitors about their particular areas of interest over the period of a year, and a questionnaire distributed to school teachers asking about their syllabus needs.

Each information sheet was produced to the same format with a standardised heading carrying the museums service's logo. The museums organised a small exhibition and a standard lecture and workshop on each of the information sheets which could be given by a number of different staff.

The information sheets were printed locally in small print runs of 200, stock and capital therefore being kept to a minimum. Additional copies were ordered when the stock fell to a specified level. As the series developed, the information sheets became a useful method of providing information to answer questions on topics which were regularly enquired about.

One of the benefits of the series was that it demonstrated the range of expertise within the museum staff. This helped to increase the status and standing of the museums service within the area.

UNIT 32   PUBLIC RELATIONS AND THE MEDIA

Related Units: 30, 31

The museum's status and standing in the eyes of the public depend on a number of factors both in and outside your control. Managing the relationship between the museum and its public is critical to success (see Unit 7). How can this be achieved successfully?

In all relations with the public – direct and indirect – it is important to develop a positive image of the museum based on success and achievement in the different aspects of its work. This is the museum's reputation. Direct contact comes in a variety of ways, some of which we have explored in sections elsewhere in this book. They include:

- reception services
- retail outlets
- displays
- exhibitions
- visitor facilities
- education services
- information services
- publications
- identification services
- buildings
- events and activities programmes
- publicity materials
- publications

Success in managing the museum's reputation with individuals/groups coming into contact with the museum depends on care and attention to detail. All museums need a strong, corporate identity which is reinforced through the museum's products, publications and services – for example staff uniforms or name badges – and which reflects the museum's mission. A corporate identity is a recognition signal, but the true identity of a museum is its personality and character. These are forged out of the quality of the services the museum provides; the quality of the relationships it has with its public; the understanding and appreciation on the part of the museum's staff of the importance of first-class public relations; and what makes your museum unique from the next, its collections.

Building a museum's reputation has to be worked at, and reputation earned. Bad publicity or poor experience on the part of the museum's visitors or users can damage the museum's reputation sometimes out of all proportion to the event itself. Contrary to popular wisdom, all publicity is not good publicity. *All* staff have to be involved in building a museum's reputation. Museum managers have therefore a key role in ensuring that staff are trained to develop a good relationship with the museum's public in all its forms.

The most effective form of publicity is good word-of-mouth publicity. A satisfied user is infinitely preferable to a dissatisfied user who can damage your museum's reputation without your knowledge.

Your users are your best advertising agents.

The media

The news media and broadcasting media have an important part to play in helping a museum develop its reputation. News or features stories about the museum can reach substantial numbers of readers. It is however important to remember that the museum does not have control over what journalists write. Their role is to sell news, not to promote your museum. It is therefore useful to develop good working relationships with the news/broadcasting media so that mutual understanding of each other's requirements is created. Careful programming and scheduling of press and media information on the museum's work can be a positive help in building the museum's reputation.

Press releases, press photocalls, interviews with journalists, appearances on radio and television, should all seek to emphasise positive success and achievement out of the museum's policies and programmes. Collect and file copies of press coverage received, and circulate these to your staff and governing committees for them to see. Many museums have a noticeboard in public areas with news items about the museum pinned up and changed on a regular basis. Make news coverage work for you in building good public relations.

Checklist for press/radio/television releases

☐ Think of the person at the receiving end.

☐ Make the release easy to read and handle.

☐ Use the best paper available, ideally good quality white paper, in the standard typing paper size used in your country.

☐ Letterhead should include name, address, telephone and fax number of museum, and the museum's logo.

☐ Head the release 'News', 'Press Information' or 'Information'.

☐ Use one side of the page.

☐ Leave wide margins.

☐ Type in double-spacing.

☐ Staple papers together; do not use pins or paper clips.

☐ Fold the release outwards with letterhead/opening of release showing in envelope.

☐ Date the release.

☐ Time the release to suit your most important outlets.

☐ At end of each page write 'MORE' or 'MORE FOLLOWS'.

☐ At end of release write 'ENDS'.

☐ Add 'For further information, contact . . .' and include one or two names with addresses, daytime and evening telephone numbers.

☐ Ask all staff to contribute ideas for news stories.

☐ Make the heading short and to the point.

☐ Make the first paragraph the most important.

☐ Remember the five W's: What, Who, Where, When, Why.

☐ What's happening; who's doing it; where it is happening; when it is happening; and why it is happening.

☐ In subsequent paragraphs expand on the introduction.

☐ Give more detail in descending order of importance.

☐ Concentrate on facts – do not use superlatives.

☐ Keep release to two or three pages at maximum.

☐ Use direct reported speech in quotation marks to add a personal note to story.

☐ Remember the media are always looking for absolutes – first, last, smallest, oldest, etc.

☐ Keep your style clear, digestible, terse, economical.

☐ Keep sentences short, avoid jargon.

☐ Be positive.

☐ Follow up the release with a telephone call to selected media if required to add extra emphasis.

STUDY EXAMPLE

A museum with a particularly large collection of local photographs needed help to identify individuals in a number of group photographs. Discussions with the editor of one of the local newspapers led to the paper featuring one photograph each week over a two-year period, and inviting readers to write in with any identifications/information about the individuals/locations featured in the photographs.

In this way the museum mobilised a very large number of people to help it in its work – far larger than its visitor numbers!, raised interest in the museum's photographic collections, encouraged new donations (of which there were many) and developed a significant audience for a range of photographic exhibitions it developed from this work.

The museum had established a mutually beneficial partnership with the newspapers.

UNIT 33   WORKING WITH OTHER ORGANISATIONS/SUPPORTERS' GROUPS

Related Units: 73–80

No museum is an island. All museums have to work with other organisations in a variety of ways. These may include other museums or museum organisations, tourist organisations, educational organisations, special interest societies and clubs, groups with special needs, arts organisations, learned societies, corporate bodies, hospitals – the list is endless. The value of working with other organisations is one of mutual benefit and an important and essential part of museum work.

In dealing with organisations outside the museum, professional standards should be observed at all times. We have seen in Unit 32 that the museum's reputation depends to a large extent on how people experience the museum. Working formally with organised groups or corporate bodies carries with it even greater responsibility than dealing with individuals. Organisational relationships can often be stronger and longer lasting. Organisations may send groups to visit the museum, or museum staff may visit them for a wide range of reasons. Contact may simply be through correspondence or by telephone.

In all dealings with organisations the museum should seek to provide a high quality and professional service, emphasise the positive aspects of the museum's work and build up support for the museum in as broad a sense as possible (see Unit 32).

Cooperation and collaboration with other organisations on projects or programmes can provide a valuable method of achieving results which might not be achieved by the museum working in isolation.

Where formal cooperation occurs, it is sensible to ensure that formal agreement is reached on the respective roles and responsibilities of the parties. It is helpful to put such agreements in writing or if necessary in contractual terms so that responsibilities are clearly defined, and results appropriately acknowledged. Lack of clarity can lead to confusion and upset, and damage to relationships can easily occur.

This is true for all forms of relationship which a museum has with outside bodies – designers, architects, sponsors, visiting groups, etc.

Few museums in the world are able to have access to all the resources which they would like to have to carry out their work. Museums therefore have to seek out active partners to help progress their forward planning and development programmes.

Supporters' groups

Supporters' groups can take different forms. Here we discuss volunteer groups and friends' organisations. Development groups are discussed in Unit 72.

VOLUNTEER GROUPS

Volunteer teams can provide helpful support to professional museum staff. Volunteers (in some cases called docents) should not be thought of as a substitute for paid staff, and their work should complement, not duplicate, that of paid staff. Volunteers can bring many skills and wide-ranging experience to a museum. It is important, however, that volunteers are carefully selected and trained for their duties, and that museum management provides clear line management and job descriptions for them. Volunteers should only work under formal supervision within the museum's policy framework. Their involvement should be decided as a matter of policy by the museum's governing body.

In museums with paid staff, it is inappropriate for volunteers to undertake core responsibilities such as entry documentation or security. Alternative tasks should be found. Remember, however, that volunteers are giving their time free to the museum, and should be afforded every courtesy, made to feel welcome in the museum and appropriately thanked for their support. Volunteers should also understand how their work relates to the museum's forward planning, and it is necessary that progress should be reported to them on a regular basis (see Unit 75).

FRIENDS' GROUPS OR MEMBERSHIP PROGRAMMES

The key difference between volunteer groups and Friends' groups lies in the type of support provided. While volunteers provide practical support – work *in* the museum, Friends' groups provide support-in-kind – work *for* the museum. Friends' groups help to create public interest in the museum by supporting it financially and politically. For example, Friends' groups may provide funds for new acquisitions or conservation programmes, host social occasions or fund temporary exhibitions. They represent an important constituency of dedicated support, but museums should guard against their becoming exclusive clubs or cliques. They should ideally reflect all sections of the community. The sort of benefits which Friends derive from their membership of a Friends' group include:

– social events and activities organised for their benefit;
– informal educational events and activities, e.g. lectures, study visits;
– discounts on publications or exhibitions;
– preview tickets for exhibitions;
– newsletters

and a sense of participation in and contribution to the life of the museum. Friends' groups need to be established on a formal footing and require a constitution, and clear lines of accountability for marketing, finances, etc. Some Friends will wish to become more actively involved in aspects of the museum's work and may also work as volunteers.

Friends' organisations play an increasingly important part internationally in museums of all sizes and all types. Information and assistance on establishing a group can be obtained from the World Federation of Friends of Museums (see Unit 85). It is worth considering establishing such a group, but advice should be taken first to ensure that it is set up on acceptable lines.

STUDY EXAMPLE

A museum with an active friends' group was encouraged to establish a fund for conservation through the group's fundraising events. The fund was able to attract additionally matching grants for specific conservation projects from government agencies and private sector sponsorship.

At the end of a five-year period, a major exhibition was mounted to demonstrate the value of the friends' support for a wide range of conservation projects, both preventive and remedial. The information presented was reused as the basis of a permanent display illustrating the role of the museum in caring for its collections.

It allowed the museum to focus on this aspect of the museum's responsibilities and encouraged visitors to give additional donations to the Fund for Conservation for further projects. The museum concentrated on the conservation process as well as the end product, and involved its friends and visitors in an aspect of the museum's work which is often carried out behind the scenes and rarely given enough attention in museum galleries.

Without the friends' support the museum would not have had sufficient funds to meet its responsibilities for the care of its collections.

UNIT 34   TYPES OF COLLECTIONS

The history of collecting and the formation and management of collections is a fascinating and complex field of study. Collections have been formed in countries throughout the world for many centuries, and collecting as a human endeavour takes place for many reasons in and outside of museums. It is possible, however, to detect general underlying trends in collecting at different periods, and to analyse collecting in a variety of ways.

Understanding the history and nature of collecting, and change and continuity in attitudes to collections is an important aspect of museum work. MUSEUM MANAGERS should be well versed in the history of collections formation in their own museums, and how in this respect their museums fit into a more general context of collecting.

Here we examine collections in four ways – by intellectual rationale, by method of acquisition, by discipline and by materials.

Intellectual rationale

People have developed and used collections through time and space for many reasons and for personal as well as public benefit. Private collections have been built up for reasons of social or political status, for academic or scientific interest, for commercial benefit and for personal 'hobbyist' interest. In many cases personal collections which have been developed out of a particular interest are ultimately acquired in whole or in part by museums. In some cases museums are built specifically to accommodate personal collections and serve as memorials to their collectors.

Collections may be developed in a haphazard way, based on the souvenir or 'curiosity' approach to collecting where items hold personal interest and meaning for the collector. They may be based on a 'fetishist' approach to collecting, where the collector is concerned to acquire many examples of similar artefacts or natural history specimens. They may be 'organised' collections where they are used to demonstrate or illustrate a particular intellectual argument or standpoint. They may be based on 'systematic' collecting in which collections are built up in a comprehensive way based on sound disciplinary approaches.

Whatever intellectual rationale underlies collecting, collecting in its widest sense is a powerful human trait which has greatly influenced the development and philosophy of museums and their work. Collecting and disposal policies for museums reflect more general attitudes to collecting, and this has been true since museums began to be developed.

Method of acquisition

Museums acquire material for their collections in a variety of ways which are described in greater detail in Units 35–41. We describe five main ways here – by donation, by purchase, by field-collecting, by exchange and by loan.

Many museum collections have been built up almost exclusively on the basis of donations. Donations take different forms and can vary in scale and importance. Items may be brought into the museum for identification and then offered to the museum, or may be left as bequests. In many cases major collections have been left to public museums as bequests by private collectors (see Unit 37).

Opportunities to purchase items will be constrained by available finance for most museums. Purchase normally takes place to complement existing collections (see Unit 37).

Field-collecting as part of a defined research programme allows for a systematic approach to collecting in line with the museum's overall collecting policy (see Unit 38). It is essentially a proactive approach to collecting, rather than the responsive approach to collecting which characterises donations and purchases.

Exchange of items or collections between museums is another method of collections development. Here collections are transferred to or exchanged with museums which can provide appropriate resources and skills to look after them (see Units 35–6).

Loans are a method of providing the public with an opportunity to see material in public or private collections which may not otherwise be accessible to the museum's users (see Unit 37).

However collections are built up over time, the museum has a responsibility to collect in the context of a defined collecting policy. It is the collecting policy which provides the framework within which collections are developed and acquired (see Unit 35).

Discipline

Collections can also be analysed by subject or discipline. Museum collections have been traditionally divided into a range of disciplines such as archaeology and anthropology, natural sciences, fine art, decorative arts, social history or technology. Such disciplines reflect academic training and approaches to the subject, and structures within higher education.

Collections analysed in this way may restrict opportunities for more interdisciplinary presentation and interpretation. The opportunities to use collections in a variety of ways and to view them from different standpoints can be lost through compartmentalisation. While academic study of collections using techniques appropriate for each discipline is necessary, it should not preclude alternative ways of using and interpreting collections.

Material categories

Collections can also be analysed in terms of the material of which they are composed such as stone, wood, feathers, leather, bone, ceramics or metals. All organic and inorganic material has different requirements in terms of collections management and preventive conservation (see Unit 46). It follows that collections may be housed or stored by material category, even though they may fall within different subject disciplines. They may also be displayed by material category in cross-disciplinary displays or exhibitions.

Understanding the nature of collecting, its historical development and its impact on museum development is an important requirement for museum staff. It provides a context within which to view your museum's collections and the history of their development. It gives insights into the changing ways in which people have used and pre-sented collections in museums, and above all makes people think about and question the approaches which they use in their work. Museums can no longer claim to be the only source of knowledge, meaning or understanding about collections. They do, however, rep-resent a significant body of expertise in the formation and use of collections. They can help users explore collections in many different ways and a good understanding of types of collections and their development is a valuable and necessary basis for their work.

UNIT 35   POLICIES FOR COLLECTING

Related Units: 34, 36, 37

What should we collect? That is probably the most important question any museum has to decide; every aspect of the museum's work will be affected by the museum's collecting policy.

Every museum should have a written collecting policy. This written policy will probably be part of the Collections Management section of a much larger Development Policy that sets out the museum's inten-tions for all aspects of its work. However, the Collecting Policy is the most important part, and is indispensable.

What should be in it? The Collecting Policy should include the follow-ing points:

■ *What* will the museum collect? This should describe in some detail the areas in which the museum intends to collect. For a large general museum this will be quite a long, complicated description; it should always be sufficiently detailed to enable a curator to decide whether or not to acquire an object.

■ *Where* will the museum collect? A regional museum will probably collect only items relating to its region, and mostly in the region itself. An art gallery, however, may buy paintings or accept donations from many different countries. A natural history museum may send expeditions to research and collect in biologically interesting parts of the world.

■ *How* will the museum collect? Will it collect through fieldwork? Will it purchase objects? Will it actively encourage members of the public to donate or bequeath things to it? Will it accept items on long loan? All these are policy decisions.

■ *Why* does the museum collect in these fields? The Collecting Policy should explain why the museum collects particular groups or collects in particular areas. It should clearly justify the museum's collecting policy, explaining how it fits into the museum's overall policy, and describing the historical collections held by the museum.

■ *When*, or in what circumstances, would the museum consider disposing of items? It is very important to ensure that no curator ever disposes of anything from the museum collection without strictly following the written procedure approved by the museum's Governing Body and set down in its Collecting Policy.

The principles which should govern every museum's Collecting Policy are set out in ICOM's *Code of Professional Ethics* (see Appendix, Section 3, pp. 301–3).

The *how* section must set out clearly the restrictions on collecting imposed by both law and ethics. Many of these restrictions will be peculiar to the country or even the museum concerned, but among those that one should see in the Collecting Policy of every museum in the world are the following:

■ The museum accepts and will obey the UNESCO *Convention on the means of prohibiting the illicit import, export and transfer of ownership of cultural property, 1970.*

■ The museum will not acquire any object unless satisfied that it can acquire valid title to the object in question.

■ The museum will not acquire any object if there is any reason to believe that its recovery involved recent unscientific or intentional destruction of an archaeological site.

■ The museum will not acquire any biological specimen whose acquisition has involved unjustified killing or ecological damage.

■ The museum will acquire only items it has the facilities and staff resources to care for properly.

The Collecting Policy may be a quite brief document, or it may be highly detailed; each museum should decide what it needs. Some museums have two documents: a quite brief policy which is formally approved by the Museum's Governing Body, and a much more detailed version to be used by the museum staff.

UNIT 36   POLICIES FOR DISPOSAL

Related Units: 34, 35, 37

When a museum acquires an object – whether by purchase, donation or fieldwork – it acquires it in order to preserve it for ever for the benefit of the public.

Even so, there are reasons why a museum might want to get rid of an object, and some of these are good reasons and some are bad:

– because the object has decayed so badly that it is now quite useless.

Are you *sure* it is useless? There are many examples of important scientific collections being destroyed by people who did not understand their value. Such a decision should never be taken without consulting at least two specialists.

– because it has been discovered to be a fake, or was wrongly identified.

But it may still be of interest and importance: many fakes have played an important part in art history, and comparing real and false will help future curators to learn. And if an object can be wrongly identified once, perhaps it can twice. Every museum contains examples of objects whose importance has been realised long after they came to the museum.

– because it does not fit into the museum's collecting policy.

At first sight this seems a very good reason for disposal, but beware! However hard we try to be rational and to be good planners, the fact is that collecting policies are influenced by fashion. In the 1960s many British museums, which used to try to collect everything, adopted policies of collecting only items of local and regional interest. Now they deeply regret disposing of foreign ethnographical material, which could illumine the connections of their regions with foreign countries, or illustrate the cultural background of immigrant communities.

– in order to sell it, and buy a better example.

This is a very dangerous practice indeed, and is contrary to the principles which govern museums throughout the world; only a few large North American art galleries regularly try to build up their collections by selling and buying. The practice is dangerous because it betrays the trust of those members of the public who give objects to museums, and because we can never be sure that our judgement will be approved by our successors. Many of the most treasured objects in museums today were once regarded as worthless.

– in order to make an exchange with another museum.

Exchange is full of dangers, for the reasons given above, but at least it ensures that the object remains in a public museum.

– because the museum already has many examples of this object.

This is sometimes a strong argument for disposing of an object, especially where the other examples are in better condition, or have more information associated with them. But it is still open to the criticism that donors may feel betrayed, and the danger that information relating to that object may turn up. Duplicates may, however, be used for different interpretive purposes; for example in handling boxes or loan boxes for School Loan Services.

– because the museum is ordered by state authorities to do so.

There are sadly many examples, from all sorts of regimes, of museums being ordered by state authorities to surrender objects so that they can be given as presents to visiting dignitaries, or (for example) to be used to decorate a presidential palace. In such a situation there is little the museum can do to resist: really this is not so much disposal as theft. It is certainly not a practice to be encouraged.

– in order to return the object to its country or people or region of origin.

Recent campaigns for cultural restitution have resulted in many museums returning to their country of origin items of special significance to that country. A number of museums, too, have returned human bones or religious items to groups to whom they are deeply significant. This is an area of intense debate and readers should refer to the further reading in Unit 85 (see Appendix, Section 4, pp. 303–5).

There are two aspects to disposal: *law* and *ethics*.

All museums are of course subject to the *law* of their countries, and in many countries whether a museum can sell, exchange, destroy or give away objects from its collections is controlled by law: either the general law which applies to all public bodies, or specific laws which govern museums or one particular museum.

It is the responsibility of every museum manager – curators, administrators and Board members – to ensure that they are familiar with the laws which apply to their museum, and to ensure that those laws are obeyed.

So far as the *ethics* of disposal are concerned, there is fairly general agreement among museum workers worldwide that:

- The principal function of a museum is to acquire objects and specimens for the public benefit and to keep them for posterity, so there must be a strong presumption against the disposal of any items in the collection of a museum.

- Any decision to dispose of an object must be made by the Governing Body of the museum, not by the curator alone.

- Any object being considered for disposal must be considered by at least two curators, one of whom should be from another museum, and their views should be given to the museum's Governing Body. Contact with a second curator may need to be made by post.

- Any donor, or anyone who contributed to the purchase of the object, must be – wherever possible – consulted.

- When the decision to dispose has been made, the object should be offered, by gift, sale or exchange, to other museums. Usually an announcement will be made in whatever journal or newsletter is most widely read in the country's museums.

- Any monies made from sale of objects must be used solely for the purpose of buying new objects for the collections. They should not be used for offsetting operating or capital expenditure.

Of course, a curator of an open-air museum of farming faced with a pile of rotting wooden tools may find it hard to take such a lengthy, complicated and formal procedure seriously. How much easier simply to wait until the museum is closed and set fire to the pile – end of problem! But that is exactly how many of the most important collections in our museums have disappeared. It is a betrayal of the trust that society places in its museums and their curators.

The best way of ensuring that a formal procedure for disposal *is* taken seriously is for the museum's Governing Body to adopt a formal Disposal Procedure, incorporating the points listed above. Such a procedure is set out in ICOM's *Code of Professional Ethics*; all museum Governing Bodies should formally adopt the relevant parts of this Code, and all museum workers should follow it.

UNIT 37   DONATIONS, PURCHASES AND LOANS

Related Units: 34–6

Here is a checklist of things that need to be done in acquiring objects for the museum.

☐ *Donations*

1. The museum hears about the offer. A note is made on an Offer Card (see Box 1).

2. The offer is investigated. The manager responsible for the collection speaks to the prospective donor, arranges to inspect the object and records the offer on the Offer Card.

3. The object is examined. The museum manager examines the object, and records all the information available about it (see Box 2).

4. The object is checked against the museum's Collecting Policy. Does it fall within the museum's collecting area? Are resources available to care for and use it? Does it contravene any ethical constraints? (see Unit 35).

5. Formal acceptance or refusal. Whoever is responsible for taking decisions on accepting objects formally decides, in the light of the collecting policy and the existing collections, whether to accept the object. Normally such decisions are the responsibility of the manager of the collection concerned. If the offer is to be refused, the donor must be thanked, usually both in person and by letter;

refusing a gift tactfully is often the most difficult job in museum work. A manager may wish to suggest another museum to which the item could be offered.

6. Taking possession. The point at which the museum takes possession of the object may be the last opportunity to gather information about it from the donor.

7. Thank-you letter. The writing of a formal letter of thanks to donors should be a normal part of the acquisition procedure of the museum.

8. Entry documentation. The entry documentation for the object is completed (see Unit 42).

9. Inspection and treatment/conservation. Any necessary preliminary treatment, for example for insect or fungal infestation, and any first-aid conservation, is carried out.

The object now goes to be accessioned, and then goes into store or on to display.

☐ *Purchases*

1. The museum hears about the object. Whoever first hears about the object completes an Offer Card (see Box 1).

2. The object is examined. The museum manager responsible for the collection examines the object, and records all the information available about it (see Box 2).

3. The object is checked against collecting policy. The object is checked against the museum's approved collecting policy. Does it fall within the museum's collecting area? Are resources available to care for and use it? Does it contravene any ethical constraints? (see Unit 35).

4. A price is negotiated. In negotiating a price with the vendor, it is important to remember the ethical considerations involved.

5. Decision on purchase. Whoever has authority to purchase objects (usually the manager up to a certain price, and the Governing Body above that) decides both whether the object is appropriate to the museum's collections, and whether the price is right.

6. Fund-raising. For more expensive acquisitions, many museums will have to raise the funds from a public appeal or other type of fund-raising campaign (see Unit 72).

7. Purchase made. The sale is formally agreed between vendor and

BOX 1

The Offer Card

The Offer Card is a system of recording objects known to the museum which *might* come into its collections. Whatever system is chosen, it is important to have a method of recording objects when they are first heard about, and which will record contacts with their owner until they are given, lent or sold to the museum.

A simple system consists of cards of a distinctive colour kept in a file which ensures that they are checked through at regular intervals.

The Offer Card should be kept very simple, but should include

— name of object
— name & address of owner
— name & address of contact
— where object is now
— nature of offer: gift/loan/sale
— dates of contacts

museum. When the sale is made by auction, the auctioneer's standard conditions of sale apply.

8. Taking possession. This may be another opportunity to find out more information about it from the person selling it to the museum (see Box 2).

9. Payment. Payment is made.

10. Entry documentation. The entry documentation for the object is completed.

11. Inspection and treatment/conservation. Any necessary preliminary treatment, for example for insect or fungal infestation, and any first-aid conservation, is carried out.

The object now goes to be accessioned, and then goes into store or on to display.

☐ *Loans*

The procedure for loans should be the same as that for donations. Too often museums accept items on loan much more readily and informally than they accept donations. This is a mistake, because the museum can become responsible for an embarrassing number of loans that it does not really need, but has the cost and responsibility of looking after. Loans should be for a finite period of time and for a specific purpose. Long-term loans should be avoided.

Agreement must be reached between lender and museum, *before* the object is collected, on all aspects of the insurance. These will include who is responsible for insuring, the sum insured for and the risks covered.

The arrangements for the loan, how long it is for and any conditions, must be carefully set out in the Loan In form completed as part of the Entry Documentation.

BOX 2

Recording information with objects

Social History and Ethnography collections have little use or significance if their objects are not accompanied by information on where they came from, how they were used, who used them, their role in the value-systems of their society and so on.

Yet when museums acquire objects, they too often miss the unique opportunity to ask the right questions to record this information. Here is a list of the questions the curator should ask when talking to the donor, lender or vendor of an object being acquired for the museum.

■ Name

– What do you call the object?
– What did the maker call the object?
– Do you know any other names for it?

■ Materials

– What is the object made of?
– Where did the materials come from originally?
– How did the maker obtain them?

■ Manufacture

– When (as nearly as possible) was it made? How do you know?
– Where was it made?
– Who made it? Please give the maker's name, address, occupation, age.
– In what circumstances did he make it? (e.g. in his spare time? at home?)
– Can you describe briefly how, and with what tools, it was made?

■ History

– Who was it made for originally?
– Did the maker sell it to them? How much for?
– Did they resell it? How much for?
– Were many such objects made by the maker, or by other local makers?
– Please can you list the successive owners, and how each obtained it?

■ Use

– How was the object originally used?
– Who was it used by?

- Was it used regularly, or occasionally?
- Where was it generally kept?
- When was it last used?
- Has it been used for any other purpose?

■ Description

- Has the object been altered at any time? Is it broken?
- Are there any parts missing?
- What colours was it originally painted?
- Does the object bear any name, initials, numbers or symbols? Can you explain them?

■ The donor

- Please give your name, address, occupation and age.
- How did you acquire the object?
- What is your relationship, if any, to the maker?
- What is your relationship, if any, to the subsequent owners?

■ Documentation

- Have you any photos or drawings showing this or a similar object, or of the makers or owners?
- Have you any documents or papers – letter, deeds, accounts, notebooks, etc. – relating to the maker or owners?

Section III
The development and care of a museum's collection

UNIT 38   COLLECTING AND FIELD DOCUMENTATION

Related Units: 35, 39–41

Collecting

Museum collecting, to be successful, must be *systematic* and *active*. It is not enough to draw up an impressive Collecting Policy and then to sit back and do nothing: every museum should also draw up an active collecting programme.

This collecting programme should not be overambitious, but it must not be so vague that no-one takes any notice of it. Too often museums leave collecting and fieldwork to the initiative of individual managers. The enthusiastic managers spend a great deal of time out of the museum, perhaps neglecting their other duties like documentation and display. The less enthusiastic ones find all their time taken up inside the museum, and the result is a static collection.

Most museums can find evidence of both faults somewhere in their history. There may have been periods when a great deal was collected and a backlog of documentation was allowed to build up, and periods when nothing seems to have been collected.

Good museum managers will ensure that their museum carries out a collecting programme that actively implements its formal Collecting Policy.

In drawing up such a programme, the museum will consider what *staff time* and *money* is available for collecting. Who will be involved in the collecting programme, and how much time can they devote to it? Are funds available to meet the programme's costs? The programme must be realistic, otherwise it will soon fail.

Then the museum must identify the *gaps* in its collections. The Collecting Policy will have identified the broad areas in which the museum needs to collect, but within those areas there will be some gaps that need filling more urgently than others.

One reason for collecting may be *rescue*. Objects the museum would like to acquire may be disappearing, and if the museum does not collect them now there may never be another chance. One example might be tribal or folk art or crafts, in a region where old values are changing and dealers are buying up every historic item they can for export.

Another reason may be the museum's *display needs*. A planned exhibition may give an urgent objective for a collecting programme.

Yet another reason may be to take part in a joint collecting and research programme with a number of other museums. Museums can be very much more successful when they cooperate in their collecting and fieldwork programmes.

The museum will need to consider what *equipment* will be needed in the collecting programme. To take an extreme example, there is no point in planning a collecting expedition that requires travel in remote regions if the museum cannot afford a vehicle!

Finally, the collecting programme should have a timetable, so that everyone can see who is expected to do what and when.

Field documentation

The collecting techniques the museum uses will of course vary greatly according to what is being collected: collecting local ethnography will demand a quite different approach and quite different equipment to collecting – say – entomology.

But one thing every type of collecting in the field does require is rigorous field documentation. Many museums, sadly, can show examples of collections acquired in the past that are much less useful than they should be. This is because the museum failed to record all the information it could have recorded when it was collecting.

It is a vital part of the collecting programme to lay down precise procedures for field documentation. The museum managers must insist that all staff follow the procedures precisely, and they should also ensure that younger members of their staff are so well trained in field documentation that it becomes second nature to them.

Read Paragraph 3.3 from the *Code of Professional Ethics* of the International Council of Museums, 1990, on page 302 of the Appendix.

The actual techniques of field documentation will, like the techniques of collecting, vary from discipline to discipline. Geology fieldwork will require rather different techniques to fieldwork in − say − industrial history. At the core of most techniques, though, will be the field notebook. Every museum worker should be trained to keep a field notebook and to enter it up every day in the field. The notebook should include sketches and diagrams as well as written notes: not everyone can be a great artist, but even the crudest drawing will preserve information which cannot be expressed in words.

Photography is another essential technique in every kind of fieldwork, and all museum workers should use a camera as naturally as they use a notebook (see Unit 40). The tape-recorder, and perhaps video-camera, will be valuable tools for many museum field-workers.

Finally, the museum must ensure that the field documentation is kept safely − for it is as important as the collections themselves − and linked to the collections so that in years to come a researcher studying a group of objects can easily find the records made in the field by the person(s) who collected them.

Remember field documentation belongs to the museum and not to the manager!

UNIT 39   FIELDWORK AND RECORD CENTRES

Related Units: 38, 40, 41

Fieldwork is a major part of the work of many museums, whether in archaeology, social history, ethnography, biology or geology. Museums are often required to store and to make available the results of fieldwork by others. Museums, for example, care for the finds and records from archaeological collections, the collections and notes of geologists, the sketches, tapes and photographs of ethnographers. In many cases museums collaborate with one another in this area because associated records are often held by more than one museum. Researchers may well combine material from many museums to create a whole picture of the topic being studied.

In addition to systematic programmes of fieldwork, the museum staff will acquire a great deal of casual information as part of their everyday work. For example, a museum manager giving a lecture to a local community group might be told about the history of an old house, about the sighting of rare animals, about traditional local customs and about a geological formation briefly exposed by engineering work.

Finally, a great deal of information will be acquired along with artefacts and specimens.

Each of these types of information must be recorded, but how?

The first step must be to formulate a policy for fieldwork and environmental recording, which should be summarised in the museum's Forward Plan (see Units 38 and 69). What level of responsibility does the museum intend to take? At the highest level, the museum would maintain an Environmental Record for its area, seeking to gather information on all aspects of the environment, including land-use, ecology, geology, historic buildings, archaeological finds and sites, and perhaps customs and traditions as well.

A museum attempting this level of environmental recording will require considerable resources, and a sophisticated computerised database. Even a simple Sites and Monuments Record will need staff qualified in information management as well as in archaeology to maintain it. A full Environmental Record will also include geological site records, species records and biological site records, as well, perhaps, as a record of historic buildings and industrial monuments and even of activities and events of ethnographic or sociological interest. Such a Record would need specialist staff in all these areas.

At the lowest level the museum would not maintain any environmental records itself, but would simply make arrangements for any information that came its way to be passed on to another, more appropriate, museum. Thus an art gallery might learn about a newly discovered archaeological site, or a history museum might be told of a threat to an important scientific site. Such museums should have formal arrangements to pass such information on, and all staff, whatever their own specialism, should be able to recognise the importance of such information.

Most museums, though, will fall between these two extremes. They will need to devise ways of recording the information they need in an accessible form.

A common method used by rural museums is to maintain files for each village in their area, into which everything is put, from photographs to field notes. Museums in towns often arrange their files by street. No arrangement is entirely satisfactory, and only if the museum maintains computerised indexes to all its information will it always be possible to find all the information the museum or an enquirer needs.

It is essential, therefore, for every museum to decide what information it will need to record, and what questions that information will most often be expected to answer. Then the museums should devise a system that will best meet those needs, but is not too complicated: a system that is simple but works is very much more useful than a system that is logical and intellectually elegant, but is so complicated that no-one uses it!

STUDY EXAMPLE

A museum with responsibility for an area which covered 100 villages, developed a system of 'village files'. Each file contained a range of standard information, which included

– a list of all archaeological finds from its area and their present location;
– a list of other finds/objects in its collections;
– a list of finds/objects held in other museums from the village;
– a list of all the architecturally significant buildings;
– location maps;
– aerial photographs;
– photographs of field monuments;
– photographs of significant buildings;
– lists and photocopies of relevant historical publications and other bibliographical material of relevance, including press-cuttings;
– transcripts of interviews held with local people;

and so on. Information was put into the files as it occurred. They formed a valuable and developing information resource for research and reference purposes.

Without recording information over time and developing appropriate filing systems, the museum would have been unable to respond effectively to enquiries or to develop other forms of service such as exhibitions, publications and displays.

UNIT 40   PHOTOGRAPHY, FILM AND VIDEO

Related Units: 38, 39, 41

Photography, film and video are used by museums in three ways:

– as recording techniques, for fieldwork and collecting,
– as original records, themselves forming part of the collections,

– as display techniques, to help interpret and present the museum's collections to the public.

In this unit we look at the first way: using photography, film and video, like notepad and sketchbook, as techniques for field recording.

Photography

In almost every country photography is now commonplace, and cheap but reliable cameras are fairly widely available. Museums should all have cameras. Staff should carry cameras with them everywhere, especially whenever they are undertaking fieldwork.

The camera should become as familiar as a pencil and notebook, and be used in the same way. Photography is a wonderful technique for field recording, and all collecting should be accompanied by the taking of photographs. Though high quality photography is still a specialist skill, anyone can take adequate photographs with a modern camera and film, and all museum workers should be able to achieve adequate results.

Museum managers should make sure that all their staff who undertake fieldwork or work with the collections receive regular training in photography, and have access to a camera and to facilities to develop and print film.

Wherever possible museum workers should use 35mm Single Lens Reflex cameras, or even a larger format. They should have a wide-angle lens (35mm or 28mm) as well as the standard 50mm lens, so that they can take photographs indoors or in restricted spaces. Not all museums, of course, will be able to afford this, and the rule must be simply to use the best camera you can afford.

Electronic flash may be useful, but museum workers should learn to take photographs in available light as far as possible, and should have a tripod.

Black and white film is more permanent than colour film, can be processed more easily and often gives clearer record photographs, but colour film can be used as well, and in many countries is now cheaper.

An invariable rule must be to make a note of every photograph you take *at the time*. Record where it was taken, who took it, when it was taken and what it shows.

Once back at the museum, the film should be processed as soon as possible, ideally in a darkroom at the museum. All museum workers should learn to develop and print black and white film, but in many museums it will be more efficient to get the processing done by someone else, perhaps a commercial studio, especially for colour film. Make sure that the technician doing the processing understands the special techniques of 'archival processing' needed to ensure that the negatives and prints last.

Finally, the museum must set up a method of storing and documenting photographs that ensures both that they are kept in the best possible conditions, and that any particular image can be found when required. The best method is to keep the negatives and one print in unique number order, and to have a series of indexes such as people, places, classified by subject to enable them to be found.

Film

Few museums will be able to use film for fieldwork nowadays, but a surprising number of museums have in their collections old documentary film – for example of ethnographic scenes, of local wildlife or of archaeological excavations – of immense historic interest.

Any museum which holds old films should get specialist advice on how to look after them, but the following points should be considered.

■ Have you any film on nitrate stock? A cellulose nitrate base was used for most 35mm film stock up to the early 1950s. It is *very dangerous* because it is highly inflammable and can spontaneously explode. Any nitrate-base films should be copied and the originals kept in a special fireproof building.

■ All films should be stored in a cool dry place, in the dark.

■ Every time a film is projected it is in danger of damage. Try to get historic film copied onto video so that the originals do not have to be used. But keep the originals safely, because video is never of such good quality as film.

Video

So far museums have used video more in displays (see Unit 20) than for fieldwork records. Video is, however, cheap, flexible and easy to use, and, although few museum workers are likely to achieve professional standards, it offers museums an invaluable recording technique.

For recording activities and processes video is invaluable. Nothing else could record so effectively the working of a machine, a craft technique, a dance or a ceremony.

Although VHS format is becoming increasingly popular at international level, there are a number of different video systems in use, and a museum considering using video – whether for fieldwork or in displays – should talk not only to specialists but also to other museums in their country which use it.

UNIT 41   ORAL HISTORY AND AUDIO RECORDING

Related Units: 38–40

In societies where most people do not regularly read and write, story-telling and the oral tradition remain of immense importance. Sadly, it seems that as literacy becomes more widespread, many of the traditions based on memory and word-of-mouth get forgotten, and oral tradition becomes despised by those for whom only what is written on paper is important.

Happily, in the last twenty years the widespread use of tape-recorders has led to a revival in respect for the oral tradition, and to a worldwide movement in favour of oral history. Alex Haley's famous book *Roots* showed how a family could preserve some of its memories from its roots in The Gambia, through the terrible experiences of slavery, to the modern urban world of the United States. His book showed, too, how oral history techniques could be combined with the evidence of historic documents to bring to life a past apparently lost forever.

Oral history is a technique and a hobby which has enlisted the enthusiasm of all sorts of people, from schoolchildren to professional historians. It is something everyone can get involved in, it can illuminate almost any aspect of life, it can create a valuable permanent record and it gives great enjoyment and satisfaction to all involved.

Many museums become involved in oral history work. Many museums are the base for groups of enthusiasts doing oral history work, while museum managers and researchers use oral history tech-

BOX 1

Hints on oral history work

The best place to interview someone is where they feel most comfortable. Often this will be in their own home. Drawing the curtains may improve the acoustics. Place the tape-recorder beside you, keep the notes on your lap and sit facing the interviewee at a comfortable distance; the microphone should be between you and the person you are interviewing.

Reel-to-reel magnetic tape is what professionals use, and it is certainly worth acquiring the equipment if you are going to do a lot of recording or if broadcasting quality is wanted. Modern cassette tape is almost as good, however, and though less versatile the equipment is much cheaper and lighter and the tapes easily obtained in most countries.

The more interviewing you do, the more skilful you will become at extracting valuable historical information from people.

niques as one of their research tools when researching books or exhibitions, or simply when researching the background of objects in the museum's collections.

Tape-recording is also used to record the sound of activities, processes and music.

Although perhaps not so good as video (see Unit 40), tape-recording will help to capture the sound and atmosphere of a huge variety of human activities, and can later be used in conjunction with photographs, written descriptions and original artefacts both for research and in the museum gallery. Examples might include the work of fishermen at sea, ploughmen in the field, ironworkers in the factory or stall-holders in the marketplace.

Tape-recording is a technique of interest to all sorts of museums, not just to history museums. Art museums can record artists talking about their work, and the environment and activities which inspired it, or can record the different views of art historians and critics. Natural history museums can record the sounds of animals, insects or birds. Industrial museums can record the sounds of machinery and the

BOX 2

Preserving the tapes

A museum undertaking even a few oral history interviews will need to give thought to how they are to be preserved and made available to users.

The first thing to create is a record system. This will probably comprise a card system similar to the museum catalogue. There will be a record card for each tape which should include

- date of interview
- name of interviewer
- name of interviewee
- age, occupation and brief family details of interviewee
- where interview took place
- what equipment was used
  copyright details and any restriction on use of the tape

The record card should also ideally contain a summary of the topics covered, preferably with a note of where on the tape they come, as indicated by the index-counter.

What indexes are required? Some sort of classified index is probably necessary, though for a small collection of tapes it may be a very simple one.

The tapes themselves should be kept in a dry, cool atmosphere, as far as possible away from any iron. Ideally they should be kept in a cupboard with brass rather than ferous-metal hinges, in order to avoid electromagnetic sources which can affect the tape.

Experts have disagreed over whether the tapes should be regularly played to keep them in good condition. Most now seem to think that this is unnecessary.

To transcribe every tape is hugely time-consuming, and should probably only be done where the interviewee was promised a transcript or where the transcript is to be published. There is, however, value in making a transcript which can be annotated by the interviewer. Much is hidden from view in a tape-recording, and the interviewer is the one person who can 'interpret' the spoken word effectively because he/she was present at the interview.

reminiscences of their operators. Musical museums can bring their instruments to life with recordings; tape-recording has revolutionised the study of folk-song.

UNIT 42   DOCUMENTATION SYSTEMS

Related Units: 37–41

There is nowadays a standard documentation system, increasingly agreed by museum workers throughout the world. It has six parts:

1   Entry

Every object or group of objects coming into a museum – whether as a gift, purchase, loan or enquiry – is recorded on a numbered *Entry Form*, which is completed (clearly, in ink) in the presence of the donor or vendor who then signs it to certify that it is a correct record. If possible three copies are made:

– one is given to the donor or lender, as a receipt,
– one stays with the object(s) until initial processing is complete, when it goes into a Supplementary Information File or into a Short-term Loans & Enquiries File,
– one is filed permanently in an Entry File arranged in entry number order.

The purpose of the Entry Form (sometimes called a Deposit Form) is both to acknowledge receipt of the object(s) and to ensure that information from the donor is not lost before a full record is made (see also Unit 37).

A *Temporary Label* is tied to the object or objects, bearing the number from the Entry Form.

2   Accessioning

Accessioning is the formal acceptance of all acquisitions (whether by gift, purchase or bequest), into the museum collection.

Each object, or group of objects, to be kept by the museum (whether gift, purchase, bequest or long loan) is entered in the *Accessions Register*. This Register is the most important part of the documentation system. It has three main functions:

– it assigns a unique number to each object,
– it describes each object,
– it gives the history and provenance of each object.

The Register must be a bound book of good-quality paper. Each page should be numbered consecutively. The Register must be kept in a safe place, preferably in a fire-proof cabinet, and a copy must be kept in another building. Entries must be written in permanent black ink only.

Each *group of objects* received at the same time and from the same source is given a permanent *Accession Number*. This may consist of the year of accession, a point and the next number available in the accessions register (e.g. 1992.28).

Each object in the group is then numbered separately (e.g. 1992.28.3). The whole is known as the *Identity Number* and is unique to that particular object.

The advantage of this two-part numbering system is that a large collection can be recorded as a group immediately, while its individual objects may have to wait for attention. Some museums may use a running number system – every object entering the collection is given a unique number in sequential order.

Most objects except for coins should be marked neatly and unobtrusively in permanent black ink; paper items should be marked in pencil. Coins should be kept in coin envelopes and details of the coin, including its accession number, should be written in permanent black ink on the envelope.

To make doubly sure, each object has a *Permanent Label* attached, bearing the permanent identity number. The temporary label is removed.

The permanent Accession Number is also written on the Entry Form.

Wherever possible or practical, the object should be photographed at this stage for record purposes.

Loans in are recorded in the same way as donations, using the Entry Form. Only if they are long-term loans, however, should they be registered (see Unit 37). Short-term loans should be recorded in a separate Loans Book.

It is polite to write to every donor to thank them for their gift, and to tell them that the object has been formally accepted by the museum (see Unit 37).

If the object has been given to the museum, it is a good idea to ask the donor to sign a *Transfer of Title Form*. The top copy goes into the Supplementary Information File, while the donor is given the second copy, signed by the MUSEUM MANAGER. The purpose of the Transfer of Title Form (sometimes called a Donation Form) is to ensure that the museum could – in the event of a dispute – prove its legal ownership of the object. The wording of the form must therefore be in accordance with the laws of the country.

3   Cataloguing

The *Catalogue* entry is then completed. The Catalogue is a complete record of everything that is known about every object in the museum's collections. It can be either held on a card catalogue, or on a computer program.

A card catalogue consists of individual cards, usually pre-printed, kept in Identity Number order in a metal card-drawer, ideally in a fire-proof lockable cabinet.

Seven types of information will be present on each card:

– name of museum
– identity number
– name of object-classification
– entry method (donation, find, purchase or lender)
– source of entry (donor, vendor or lender)
– date of entry
– history of object

Other types of information may be useful as well, but the above are usually considered essential.

The cards should be filed in Identity Number order. (It is almost always a mistake to file them in any other way.)

A *Supplementary Information File* contains all the documentation

---

BOX 1

Materials needed for documentation

- Entry Forms
- Exit Forms
- Transfer of Title Forms
- Accession Register
- Labels
- Supplementary Information File
- Permanent black ink
- Pens
- Catalogue cards
- Index cards
- Card cabinets
- Fire-proof safe

---

relevant to the object. It will contain the Entry Form and Transfer of Title Form for each object, and may also contain invoices, receipts, letters, newspaper cuttings, conservator's report, photographs, excavator's notes, etc.

4   Indexing and retrieval

Indexes enable the manager to find information in the catalogue without reading every single card! The museum must decide what questions are most often asked, and therefore what indexes are needed. The most commonly used indexes are:

- names and details of donor
- classification
- location
- provenance
- artist

In a manual system, there will need to be a separate set of cards for each index. A computer system will permit vastly more sophisticated indexing.

5   Movement control

Movement control means the recording of movements of objects from the collections, both within and in and out of the museum. The bigger the collections, the more important it is for the museum to have a good movement control system.

In the simplest system, every time an object is moved permanently, or for a long period, a note is made on its catalogue card, showing the date it was moved, who by and where to. Every time it is moved temporarily, for a short time, a *Proxy Card* is left in its usual place, showing when it was moved, who by and where to.

6   Exit documentation

Exit documentation records every movement of an object out of the museum building.

A good system to use is an Exit Form similar to the Entry Form. One copy of the form is kept in a Loans Out file until the object comes back, when it is put permanently in the Supplementary Information File. The second copy goes to the borrower or recipient.

BOX 2

Computerisation

Computerising the museum's documentation will save the museum neither money nor time. It will certainly cost rather more than a purely manual system, and will almost certainly need as much staff time to manage.

A poorly-designed or badly-managed documentation system will not be improved by being computerised.

What computerisation *will* do is to allow the museum staff to achieve far more than they could achieve with a manual system. If well-planned and well-managed, it will give the museum much greater control over its collections and its information.

Remember that there are many additional costs involved in managing computers, which require software, disks and other 'consumables' as well as regular maintenance. They will also require a reliable power supply, and will only operate within a specific temperature range, usually 50°F to 104°F (10°C to 40°C). If the range in your museum is outside this range, you may need specially prepared equipment.

How can a museum computerise its documentation? The first step must be to ensure that the museum's basic manual documentation is efficient, well-designed and to modern standards. Computerising will quickly show up problems in the basic system.

The second step must be to seek advice. If at all possible, initial advice should be from someone who understands both computers and museum documentation. Many museums have run into problems because their adviser understood computers, but did not really understand the requirements of museum documentation. Computerising museum documentation and classification is a highly complex field.

If good advice is not available locally, CIDOC, the ICOM International Committee for Documentation may be able to help. The range of reference books cited in Unit 86 is a valuable source of information.

UNIT 43   THE ROLE OF COLLECTIONS IN RESEARCH

Related Units: 35, 36, 38–41

Museum collections of all types have a vital role to play in research. Indeed one of the justifications of collecting material for museum collections is that it forms a permanent body of research material for future generations. Hence it is of critical importance that collecting is not carried out in an arbitrary or aimless way. It must be done within the framework of a carefully constructed collecting and disposal policy, and through well-organised collecting programmes.

Managing collections effectively and efficiently, and making the necessary investment in them over time, will ensure that the collections are maintained for research purposes in the future. It is often the case that in the light of new scientific techniques, new discoveries or new methodologies, researchers will be able to approach and use museum collections in ways which had not previously been considered. The recent advances in the analysis of animal and human bone for DNA is a contemporary example.

In considering the role of collections in research it is also necessary to remember that researchers will often be examining classes of material held in more than one museum. Your museum may be one of a number managing, for example, archaeological material or geological material.

In such cases the body of material as a whole may be of interest, the sum of the parts. If some of those parts have been poorly managed and have suffered neglect or degradation, the quality of research is impaired.

Collections in a museum therefore should not be thought of in isolation from other collections. It is essential that the museum is itself able to compare and contrast its own collections with the wider resource. If it does not have the expertise in-house to encompass all fields, it should seek to obtain it from other institutions, such as universities, colleges, other museums.

The responsibility of the museum is to assemble as much information about its collections as possible with outside help if or as required.

Carrying out research on collections in-house, or making collections available to outside organisations or individuals for research purposes, illustrates the importance of effective documentation in collections management. Without high-quality records the value of collections is substantially reduced.

The museum should create filing systems and documentation procedures which allow for information about items/specimens to be systematically kept and maintained. Whenever researchers have used information or collections held by the museum for publication purposes, the provision of copies of their published work for the museum should be made a condition of access. In this way the museum actively builds up an information resource of direct benefit to the collections.

In Unit 33 we discussed the opportunities for museums to work with other organisations. In the field of research, museums have good opportunities to create joint research programmes with other museums known to be collecting or to hold collections in the same subject areas. Collections research projects of this type can often lead to improved understanding and awareness of the importance of particular holdings, throw new light on collections through documentary research and lead to joint publications, exhibitions and complementary collecting and research projects. The study example below is based on a large-scale, national research programme, but the principles could be applied for any subject area with relatively small numbers of museums at local or regional level.

STUDY EXAMPLE

A two-year collections research programme was established to record all natural history collections held in museums in one European country. Some 300 museums were surveyed by postal questionnaire, and study visits were made to 100 museums over the two-year period to record selected collections in more detail. The results of the project were recorded on micro-computer, and a report and digest published.

The computer database was used to 'reassemble' collections which had been fragmented across a number of museums and to throw more light on the natural historians in the nineteenth century who had initiated many of the collections. The published report was also able to identify how to improve collections management for the collections, in particular storage and documentation. A number of museums used the report to mount new displays on their natural history collections.

Collaboration in assessing a national resource provided the basis for developing long-term strategies for research and conservation.

UNIT 44   CONSERVATION PLANNING

Related Units: 45–58

Conservation is only one aspect of museum and collections management, but it is in many ways the most important. The collections in the care of the museum form the primary resource from which all other activities flow. The museum's responsibilities to its collections should be paramount above all others. Without collections there is no museum. The duty of care is thus central to the museum's work and should be implicit in the museum's stated mission or purpose and its functional objectives.

We have emphasised throughout this handbook that you should establish policies for the different aspects of your museum's work, and draw up a management plan to help you implement those policies. A key component of the museum's overall forward plan is a conservation plan forming part of the museum's collections management strategy. A conservation plan will help to provide a framework for establishing and maintaining appropriate standards of collections care and for setting priorities for remedial conservation work. What sort of components should there be in a conservation plan and what steps do you need to take to draw up a plan?

Your plan will cover such matters as a strategy for dealing with disasters and emergencies such as fire, flood, civil unrest, war, earthquake (see Unit 56); conservation guidelines in your museum's policies on loans; conservation assessments by conservators; environmental monitoring programmes; buildings inspection and maintenance programmes; and documentation for conservation.

What steps do you need to take to draw up a conservation plan? The following checklist provides some guidelines:

1. First ensure that the conservation plan is drawn up on the basis of the museum's policies towards its collections.

2. The MUSEUM MANAGER then commissions a written assessment of the state of the museum building(s) from a buildings surveyor.

3. The buildings surveyor reports on the structural condition of the

museum building(s), making recommendations for improvement and providing indicative costs.

4. In the light of this report, the MUSEUM MANAGER commissions a written report on the collections in the care of the museum from a conservator.

5. The Conservator reports on:

- environmental conditions in display and storage areas following a programme of monitoring relative humidity, temperature and particulate pollution;
- the state of preservation of the objects or specimens in the collections;
- the methods of storage and display;

and makes recommendations in a written report to the MUSEUM MANAGER on the necessary steps to improve conditions. The report indicates costs and sources of supply, and identifies additional specialist conservation advice which may be needed to supplement the collections report for particular items or specimens.

6. The MUSEUM MANAGER coordinates a curatorial assessment of objects or specimens within the collections to ensure that the museum is aware of the historical or scientific significance of the material held in care. This may necessitate bringing in specialist advice to the museum from individuals in other museums or institutions.

7. In the light of this information, the MUSEUM MANAGER prepares an overall statement of conservation policy for the museum, relating this to other policy statements, e.g. the museum's collecting and disposal policy.

8. The MUSEUM MANAGER then prepares a conservation plan which covers the following aspects:

- the specific improvements necessary to the fabric or structure of the building(s);
- the specific improvements needing to be made in preventive conservation and storage, and the priority order in which these should be carried out;
- the establishment of effective monitoring procedures; for buildings maintenance purposes, for environmental conditions in storage and display areas and for the control of artefacts in the care of the museum;
- priorities for remedial conservation of items/specimens in the collections in the light of the curatorial and conservation assessments;

   – arrangements for training staff in the care of collections, e.g. handling, storage control, documentation, environmental monitoring.

The MUSEUM MANAGER includes in the plan estimates of costs and indicates the timescale over which the work will be carried out.

   9. The MUSEUM MANAGER in consultation with the museum's Governing Body seeks the requisite funds to carry out the necessary work over a defined period.

10. The MUSEUM MANAGER produces a procedure manual for staff engaged in preventive and remedial conservation to ensure that agreed management procedures and standards are adhered to.

You will note that the MUSEUM MANAGER has a central role in this work. It is the Manager's responsibility to ensure the long-term safekeeping and safeguarding of the museum's collections. A conservation plan is a powerful method of achieving this objective.

UNIT 45   WORKING WITH CONSERVATORS
Related Units: 46–53

Few museums have in-house conservators, and many rely on contracting conservators to carry out collections surveys and reports, environmental assessments and remedial conservation work. The availability of trained and experienced conservators working in different disciplines varies from country to country. Consequently museums have to decide how most effectively to obtain and use available professional conservation services to meet their needs.

We have explored the process of conservation planning in Unit 44 and looked at the role of conservators in that process. Wherever possible conservators should be used in environmental assessments of storage and display areas, although through effective staff training programmes and with appropriate equipment other staff can be used to carry these out. Their work should be monitored by a conservator, however, on an agreed schedule.

Collections surveys and reports should also be carried out wherever possible by trained conservators, either generalists or specialists in their fields. General surveys and condition reports on collections may be carried out by other staff following training, where conservators are not easily available.

However, remedial conservation is another matter. Here it is essential to use trained conservators to conserve or restore items. Irreparable damage can be caused by well-intentioned, but unskilled or inappropriate 'conservation' methods.

Some categories of artefact can be cleaned and protected under the supervision of a trained conservator, but in general unless guidance and supervision is readily available this is not recommended. Conservators therefore have an important and continuing role to play for the museum, and establishing good working relationships is vital.

Apart from remedial conservation work, museum managers should also use conservators to help train staff in preventive conservation methods (see Unit 46).

In establishing work programmes for in-house or contract conservators, a detailed, written brief should be developed by the curator together with a schedule for the work programme. Both parties should agree the brief and schedule, and work should be undertaken within this contractual framework.

Conservators are skilled professionals and their work, advice and expertise should be highly regarded by the museum. They should be involved wherever possible or practicable in discussing or planning for exhibitions, displays, storage facilities, new buildings, etc. – wherever collections are to be used or housed. Their advice should also be sought in developing information resources for the museum on conservation, i.e. relevant books/journals about conservation, suppliers of materials for storage or display, suppliers of conservation equipment and names/addresses of other specialist conservators. They should also be used to identify the sort of practical, remedial conservation work that can be legitimately carried out under supervision by trained museum staff/volunteers.

STUDY EXAMPLE

A museum manager newly appointed to a museum contracted a generalist conservator to visit the museum for a week. The conservator worked in a large urban museum and was able to visit the museum as part of a recently established support programme for small museums. The first day was taken up with a survey of preventive conservation measures and necessary improvements, and the remaining four days examined four priority collections and their storage.

Every lunchtime, different groups of staff and volunteers underwent training carried out by the conservator in preventive conservation methods, especially handling and storage methods. The conservator provided a detailed report on the necessary improvements to preventive conservation – new blinds and shutters in the windows, environmental monitoring systems, etc. – and storage, together with special reports on the priority needs for remedial conservation on the four collections and their special storage requirements.

The reports then formed part of the collections management section of the museum's forward plan. The plan also included a new training regime for museum staff and volunteers in the principles and practice of preventive conservation, and refresher courses for senior staff.

Because the reports had been commissioned from an expert outside the museum, the governing body provided additional resources to implement the recommendations.

UNIT 46   PREVENTIVE CONSERVATION: PRINCIPLES

Related Units: 44, 45, 47–53

The essential difference between preventive and remedial conservation is that good preventive conservation should avoid the need for remedial conservation. Preventive conservation is about ensuring that the museum's collections are stored, displayed, handled and maintained in ways which do not lead to deterioration. Remedial conservation is about repairing damage or decay to collections, using techniques which are reversible.

In many cases, preventive conservation is a matter of basic common sense and we explore different aspects of preventive conservation in the succeeding units. It is important to recognise however that efficient preventive conservation is about meeting the museum's responsibilities to care for the collections it holds.

It seeks to ensure that expensive and complex remedial conservation is not required for the future, and can therefore be seen as a form of insurance policy against incurring costs in the future. Preventive conservation and security go hand-in-hand in ensuring the long-term well-being and safeguarding of collections.

These are fundamental responsibilities of the museum's governing body, which must be made aware of the importance of preventive conservation. The MUSEUM MANAGER must exercise skilled diplomacy to persuade and to encourage his/her governors to give priority to this aspect of collections management.

Investment in preventive conservation is now seen as a key priority for museums of all types and sizes internationally.

Different types of collections need different forms of care. What is appropriate, for example, for the storage of metallic objects is not necessarily appropriate for textiles or photographic collections.

Museum managers should therefore be trained in understanding the special needs of different types of collection. In particular, they should be aware of the effects of different materials used in storage and display on museum collections and their special requirements in terms of light, temperature and relative humidity levels. They should be particularly trained in the appropriate handling of items in their collections. Poor handling, packing and transport is a major source of damage to collections, and there can be no excuse for museum staff damaging material in the collections through lack of care in these areas.

Common-sense precautions include:

- ensuring that relative humidity and temperature in storage and display areas are kept stable and at an appropriate level for items;
- ensuring that light levels are at an appropriate level for items on display;
- keeping storage areas unlit when access is not required;
- checking that materials used in storage and display – wood, fabrics, paints, adhesives, plastics and rubber – are not harmful to items; keeping storage areas clean, tidy and uncluttered;
- providing sufficient space in storage containers to avoid crushing or abrasion of items;
- not storing items on top of or inside one another;
- raising stored items/storage containers off the floor of storage areas in case of flooding;
- cleaning items only following expert advice;
- storing items in secure areas;
- checking collections on a regular basis against pest infestation;
- avoiding handling wherever possible, and then only using cotton gloves;
- not smoking, eating or drinking in the vicinity of collections;
- ensuring all staff understand the principles and practice of preventive conservation.

STUDY EXAMPLE

As part of its procedure manual (see Unit 82), a museum established a range of induction procedures for all new staff. Included in these procedures was a two-day course on preventive conservation. As a basis for this in-house course a training manual was developed so that the course tutor(s) could ensure a consistent and standardised approach to the training.

Use was made of existing publications, videos and conservation reports. All staff in the museum were also required to undertake a one-day refresher course each year on preventive conservation techniques. The training manual was extended to include this course.

The training programme was so successful that it became used by a number of small museums in the area.

KEY WORD

PREVENTIVE CONSERVATION – the processes by which a museum's collections are stored, handled, displayed and maintained in ways which do not lead to deterioration and the need for remedial conservation.

UNIT 47   ENVIRONMENTAL MONITORING AND CONTROL: LIGHT

Related Units: 44–6

Light can create serious damage to museum collections, and is one of the greatest threats to the long-term care of collections. Light is a form of energy and can cause colour fading as well as deterioration in the materials from which a museum object is made. All museum objects are to a greater or lesser extent affected by light although metals and ceramics are not affected to the same extent as other materials. While damage from light can never be completely eliminated, it can be reduced by:

– reducing the amount of time an object is illuminated;
– reducing illumination to a level necessary for comfortable viewing by visitors;
– eliminating ultra-violet (UV) radiation (see below).

Light levels

Any light, however strong or weak, causes damage. A strong light produces approximately the same amount of damage in one year as a weak light one-tenth the strength will produce in ten years. The intensity of light is measured by a *light meter* using units of measurements known as *lux units*. Recommended maximum levels of illumination range from 50–200 lux. The following levels should not be exceeded for the categories of material shown:

- 200 lux – oil/tempera paintings, undyed leather, lacquer, wood, horn, bone and ivory, stone.
- 50 lux – costume, textiles, watercolour paintings, tapestries, furniture, prints and drawings, postage stamps, manuscripts, ephemera, miniatures, wallpaper, dyed leather and most natural history and ethnographic items.

Special care should be taken to protect museum items made of more than one type of material. Light levels should be regularly monitored in all areas where collections are displayed or kept, records kept, and staff trained to measure light levels using appropriate equipment. All museums should own light meters for regular use.

It is difficult to reduce the level of illumination to 200 lux when the museum gallery displays are lit by daylight. For a value of 50 lux, daylight is too variable and artificial light will be needed for museum displays containing items which need to be lit at or below that level.

Display and exhibition galleries need to be designed and used with light levels firmly in mind. A combination of artificial light and daylight, which can be controlled by a variety of methods depending on the nature of the material to be displayed, will provide the flexibility a museum needs. The museum has to reach a compromise between the needs of the object (total darkness!) and the needs of the visitor (enough light to see the object). There are a number of methods which can be used singly or in combination by a museum to reduce light levels:

SIMPLE AND CHEAP METHODS

- curtains;
- moving items on display away from window areas;
- fitting screens or covers to display cases;
- installing blinds with horizontal or vertical louvres, curtains or shutters – and closing them when the museum is closed to the public;
- reducing the number and wattage of light bulbs;
- cutting out illumination when the museum is closed to the public;
- fitting dimmer or cut-out switches to room/case lights;

- blocking out windows;
- siting display cases/display screens out of strong daylight zones.

SOPHISTICATED AND MORE EXPENSIVE METHODS

- installing photocells to control blinds automatically;
- fitting time switches to case-lights;
- fitting *diffuser panels* over lighting systems;
- installing 'grey' or light sensitive glass in windows.

Ultra-violet light

The ultra-violet (UV) component of light is particularly damaging, and must be eliminated by using UV absorbent filters. Daylight and fluorescent lamps emit high levels of UV radiation. Tungsten incandescent lamps do not need UV filters, but tungsten halogen (quartz iodine) lamps should only be used with ordinary glass filters to eliminate short wave length UV.

Ultra-violet levels are measured by a *UV-monitor* which measures the proportion of ultra-violet falling on an object. Levels over 75 microwatts per lumen (uw/lm) are considered excessive for light-sensitive objects and the UV-light must be screened out by UV-absorbent film or glass in one of the following ways:

- laminated glass UV filter;
- acrylic/polycarbonate sheets;
- UV varnish applied to window or display case glass;
- polyester film applied to window or display case glass;
- plastic filter sleeves for fluorescent lamp tubes.

Advice should be sought from conservators and manufacturers as to the most appropriate form of protective material for the museum. Check for life expectancy, and length of manufacturers' guarantees.

Radiant heat from lights

Museums should guard against mounting tungsten light fittings too near to museum objects. Heat build-up from tungsten lights can have an adverse affect on the moisture content of sensitive materials, and surface heating can create cracking and splitting. Light fittings of all types should therefore be mounted *outside* display cases wherever possible to avoid radiant heat problems.

Beware, too, of shining spotlights directly on light-sensitive materials as this can cause localised heat build-up and damage.

STUDY EXAMPLE

A museum wishing to show a large collection of postage stamps developed a system of horizontal sliding display units made by a local joiner using appropriate and acceptable materials. The units slid into a cabinet which provided protection from light when the stamps were not being examined, and the unit could also be locked for additional security when the museum was closed. Visitors wishing to see the stamp collection simply slid out each of the 20 display units, which were glazed on both sides, for viewing, and slid them back after study.

The technique described is suitable for a variety of light-sensitive paper items, such as engravings, water-colours and drawings or flat textiles.

Museum display and storage units of this type can be copied or adapted by other museums. A neighbouring museum soon adopted a similar system to store sheets of music.

UNIT 48   ENVIRONMENTAL MONITORING AND CONTROL: TEMPERATURE AND HUMIDITY

Related Units: 44–6

Like light, *temperature* and *humidity* are key agents of deterioration in museum collections. *Relative humidity* (RH) is a ratio of water vapour in the air to the amount that it could hold if fully saturated – and is expressed as a percentage. Low levels of relative humidity imply dry conditions since the air is then capable of taking up moisture. High values are recorded when the air is already humid and unable to take up much more moisture, for example in humid or wet weather. RH is measured with a *hygrometer*.

Stable relative humidity is critical for museum objects. Changes in relative humidity create dimensional changes in organic museum objects, e.g. wood, leather, textiles, ivory, bone, paper, etc. These changes cause expansion and contraction of materials and irreparable damage can result. Organic materials are also liable to attack from moulds/fungi if conditions are humid, over 65 per cent RH (see Unit 49). Metallic objects can also be adversely affected by high levels of

167

RH which encourage corrosion, and as low an RH as possible needs to be provided for all metal objects.

Museums should aim to have a constant RH all year round in storage and display areas. Ideally it should not rise above 60 per cent or fall below 40 per cent, and should be stabilised at 50–55 per cent for a mixed collection.

In older buildings where condensation can occur at this level, 45–50 per cent RH is an effective compromise.

It is perfectly possible of course – and may be a practical solution in many small museums in tropical climates – to provide micro-environments or more controlled areas for special categories of material in the collection.

Museums should be aware however that in certain countries items which have adjusted over a long period of time to particular environmental conditions may be irreparably damaged if introduced into a controlled museum environment too rapidly.

Temperature

Temperature is measured with a *thermometer*. It is associated with relative humidity. The ability of air to hold water vapour increases with higher temperatures, and decreases with lower temperatures. Change in temperature in a storage or display area can therefore affect levels of RH. Changing temperature can also speed up the rate of biological/chemical deterioration. Museum collections do not require high temperatures – a temperature of 18°C (+/– 2°C) is an acceptable temperature for the display of a mixed collection; a temperature of 15°C is adequate for storage areas. Beware of localised high temperatures created by heaters or spotlights.

Measuring environmental conditions

Temperature and relative humidity must be recorded on a regular basis to build up a picture of environmental conditions and problems in the museum. A thermometer and a hygrometer should be installed in those locations where environmental conditions need to be checked. Ideally, an *electronic hygrometer* can be used for taking spot checks on conditions and for calibrating continuous recording instruments. These are called *recording thermohygrographs* and record tempera-

BOX

Conversion chart Centigrade/Fahrenheit

°C	°F	°C	°F	°C	°F	°C	°F	°C	°F	°C	°F
−20	−4·0	1	33·8	22	71·6	43	109·4	64	147·2	85	185·0
−19	−2·2	2	35·6	23	73·4	44	111·2	65	149·0	86	186·8
−18	−0·4	3	37·4	24	75·2	45	113·0	66	150·8	87	188·6
−17	1·4	4	39·2	25	77·0	46	114·8	67	152·6	88	190·4
−16	3·2	5	41·0	26	78·8	47	116·6	68	154·4	89	192·2
−15	5·0	6	42·8	27	80·6	48	118·4	69	156·2	90	194·0
−14	6·8	7	44·6	28	82·4	49	120·2	70	158·0	91	195·8
−13	8·6	8	46·4	29	84·2	50	122·0	71	159·8	92	197·6
−12	10·4	9	48·2	30	86·0	51	123·8	72	161·6	93	199·4
−11	12·2	10	50·0	31	87·8	52	125·6	73	163·4	94	201·2
−10	14·0	11	51·8	32	89·6	53	127·4	74	165·2	95	203·0
−9	15·8	12	53·6	33	91·4	54	129·2	75	167·0	96	204·8
−8	17·6	13	55·4	34	93·2	55	131·0	76	168·8	97	206·6
−7	19·4	14	57·2	35	95·0	56	132·8	77	170·6	98	208·4
−6	21·2	15	59·0	36	96·8	57	134·6	78	172·4	99	210·2
−5	23·0	16	60·8	37	98·6	58	136·4	79	174·2	100	212·0
−4	24·8	17	62·6	38	100·4	59	138·2	80	176·0	101	213·8
−3	26·6	18	64·4	39	102·2	60	140·0	81	177·8	102	215·6
−2	28·4	19	66·2	40	104·0	61	141·8	82	179·6	103	217·4
−1	30·2	20	68·0	41	105·8	62	143·6	83	181·4	104	219·2
0	32·0	21	69·8	42	107·6	63	145·4	84	183·2	105	221·0

ture and humidity levels on a weekly or monthly chart. They should be sited in all areas of display and storage where conditions need to be measured. Small case meters or recording strips can also be used to monitor conditions within display cases.

Preventive measures

EQUIPMENT

Various methods of controlling RH conditions exist. Specialised equipment can be used to humidify or dehumidify areas operated by a humidistat. The key requirement is to level out fluctuations in levels of relative humidity. Seasonal change can affect conditions radically. In some countries, a high priority may be to install a permanent heating or cooling system so that constant temperature conditions can be maintained through the year. It can be fitted with individual thermo-stats allowing for adjustment to suit collections in different areas of the museum.

Standards of environmental control will undoubtedly vary from museum to museum depending on resources. At a minimum, museums should aim to eliminate too high or too low levels of relative humidity and should avoid all sudden changes in humidity. A higher standard will require constant RH control throughout the year. It may not be possible to control humidity levels simply by a heating system. Freestanding units – *humidifiers* where conditions are too dry or *dehumidifiers* where conditions are too damp – may need to be used. An optimum approach is to use a full air-conditioning system, but this will be too expensive for many smaller museums to contemplate.

CONTROL MEASURES

Where money is short, the museum will need to improvise. Windows can be opened in good weather to help ventilate the indoor climate and to introduce warm air into damp or cold rooms, but avoid periods of high atmospheric pollution especially in urban environments or desert areas. Fans can also be used to circulate air and artificial heat can be used to dry out damp environments. Oil or paraffin burners should *not* be used as their gases are harmful. If humidity levels are too low, introduce trays of wet cotton wool and fungicide in different parts of the display or storage areas.

Other basic precautions include:

– keeping all objects off floor level in case of dampness;
– keeping all objects away from outside walls in case of condensation;
– providing space for free air-flow and adequate ventilation;
– specifying individuals to be responsible for monitoring environmental conditions;
– ensuring that the museum has control over heating systems in use in storage and display areas. Sometimes where a museum is in a building shared with one or more organisations, lack of control can be a problem;
– maintaining equipment and climate control systems on a regular maintenance schedule;
– not introducing amounts of water into display and storage areas, e.g. for cleaning purposes, without due care and control.

UNIT 49   ENVIRONMENTAL MONITORING AND CONTROL: AIR POLLUTION/INSECT AND PEST ATTACK

Related Units: 44–6

Air pollution

Air pollution is mainly associated with urban areas and industry, and it is mostly caused by the burning of fuels. In urban areas dirt particles move in the air. Particles vary in weight and therefore settle in different ways and in different densities.

Dirt particles in the air outside the museum include sooty and tarry material. They are usually acid from having absorbed sulphur dioxide – especially where fuels have been burnt in power stations or in vehicle engines – and can contain traces of metal, e.g. iron which can create deterioration. Dust and dirt particles therefore can absorb moisture and acids from the air and in contact with museum objects set up undesirable chemical reactions – the corrosion of metals being a particular difficulty. In desert regions, sand or dust storms are an additional hazard.

Other forms of air pollution derive from furnishing materials such as carpets and curtains in the museum; salt in the air in coastal regions which can cause severe deterioration in metalwork; and gaseous pollution which, like particulate pollution, is caused by burning fuel in factories, cars, machinery, power stations and chemical plants. A typical city atmosphere includes:

– 20 per cent Oxygen O_2
– 78 per cent Nitrogen N_2
– Carbon Dioxide CO_2
– Water Vapour H_2O
– Argon Ar
– Contaminant gases

The worst contaminant gases are

– Sulphur Dioxide SO_2
– Sulphur Trioxide SO_3
– Ozone O_3
– Nitrous Oxides NO_1, NO_2, NC_2O_3

Sulphur is released by burning petrol. Sulphur plus Oxygen gives

Sulphur Dioxide; Sulphur Dioxide plus Oxygen gives Sulphur Trioxide; Sulphur Trioxide plus water gives Sulphuric Acid. In a similar reaction Ozone and Nitrous Oxides produce Nitric Acid. Both acids are strong, powerful and attack many materials including stone, metal and organic materials.

For museums in towns or industrial areas, or in areas which are at risk in other ways, museums should ideally invest in air filtering or conditioning systems. This is expensive, and for many museums not a possibility. The problem of dirt and dust must therefore be minimised in other ways. Dirt on museum objects not only looks unsightly, but also requires to be cleaned off. Cleaning carries with it certain dangers and risks if not carried out appropriately. No object should ever be dusted.

Techniques include:

- avoiding putting objects on open display;
- using well-made, dust resistant display cases;
- keeping objects wrapped in acid free tissue paper in closed storage units or boxes with lids;
- using dust covers for large objects;
- keeping doors and windows shut and sealed where possible or desirable;
- ensuring public and staff areas of the museum are kept as clean as possible;
- cleaning museum areas with vacuum cleaners, not dusters.

Insect/pest attack

Insect and pest attack, especially rodents, can be a particular problem for museums. The control of rodents is relatively simple, although commercial companies may be needed to protect against the problem or eradicate nests, etc. Advice should be sought in appropriate methods. Don't disregard traditional methods of controlling insects and other pests. For example, the museum cat is a cheap and simple method of reducing rodent problems! Rodents can not only damage museum items, especially where these are made of organic materials or are natural history specimens, but also packaging materials, electrical wiring circuits, etc. Storage areas in particular should be regularly checked for any signs of rodent presence.

Insects are a more complicated matter. All organic material, especially wood, entering the museum should be first inspected for insect infestation. Insects are notoriously difficult to kill especially where they have to be controlled in areas such as public display galleries where only 'safe' measures can be taken.

The normal life cycle of insects passes through three stages: egg, larva and adult. It is often the larva which damages items, but cannot always be detected until the adult stage is reached. Signs of attack vary from insect to insect – active woodworm, for example, produces little piles of sawdust, while insect attack on natural history specimens produces disturbance of bird feathers or fallen hair in mammals. Termites are a particular menace in many countries. Professional advice needs to be taken and a regular control programme established.

Various proprietary brands of chemical treatment against beetles and moths are available, which can be absorbed onto inert pads and put into showcases and storage areas as a preventive measure. Fumigation of items, which may be necessary to kill eggs or larvae, is a hazardous procedure, and appropriate equipment and safeguards are essential. In all cases, health and safety measures should be closely observed (see Unit 81).

As with all conservation, prevention is better than cure, and vigilance and regular inspection are required to avoid damage to collections.

UNIT 50   MATERIALS TESTING

Related Units: 44–6, 51–3

Materials which may be convenient or look attractive for storage or display purposes can cause serious physical or chemical damage to museum collections. Materials for display cases and storage containers/shelves should be inert, especially as these may be reused for different objects at a later date.

Chemical damage

One of the main causes of chemical damage in museums is from materials which release compounds into the air in vapour form. We have already noted, in Unit 49, how dangerous such gaseous pollution can be to collections. In confined spaces, such as display cases or storage cupboards, vapours generated from materials can build up to a serious level very rapidly and affect items. Metals are particularly liable to attack and can corrode very quickly.

Organic acids can act as a catalyst for the reaction between lead and carbon dioxide. The reaction causes the surface of lead to be covered by a white powdery layer of lead carbonate. If the reaction is allowed to continue loss of surface detail and ultimately disintegration will follow. While this type of damage is easy to see, other types of decay are not usually obvious such as the effect of formaldehyde on leather which makes it brittle.

Materials should be tested before use, and manufacturers asked to guarantee the suitability of their products for the use(s) intended by the museum. Money can be wasted if inappropriate materials are used, and collections can be put at risk or suffer irreparable damage. Take care to ensure that manufacturers have not changed the composition of their products without notification since previous testing.

Problems

WOOD

All woods produce vapours harmful to objects – some are worse than others. Unseasoned wood produces more than seasoned wood. Least harmful woods include mahogany, obeche and well-seasoned soft woods; most harmful include oak, chestnut and Douglas fir.

Composite boards, chipboard, plywood and hardboard emit organic acid vapour, as well as producing vapours from their bonding adhesives. These are usually formaldehyde-based resins, which can tarnish metals, and damage materials containing protein – leather, wool, fur and bone. Marine and exterior plywood are usually bonded by adhesives which release lower forms of formaldehyde and are therefore safer to use.

To minimise dangers from wood/resin vapours, wood should be sealed with suitable paints, varnishes or lacquers. These cannot stop the emission of vapours completely, and impermeable membranes such as aluminium foil can be used to supplement sealants. Remember to seal the edges of composite boards which emit vapours at a higher rate than surfaces.

FABRICS

Woollen textiles and felts contain sulphur compounds and can tarnish metals. They can also take up moisture in the air. Cellulose-based materials – cotton, linen, hessian – do not create this problem. Where cellulose-based materials have been dyed, it is worth having the material tested by a conservator before use as some dyes have sulphur in them.

PAINTS

Oil-based paints will produce organic acid vapour as they dry, so ensure that these paints are dry before use and the smell has disappeared. Allow plenty of time for emulsion paints to dry before use. It is preferable to use as little paint within display cases as possible. Seal wood and cover it with a safe fabric where possible.

ADHESIVES

Many synthetic adhesives have complex chemical formulae and should be avoided near objects. Advice needs to be taken from professional conservators before use.

PLASTICS/RUBBER

Some poly-foam and sheeting is stable and can be used as lining boards and display mounts in display cases. Stable forms of polyester are used for envelopes for archival material and packing tissue.

Polyurethane or rubber-based materials should be avoided. Rubber is not a stable material and can perish under adverse conditions.

Problems associated with chemical damage can be more acute in high temperatures or high relative humidity (see Unit 48).

MATERIALS IN CONTACT WITH OBJECTS

- Never use 'plasticine' or proprietary putty-like substances for fixing objects. Staining and tarnishing can result.
- Never use rubber bands for attaching labels or mounting objects. Rubber tends to age and stick to objects.
- Never use metal pins or wire in contact with metal objects as corrosion will occur. Use perspex rods or nylon wire or thread.
- Never use metal pins in contact with textile, leather, bone or organic moisture-holding materials as the pins corrode and stain objects and materials.

If in doubt, contact a conservator and the manufacturer/supplier. Where possible, carry out tests to ensure that appropriate materials are used at all times.

A museum had used 'drawing pins' or 'thumb-tacks' to fasten a number of original photographs to a display board covered by felt. Because the relative humidity in the display room was high, the felt had absorbed moisture and the pins gradually rusted. The rust damaged and discoloured the corners of the photographs through which the pins had been pushed – a practice to be avoided at all times!

The photographs had been lent for a special exhibition, and when the lender saw the way in which the museum had not cared for the photographs properly, she withdrew them from the exhibition. The photographs had been the central feature of the exhibition.

The museum had demonstrated that it was not able to look after collections responsibly, and its reputation was severely affected by the subsequent embarrassment.

UNIT 51   STORAGE: LARGE AND HEAVY OBJECTS

Related Units: 44–50, 52, 53, 57, 58

Storage of large and heavy items carries with it special needs. As with all collections storage, a suitably secure building is required; environmental conditions need to be controlled; systems and procedures need to be developed for documenting the entry, exit and location of items, and for audit and stocktaking; handling procedures and equipment need to be developed and provided; regular conservation assessment needs to be undertaken; and access and accessibility need to be assured.

Storage buildings

Buildings used for the storage of large or heavy items – industrial and agricultural collections, transport collections, monumental or architectural items – or the bulk storage of collections, such as excavated bone or ceramics, should be secure, weather-proof, well-lit and adequately provided with an electricity supply.

Most museum objects are likely to be accommodated in a building with a headroom of 5–6 metres, suitable for a lorry to be unloaded with the aid of a mobile crane or fork-lift truck. If the building has columns, a spacing of $c4$ metres is likely to be the minimum acceptable. The main access door should be the full height of the building and not less than $c4$m wide.

For unloading and moving purposes, there should be a concrete platform or apron outside the main access at floor level. Heavier items can then be unloaded outside the building and pulled or winched inside. It is helpful to have anchor points set into the floor for pulling devices. Large items which have to be stored outdoors, should be protected with tarpaulins or covers. Wherever possible, and in whatever climate, it is preferable to store all items inside the storage building. Even large items of machinery which have been working in the open can deteriorate if left stored open to the elements.

Environmental conditions

Creating appropriate environments for stores holding large items is complicated. Sufficient heating or dehumidification must be provided to ensure that condensation is avoided, otherwise even with the application of preservatives metalwork will rust. With large items made of wood, or a range of materials, too low a level of humidity or fluctuating relative humidity will cause damage. A stable environment should be aimed at (see Unit 48) with an RH level of 50–55 per cent.

As we noted in Unit 49 stores should be kept as clean as possible at all times. Concrete floors should be sealed to avoid concrete dust being thrown up. Items should be covered with dust sheets; polythene sheeting, however, should not be used as it can easily cause condensation.

Care of collections

Equipment needed for large and heavy item storage includes a variety of mechanical handling systems. Where possible items should be put on wooden pallets, stored in heavy duty racking and moved with a fork-lift truck or hydraulic lift. Special care should be taken in terms of health and safety. The lifting and manipulation of heavy items should be very carefully planned and carried out to avoid any danger to museum staff.

It is worthwhile reassembling industrial items or machinery where possible. It is easier to store a machine in a made-up form, than in many component parts. It is very easy for machine parts, for example, to be muddled up or to be damaged. Many large/heavy items can be severely damaged by poor handling. Just because they are large and heavy does not mean that they are robust! Stone items in particular can be much more fragile than they look. Every care should be taken in handling and storage not to put stress on weak parts.

Large and heavy items being stored or moved in a museum building – stone, sculpture, paintings, mummy cases, furniture – need very careful handling and support (see Unit 53).

UNIT 52   STORAGE: SMALL AND LIGHT OBJECTS

Related Units: 44–51, 53, 57, 58

The large majority of museums are responsible for collections which do not include particularly large or heavy items. The storage of collections is often poorly considered and inappropriate. A key responsibility of museum managers is to ensure that adequate storage facilities and methods are provided for the museum and its collections.

In most museums, the bulk of the collections are in store rather than on display. The same standards of care, however, need to be exercised for material on display or in store, and more space for storage is likely to be needed than for display. There is no set prescription for storage facilities but general principles are outlined here with some advice on caring for individual types of material in store.

Storage systems and facilities

As with the storage of large items, storage facilities need to be secure and housed in a suitable building. Environmental conditions need to be controlled (see Units 47–9). Systems/procedures need to be developed for the entry, exit and location of all items, and for audit and stocktaking. Safe handling procedures need to be developed, and regular conservation and security assessment needs to be undertaken. Unauthorised personnel should never be allowed in storage areas or facilities.

Space needs to be provided for the movement of people and collections, and space for expansion as more items enter the collections needs to be provided. Written procedures for logging staff in and out of storage areas, and for ensuring that equipment such as humidifiers or thermohygrographs are maintained on a regular schedule should be established.

There are no simple prescriptions for storage facilities for small/light museum collections. Different categories of material require different attention, however, and each have special requirements – some of these are noted below. In general terms, storage facilities need to maximise space without overcrowding or creating hazards for the movement of items or people.

Racking systems and cupboards are commonly used for a wide range of items which may be boxed, covered or kept in drawers. Great care needs to be taken with racking systems and storage cupboards to ensure that items do not touch each other, where not otherwise protected by individual containers, and that items are never piled on top of one another. Racking systems and cupboards therefore need to be of an adequate size to cope with the collections and should have adjustable shelving to allow for changes in use. Racking/shelving systems can be built as free-standing units, or in roller systems to maximise limited space and to allow for increased security.

Cupboards – metal or wood – have the benefit of being lockable, although care needs to be taken to ensure adequate ventilation. The use of acid-free storage boxes/containers and acid-free tissue paper as a padding and packaging medium is recommended for all types of collections.

It is helpful to have lists of items in any one storage container – box, shelf, cupboard – attached to the outside of the storage container for ease of reference and security checking. This helps to prevent un-necessary searching for items which may lead to damage. These checklists can form part of the documentation systems for entry, exit and location as well as helping in audit and stocktaking.

Storage methods

METALLIC OBJECTS

Iron objects should ideally be stored at a relative humidity of 40 per cent or less, although for mixed material objects or mixed collections an RH of 50–55 per cent is acceptable. Iron will corrode if relative humidity levels are too high, and every effort should be made to create adequate conditions for storage by providing suitable micro-environments within general storage areas.

Iron objects from excavations on land or underwater can often be unrecognisable and it is only through X-ray that their function or form becomes apparent. It is therefore essential that all iron is treated carefully, and stored in inert containers with acid-free tissue or packaging materials such as inert foam to avoid movement within the storage container.

As with iron objects, copper alloy or bronze items should be kept in conditions of low relative humidity, at 40 per cent RH or less where possible, to avoid corrosion. Other metal objects, silver, lead, gold should be stored in inert plastic or metal cabinets or containers. Dry silica gel, a desiccant agent, can be used in storage containers to help provide localised control of relative humidity. It absorbs moisture from the air and helps to achieve a balanced environment. The manufacturer will supply details of the amount of gel needed to provide good protection for the objects.

CERAMIC COLLECTIONS

All ceramics should be handled as little as possible and with great care, and should be stored in their normal upright position in secure, dust-free cupboards, one row deep on a shelf. If space does not allow, store smaller items in front of larger ones. Never overcrowd ceramics in store, and always see that there is sufficient clearance for withdrawal or when closing the door. Never stack cups and bowls inside one another, and never stack too many plates in a pile. Where plates are stacked, use folded tissue paper or insert foam or paper between them. Wherever possible, store ceramics on lightly padded shelves to minimise the shock of any vibration or movement, and make sure that lateral movement is minimised by padding.

ETHNOGRAPHIC COLLECTIONS

Ethnographic collections include complex objects which are often made from organic materials, leather, hide, skin, grass, wood, fur, feathers, shells, etc. All of these materials are sensitive to RH fluctuation and prone to insect/pest attack (see Units 48–9). Storage conditions should be 50–55 per cent RH wherever possible. Where storing items on shelving aim for a free movement of air around the object to inhibit possible mould growth, and a dust-free environment. The best packing material for most ethnographic collections is acid-free tissue paper, used in conjunction with acid-free storage boxes.

PAINTINGS

In general, problems with the storage of paintings occur with overcrowding, stacking of paintings on top of each other and inadequate space for movement. Strong, secure racking, using wood or metal, should be padded to reduce the danger of frames being chipped or damaged. Care should be taken to ensure that the surfaces of paintings are not in contact with glass or perspex. Sliding storage racks on which paintings or frames can be hung, while expensive, provide a good solution to storage provided that paintings are securely fastened to the racking and are well supported.

Watercolours, prints and drawings which are particularly sensitive to environmental changes, and light, are best stored flat in boxes or drawers with acid-free tissue used as padding. Acid-free storage boxes specially designed for these items should be used. Watercolours, prints and drawings should be stored out of their frames wherever possible.

NATURAL HISTORY COLLECTIONS

As with paintings, care should be taken to avoid overcrowding or stacking in storage containers, on shelves or in cupboards. Damage can too easily occur in these conditions. Sufficient space therefore needs to be given to mounted specimens of birds or animals on shelving, and where stored in boxes sufficient acid-free tissue paper should be used to pad the specimen enclosed.

Study collections of insects, butterflies or moths, etc. need specialised storage and advice should be sought from a trained natural history conservator in their care. Special care needs to be taken to check natural history specimens for pest/insect infestation regularly in storage areas.

TEXTILE COLLECTIONS

Textile collections can be divided into two groups – flat and three-dimensional. Flat textiles include: tapestries, wall hangings, carpets, household linens, bed covers, curtains, flags and banners, embroideries and lace. Three-dimensional textiles include costume, accessories and upholstery.

Flat textiles should be stored flat in trays or acid-free boxes interleaved with acid-free tissue. If the objects are too large they can be rolled onto cardboard or plastic tubes. Cardboard tubes are acidic and should be first protected by wrapping in aluminium foil and acid-free tissue paper. Once rolled onto the tube, the textile should be wrapped in pre-washed calico or closely-woven cotton fabric and tied with wide tapes. Tubes should be stored suspended in racking, and rolled textiles should never be stacked on top of each other.

Three-dimensional textile items should be hung on prepared and padded hangers and well spaced in cupboards with protective cotton covers, where the item is robust enough. For more delicate items, as well as costume accessories, storage in boxes with acid-free tissue padding is recommended. Upholstered items such as chairs, sofas, screens should be covered with pre-washed closely woven cotton to protect them from dust and dirt. Textile conservation is extremely time-consuming and therefore expensive, and good storage will help to prevent damage occurring.

PHOTOGRAPHIC COLLECTIONS

Photographic prints and negatives should be enclosed in archival quality, acid-free paper sleeves, envelopes or wrappers, placed within a box and sited on a shelf or cabinet. Slides are best stored in acid-free paper sleeves in a hanging file in a cabinet. Glass plate negatives should be stored individually in neutral paper enclosures, and put vertically in strong acid-free boxes.

ELECTRONIC MEDIA

Computer discs, audio and video tapes should be stored away from sources of electro-magnetic radiation.

GLASS COLLECTIONS

As with ceramics, never overcrowd storage shelves and never let glass objects touch one another. Never place small objects inside larger ones, and always place smaller items at the front of shelves where more than one row of objects has to be stored. Glass fragments should be stored in boxes with supportive padding made from acid-free tissue or foam plastic. Great care should be taken when handling or moving glass, especially fragments.

GEOLOGICAL COLLECTIONS

Materials used in storage containers should be tested in advance of their use with geological collections. It is commonly and mistakenly thought that geological collections are stable. This is by no means true. Oak cabinets will release organic acid vapour which affects carbonate specimens; lead specimens can be corroded by acetic and formic acid from composite boards and boxes. Specimens should therefore be stored with due care to their packing.

Poor handling or inadequate packing is often the cause of damage to geological specimens. Specimens should be placed in trays or in acetate topped boxes so that they are held gently but firmly, and cannot knock or rub against each other. Acid-free tissue paper can be used for additional packing. Drawers in cabinets should be of a size that allows them to be easily lifted when full of specimens.

Don't forget: geological specimens are heavy!

UNIT 53   HANDLING AND PACKING

Related Units: 44–6, 50–2

Handling museum artefacts or specimens of all types and of all sizes in the primary collections should be kept to a minimum at all times. Apart from the damage handling itself can do to artefacts, they are exposed to many more risks when handled. Most damage to museum collections comes about through careless handling and transport, or poor storage.

It is important to think ahead and plan before handling and packing artefacts. The checklist below is designed to help raise as well as answer questions which are relevant to handling and packing collections of all types.

☐ General points

– If an artefact needs to be handled for study, transit, restorage, display, etc., only allow designated, responsible persons to handle material.
– Never let persons handle collections, e.g. students/researchers, without express guidance and supervision at all times.
– Understand the special needs of different artefact types before handling.
– Use lintless cotton gloves to handle artefacts to avoid leaving residue from fingers/hands.
– Concentrate when handling objects; do not carry on conversations, attempt to write with one hand, answer the telephone, etc.
– Special care should be taken when handling certain types of object, e.g. old bird/animal mounts which may have been treated with arsenic, or radioactive materials. Appropriate gloves, masks, eye-masks and protective clothing is required.
– Wear protective clothing where necessary, e.g. a cotton laboratory coat or the like when handling material.

- Use pencils, not ink, in the vicinity of artefacts, or natural history specimens.
- Never eat, drink or smoke in the vicinity of an artefact or natural history specimen.
- Know and carry out all relevant health and safety requirements.

☐ When studying

- Never reach across artefacts or carry one artefact across another in case of accidents.
- Never pile material on top of other material.
- Remember that lightweight items, e.g. glass, can be easily knocked over. Take necessary precautions to create cushioning wherever possible.
- Never leave material out of storage containers, for example on a table, for any length of time unattended.
- When working with items, work on a clean, uncluttered table or desk or in a clean area. You may need to pad work surfaces for certain types of artefact.
- Never lift fragile material by weak points such as the rim or handle, but use both hands to cradle the item.

☐ In the stores

- Keep stores uncluttered, tidy and clean to avoid accidents when material is being carried or moved.
- Use both hands to lift material.
- Do not overload drawers, storage boxes or containers – too much weight can create difficulties in lifting or sliding.
- In storage areas, on racking and in boxes and containers, ensure material is spaced effectively to avoid items rubbing against each other.
- Ensure that objects are relocated in the correct position, following study or display, when re-entering stores.
- Carry one object, drawer or box at a time.
- Do not carry material stacked on top of other material.
- When carrying smaller items, use a padded container or basket.
- Make sure that doors are opened for you if required, rather than trying to open a door while carrying material or putting material temporarily on the floor to open the door.
- Never put material down in a location where collections are not normally held.
- Make sure that you have enough people to help, or appropriate equipment, e.g. trolleys, hydraulic lifting apparatus, carrying straps, glass-lifters to assist.
- Use trolleys in stores where possible or practical to avoid carrying.

☐ **Packing and transit**

- Pack or store material wherever possible using inert, tested materials such as acid-free tissue paper or acid-free storage boxes.
- Packing for transit implies movement, vibration and shock, and artefacts need to be carefully protected and cushioned. Use experienced and trained technicians where possible or ask for advice if uncertain.
- When moving three-dimensional artefacts, make sure the rear and sides are protected well.
- When moving items, make certain that corners are well protected.
- Label all items in transit with FRAGILE/THIS WAY UP notices and put red warnings on vulnerable parts.

There are many useful publications on transport of museum collections and special packing systems. Museum managers should be fully aware of all the risks inherent in handling, movement and transport of collections.

With careful forward planning, and effective preparation, risks can be minimised. Without due care and attention, and consideration, museum collections are at their most vulnerable when being handled or moved. Museum managers must make certain that all staff designated to handle collections are fully aware of procedures and risks, and training should be provided in this crucially important area.

UNIT 54   REMEDIAL CONSERVATION: PRINCIPLES

Remedial conservation is the process by which the deterioration of an object is halted and its survival in a stable condition is assured. Conservators are highly skilled individuals and will have, or develop through training, a close understanding of the make up of an object and its physical condition. It is their job to analyse the needs of an object and to treat it in an appropriate way. Wherever possible, the conservator will use materials, or employ methods of treatment which can be reversed at a later date if required.

Different materials require different conservation treatments and remedial conservation can often be a very time-consuming and costly matter. New, often highly sophisticated, scientific techniques are now employed by conservators to examine and analyse objects before treatment. It follows that items which have undergone remedial conservation must be returned to conditions of storage or display which will ensure their survival in the long term. Remedial and preventive conservation therefore go hand in hand.

Where a museum has identified a programme of remedial conservation (see Unit 44), the conservator should provide estimates for the work to be carried out. While these estimates may need to be revised once work in the studio or laboratory begins and the conservator can examine the object(s) in appropriate conditions, they provide a basis on which the museum can plan and budget for the conservation programme.

Detailed records, including photographs, should be taken of the remedial work carried out on the objects, and copies should be returned to the museum with the conserved items. If in the future work is required, these records provide a valuable part of the 'conservation history' of the object. Cross references should be established to the museum's collections documentation system, so that a record of all work that has been carried out is easily accessible.

Curator and conservator should work closely together in the remedial conservation process. The conservator will benefit from having detailed information about the object to be treated, and the curatorial staff should take an informed interest in the work which the conservator carries out on the object.

Conservation or restoration?

The difference between the terms 'conservation' and 'restoration' is an important one for museum staff to understand. In some countries the processes are barely distinguished from each other. But the distinction is important. While remedial conservation seeks to halt the deterioration and stabilise an object, restoration aims to return an object to as near its original position as possible. In museum work, restoration may follow from conservation if there is a need, for example, for the object to be meaningfully displayed.

Different objects will require different approaches. If restoration work is carried out, it should be undertaken with the same attention to detail as remedial conservation. Over-restoring an object can damage its historical and aesthetic value. Restoration will require often detailed comparative research with other objects of similar type, and the processes used must always be capable of reversal if at some future time new techniques or new research findings require modification or alteration to the restored object. Detailed records of process and the approach used in any restoration must be fully documented, and supplied to the museum when the work is completed.

The balance between conservation and restoration is often a difficult matter. Some objects, such as vehicles, for example, may need to be fully restored if they are to be displayed in working condition. It is essential for conservators/restorers and museums alike to be able to identify and explain to the public the extent of restoration on a museum object.

Conservators have undergone intensive professional training and work within the framework of a professional code of ethics. No remedial conservation should be undertaken by unsupervised museum staff as such work always causes irreparable damage to collections. Always take guidance from a professional conservator.

If your museum does not employ conservation staff, and you wish to have remedial conservation carried out, select conservators on the basis of their experience, qualifications and the type of work they have carried out. Ask colleagues in other museums what quality of service they have received, and visit conservators at their workplace to discuss their work, and the range of documentation or photography they will provide.

Developing a good working relationship with the conservator will be of the utmost importance in any conservation programme which you undertake.

KEY WORD

REMEDIAL CONSERVATION – the processes involved in repairing damage to collections, using specialist conservation techniques which are reversible. The need for remedial conservation is often due to poor collections' management and inadequate preventive conservation measures.

UNIT 55   REMEDIAL CONSERVATION: PRACTICE

Related Units: 44–5

In general terms, only experienced and professionally trained conservators should carry out remedial conservation on museum collections. An enormous amount of damage can occur if untrained or unsupervised individuals attempt to carry out remedial conservation, and museum managers should guard against this happening. It is often the case that well-meaning intentions can lead to irreversible damage to museum items. Inappropriate cleaning techniques or materials may be used, adhesives may affect material adversely because of their chemical composition or physical damage may occur which cannot be undone.

In practice, museum collections are extraordinarily wide-ranging – different types of objects and different types of material have different types of needs (see Units 46–53). It is this range of need that requires expert knowledge, and few conservators can be expected to have expert knowledge across all specialist areas. However, conservators can advise on what *not* to do in a general sense, or help create a scheme within which conservation can be carried out.

The key element is skill. In many areas, highly skilled traditional craft workers (with, say, textiles or wooden objects) may be the best people to undertake the actual work of restoration, but always under the supervision of the conservator and the museum manager.

Some limited basic conservation, or repair and restoration (see Unit 54), can be carried out on museum collections by people who are not trained conservators, but the museum manager must always work with conservators to define precisely what can and what cannot be done by unskilled people. They must, of course, be fully briefed as to what are the limits of their work; and they should be reassured that it is always better to ask for advice from the museum manager than to make a mistake with a museum object. Once the museum manager has established these procedures, it may be possible, under skilled supervision and guidance, for much useful work to be carried out in this way.

There are risks, even with good procedures, to using unskilled workers. For example, metalwork can be cared for by using appropriate methods. But what on the surface of things may appear a straightforward process to the untutored eye, such as cleaning and polishing, can have long-term damaging effects on objects unless suitable materials and techniques are always used. Constant support and guidance are needed, and regular discussions with workers should be held, as methods can and do change, and they need to be kept fully informed.

In particular, delicate objects such as textiles, ceramics, glass objects, clocks and watches or paintings can be irreversibly damaged if treated in an inappropriate way. Many 'amateur' conservators will not necessarily appreciate the damage they can cause.

Techniques, methods and materials may vary through time. A professional conservator will be able to keep the museum manager up to date and advise on the best possible way to approach the collections.

Museums have a key responsibility in caring for collections. Never attempt to conserve or restore an item without guidance from a professionally trained conservator.

UNIT 56   DISASTER PLANNING/ INSURANCE

Related Units: 44–6, 53, 57, 58, 63

Disasters can and do occur at any time and in any place. Museums are not immune to fire or flood, earthquakes or explosions, civil unrest, vandalism or war damage. The disaster may be small- or large-scale, due to neglect, error, human agency or forces of nature. How can museums cope with disasters?

First, any disaster requires a speedy reaction to reduce or limit damage to collections, buildings/equipment or people. Controlling a disaster is only likely to be effective if systems and procedures have already been put in place. This means planning ahead for possible eventualities and producing a *Disaster Control Plan* for the museum. Where possible the museum should ensure that its Disaster Control Plan relates to national or local disaster planning.

A Disaster Control Plan should set out the steps for *preventing disasters* and *reacting to disasters* efficiently and speedily. Museum staff should be trained to deal with disasters; the museum should have disaster control equipment and supplies; and planned procedures. Such measures should be considered in relation to a museum's insurance policies.

Preventive measures to combat security and conservation problems are discussed elsewhere in this book (see Units 46–9 and 57–8, for example). Here we identify a series of steps to take in planning procedures and reacting to disasters.

1 THE DISASTER REACTION TEAM

A Disaster Reaction Team is made up of about six capable individuals, not necessarily all from the museum's staff, who are readily available in the event of a disaster. Many disasters occur when museums are closed and there are no staff on the premises. The team should therefore include people who have collections management and conservation skills with at least one person knowing the museum's collections. The team leader should have an understanding of conservation requirements.

They should be trained and briefed on the layout of the museum building(s) and its emergency points, for example, fire extinguishers, disaster boxes, telephones, alarm points and service control points. Each member should have a copy of the museum's Disaster Control Plan which should be updated on a regular basis. The size of the museum will determine the number of teams necessary.

2 DISASTER CONTROL EQUIPMENT

Basic equipment/supplies should be readily at hand in the event of a disaster. The museum should create Disaster Boxes containing protective clothing, emergency equipment, cleaning and packing equipment, storage containers and damage recording supplies. Disaster Boxes should be clearly labelled, sited near high priority/irreplaceable collections, and not used for any other purpose at any time. At least one Disaster Box should be maintained off-site.

Remember that communications is one of the keys to effective disaster control. Telephone systems may well be put out of action in a disaster. Alternative channels of communication, for example radio telephones or couriers, will need to be available or on standby.

3 SUPPORT SERVICES

The museum may need the support of other specialist or allied services such as libraries or archive offices, in the event of disaster. Lists of organisations/individuals providing specialist services, including conservation services, should be kept together with emergency telephone numbers in the Disaster Control Plan. Remember that suppliers of emergency equipment such as pumps, hoses or crates are likely to charge for services.

However, some large and multi-national companies may be prepared to work with the museum in disaster planning and supply equipment or communications system at short notice as part of their service and responsibility to the local community. So, too, will emergency services such as glaziers, plumbers and builders. Insurance companies should be contacted as soon as possible, after a disaster has occurred.

4 DISASTER PROCEDURES

If a disaster strikes a museum during working hours, the procedure for raising the alarm must include contact with the leader of the Disaster Reaction Team. Out of working hours, the relevant emergency services should be provided with full details of whom to contact. The museum should liaise closely with the emergency services on a regular basis to ensure that each is aware of each other's responsibilities.

The leader of the Disaster Reaction Team should ensure that the members of the team are gathered at an appropriate point, together with key museum staff responsible for the collections damaged or under threat. Services such as gas, water, electricity should be disconnected as and when appropriate.

5 DAMAGE ASSESSMENT

When the disaster area is safe and accessible – and not before – the extent of the damage should be investigated, and photographed where possible. Only when this investigation has been carried out carefully can a salvage plan be drawn up. Each member of the team should then be clearly briefed on his/her tasks, issued with protective clothing and set to work. Access to and movement within the disaster area should be controlled by the team leader. Areas should be designated for sorting, cleaning, labelling and packing damaged material.

Remember that security is of critical importance when normal security procedures may not be working normally.

6 REMOVAL OF MATERIAL

This is the most important part of the disaster reaction procedure. Speed is likely to be important, but care is essential. Material must be removed, cleaned, packed and transported to areas of safety and conservation facilities. Early contact should be made with specialist conservation facilities to ensure that material can be treated in the event of disasters.

The following points should be noted:

– items should be removed with the minimum of damage.
– items should be identified and a damage list drawn up.
– where possible items should be photographed.
– where appropriate, items should be cleaned.
– items should be labelled, and packed as appropriate.

— containers should be clearly marked.

— conservation assessment and treatment should be carried out as appropriate (see Units 54–5).

7 THE DISASTER AREA

The speed with which the disaster area can be returned to normal will depend on the nature of the damage. With flood or water damage from fire hoses (a common problem), the area will need to be dried out and ventilated. Care should be taken to inhibit mould growth with fungicides. RH levels should be regularly monitored.

8 DISASTER PROCEDURES ASSESSMENT

Lastly, review the Disaster Control Plan. Did the Plan work well? Did the team(s) carry out their tasks efficiently? Was the Disaster Box properly equipped? What lessons were learnt for the future?

STUDY EXAMPLE

A museums service responsible for twenty museums in its area established a series of disaster supply stockpiles in different locations. Each stockpile consisted of a series of bags of equipment and tools. (The numbers of items in each stockpile varied, depending on the extent of the likely risks.)

The resources included:

— A personal emergency bag kept by each member of the disaster team.
— Protective suit, safety helmet, head torch, safety torch, batteries.
— Bag 1 – Tool bag
— Hammers, pliers, saws, screwdrivers, extension lead.
— Bag 2 – Initial entry equipment
— Safety helmets, protective clothing, protective glasses, leather gloves, polythene sheeting, nylon ropes, first-aid kit (see Unit 81), respirators, safety masks, webbing lifting straps.
— Bag 3 – Wet recovery materials
— Mops, plastic buckets, sponge cloths, blotting paper, dustpans, brushes, rubber gloves, water spray bottles, bandages, safety-pins.
— Bag 4 – Recording and packing equipment
— Hand cleaner, lightweight vinyl gloves, plastic aprons, pencils, notepads, tie-on labels, string, clipboards, self-adhesive labels, stapler/staples, plastic bags, adhesive tape, scissors, rubber bands, paper towels, paper for packing.
— Loose items
— Folding tables, wrapping materials, polythene sheeting, waterproof clothing, salvage blankets.

These bags provide the basis for a disaster supply kit. Their contents, however, can be adapted to local circumstances and the availability of supplies.

UNIT 57 COLLECTIONS SECURITY: PHYSICAL AND ELECTRONIC

Related Units: 44, 45, 58, 63

Physical security

Museum collections, whether behind glass or on open display, are automatically at risk of theft/damage when the museum is open to the public. Increasing market prices for museum items of all types means theft is increasing in museums worldwide. Damage, whether intentional or accidental, through fire, flood or other disasters (see Unit 56), also needs to be protected against.

Collections security depends on:

– effective protective measures;
– appropriate security procedures (see Unit 58) and
– good buildings security (see Unit 63).

Here we examine some protective measures for collections:

1 DISPLAY CASES

Do not assume that a display case, whatever material it is made from, provides complete security – it does not! Two areas of weakness exist – the case glass and the frame, which can be broken/damaged by force; and the locking system which is often easy to overcome. Museum managers should check display cases for weak points – are the case locks visible and accessible to a would-be thief? How strong is the frame? Are wall cases securely attached to the wall system? Can display cases be easily moved or shaken? Do joints provide entry-points for screwdrivers or metal bars? Is the case alarmed? Is it regularly checked by security staff?

2 FRAMED PICTURES

Pictures are vulnerable from theft and damage. Framed pictures should be fastened to walls/screens with mirror plates and screws. Screws should be strong and of suitable length, and the screwheads

193

covered to obscure the type of screw used. Use different sorts of screwhead to increase security. Rod hanging systems are normally supplied with security screws/fastenings for height adjustment. Where required, portable alarm systems can be used for individual pictures, or pictures can be linked to the museum's alarm system (see below).

3 OPEN DISPLAYS

Where collections are on open display, discourage touching/handling by physical barriers, such as ropes or information panels on barriers and by putting items beyond arms reach. Use psychological deterrents such as different floor coverings/textures for visitor routes; notices; and requests in information leaflets. Never leave damage 'on display', for example graffiti on a display board, as it encourages repetition.

Electronic security

Some museums will not be able to afford electronic security and it is worth remembering that alarm systems do not prevent theft or catch thieves. They can be components of your overall security system, which includes effective buildings security, physical security and security procedures. Alarms alert the museum's security staff, and/or an alarm company's station.

Remember that a handbell or a whistle can often be just as effective in alerting security staff to a problem as expensive electronic equipment. Thieves and vandals will only be apprehended if the response time to the alarm is rapid, and the physical/buildings security helps to slow or halt their escape.

Wherever possible, alarm systems should be linked to an alarm company's station to ensure an immediate response, especially when the museum is closed. They should be installed by a reputable alarm company, and regularly checked and maintained. The control panel should be sited in a secure place in the museum, and only a limited number of people should have access to it.

Electronic detection systems include:

■ *magnetic contact* – if a magnetic contact, e.g. on a window, door or a display case is broken, the alarm is sounded.

■ *wiring* – the alarm wire is bedded in a door or shutter, and is only triggered if the door/shutter is cut into.

■ *vibration detectors* – these are set on doors, windows or display cases and activated by abnormal levels of vibration.

■ *break-glass detectors* – these detect the frequency pattern of breaking glass, e.g. in windows and display cases, or rooflights.

■ *passive infra-red sensors* – these sensors are designed to detect body-heat and provide an area such as a corridor or part of a gallery with an alarm screen.

■ *activity detection sensors* – microwave or ultra-sonic sensors detect movement within a detection area. These can be used in conjunction with passive infra-red detectors to provide a cross-checking safeguard in case of a false alarm from one system.

■ *smoke detectors* – sensors detect smoke, trigger alarms and if required water sprinkler or gas prevention systems.

■ *closed circuit television (CCTV)* – CCTV is not a replacement for security staff. It must be watched continuously if a response is to be made to a security threat, and the watcher needs to be in immediate contact with security staff on the ground, for example through two-way radio. Some CCTV systems can be linked to passive infra-red sensors or activity detection sensors, and alert the watcher to possible threat and/or activate recording videotape.

The choice of alarm system will depend on the size of museum, the level of risk and financial resources. Significant advances are being made in micro-electronics every year and systems need to be reappraised on a regular basis.

UNIT 58   COLLECTIONS SECURITY: SYSTEMS AND PROCEDURES

Related Units: 44, 45, 53, 57, 63

Security staff

Security staff deter criminal or anti-social behaviour in the museum and security staff are an essential part of a security system. Security staff should be properly trained and regularly updated in security procedures, and how to respond to emergencies. Where possible in small museums there should be a minimum of two security staff on duty at any one time for personal safety. Security staff should have ready access to an emergency alarm system, for example an alarm button at the reception desk, two-way radio where appropriate and an emergency telephone. Emergency telephone numbers should be immediately at hand (see Unit 56).

Security staff will have a range of duties amongst which should be:

– checking that doors and windows are locked and intact;
– regular, but random patrolling of galleries and other public areas of the museum;
– checking displays and display cases on a daily basis;
– reporting damage or other problems such as the need for replacement light-bulbs, or the need for cleaning;
– and being alert to possible problems with visitors such as rowdiness or suspicious behaviour.

In many small museums, museum staff often have to carry out other tasks as well as providing security cover, for example answering telephone enquiries, or selling items in the museum shop.

The MUSEUM MANAGER will have to give careful thought to how the security and customer care/service aspects of the museum's work can be effectively carried out. The MUSEUM MANAGER should also ensure that the security staff are fully under his/her management.

In far too many museums, theft has been carried out by museum security staff who are often poorly paid and insufficiently trained and managed. On appointment, as far as the laws of the country allow, their personal records should be checked for any previous criminal activity.

Security staff should be regarded as key members of the museum's staff. In some countries, security staff act as excellent guides to the museum's collections. Their interpretive and security duties, however, need to be carefully balanced.

Security procedures

The museum should develop, as part of its procedure manual, clear security procedures which all staff should adhere to (see also Unit 56). The checklist below includes a number of points to build into the procedure:

■ *All* staff should sign in and out of the museum on entry and exit in a daily record book. This provides a checklist of people in the museum in case of fire or other emergency requiring evacuation. All staff should enter/exit from the museum only through official control points.

■ Visitors to private areas of the museum should also sign in and out of the museum, and should be given security badges to wear and be accompanied by a member of staff. Anyone not wearing a badge can thus be challenged if seen in private areas.

■ Key control is an essential part of the security procedure. No internal keys should leave the museum, and keys should be checked and present before the museum closes at the end of the day. One person should have responsibility for key control on a day-to-day basis, record them in a log-book on issue and check them on return. Keys should be kept in a locked cabinet at all times and never left unattended, or lent to unauthorised persons. Keys should be provided to those staff who need them and for no other reasons.

■ Supervision of students and researchers is essential. Always check the credentials of a researcher before allowing access to collections, and ask researchers to write to the museum in advance to make an appointment. Make certain that the items and the supporting documentation to be examined are listed, that the list is signed by the researcher and member of staff supervising at the outset of the period of study and the items are checked off against the list at the end of the period of study. Never leave a researcher or visitor unsupervised, especially in an area where there are collections accessible.

■ Where contractors/delivery firms are entering the museum, stringent security precautions should also apply. The museum manager and security staff should be aware of their arrival and the reasons for their being in the museum. In many cases contractors will be working in sensitive areas of the museum internally and externally. Every care should be taken to ensure that security systems and procedures are not bypassed, that dangerous or inflammable materials are not left in vulnerable areas and that equipment such as ladders is not left unlocked and accessible.

■ Responsibility for the alarm system, its maintenance schedule and testing should be assigned to an appropriate member of staff. The procedures for closing and locking the museum at the end of the day, setting the alarm system and opening the museum at the beginning of the day should be clearly defined, and the responsibility of designated staff. Museums can often be at their most vulnerable at opening and closing times.

■ Adequate procedures for emergency evacuation in case of fire or other disasters should be in place and regularly tested. Staff should of course be trained in carrying out evacuation procedures efficiently.

Unit 58   Collections security: systems and procedures

It is the MUSEUM MANAGER's or security manager's responsibility to ensure that effective security procedures are in place, are monitored and updated where required, staff are adequately trained and risks are contained.

It is better to be safe than sorry.

Section IV
The museum and its building

UNIT 59   MUSEUM BUILDINGS: FORM AND FUNCTION

Related Units: 1, 3–5, 60, 66

Museums in all countries are housed in an extraordinarily wide range of buildings. Museum buildings fall into two general categories – conversions and purpose-built. They include:

– important historic or contemporary buildings, originally used for domestic, public service/state, commercial, industrial, religious or military purposes, converted wholly or in part for museum use.
– historic, purpose-built museum buildings.
– redundant buildings of limited architectural significance.
– contemporary/new, purpose-built museum buildings.

The form which museums take at their establishment is conditioned by their social, economic and political context, available locations, the financial resources available and the objectives set by the individual or organisation developing the museum, and their funding partners. Many existing museums have been altered, adapted and extended through time as the contexts within which they operate have themselves changed.

Few museums are or should be static, and they should be established or managed in the knowledge that both their form and function are likely to change over time as attitudes and policies, values and emphases change and evolve. It follows that museum architecture and design, both internally and externally, not only reflect changing museum needs and attitudes to collections management, user services and administration and management, but can also act as a constraint when and where necessary change is difficult to accommodate.

The form of a museum building whether converted or purpose-built must relate to its mission and objectives (see Unit 69). The allocation of space depends on a close understanding of the individual museum's aims and objectives, and on the priorities which the museum sets itself in the light of its resources and policies – financial, staffing, collections, services, etc.

There are three main considerations to bear in mind – the public using the museum and its visitor facilities; the collections/information available for the public; and the range of services supporting the museum – technical, managerial, administrative and educational.

The simplified checklists below indicate the elements which might be included in discussing space allocation. The amount of space, the disposition of space and the requirements of that space for these different functions will differ from museum to museum, but it is essential that adequate space is given to priority functions. These are asterisked on the checklists.

☐ **Public space/services**

- Visitor entrance*
- Reception*
- Orientation*
- Visitor information*
- Cloakrooms
- Assembly area
- Rest areas*
- Lavatories*
- Catering facilities
- Audio-visual theatre
- Education room(s)*
- Lecture theatre
- Meeting rooms
- Retail facilities*
- Security office/desk*
- Telephones/post boxes
- Donations box

☐ **Public space/collections**

- Temporary exhibitions*
- Displays*
- Resource centres
- Library
- Documentation/information*
- Archives/records
- Study collections*
- Collections management staff offices*
- Duty staff offices

☐ **Storage**

- Collections storage*

☐ **Supporting services**

- Management*
- Administration/finance*

- Security*
- Cleaning*
- Technical workshop(s)*
- Photographic studios
- Design/display studios
- Publications/shop stock stores*
- Publications office
- Information/PR/publicity office
- Research/fieldwork*
- Collections storage*
- Conservation laboratories
- Technician's stores*
- Exhibitions storage*
- Staff rest room(s)*
- Heating/air conditioning plant*
- Garage(s)/parking areas
- Delivery bay

A museum building should function cost-effectively and cost-efficiently, use environmentally appropriate materials and make a firm architectural statement about the museum. Buildings should be sound and well maintained. They should be well-sited in terms of access and accessibility, and provide adequate space for existing requirements, and later expansion.

The relationship of one element to another needs very careful consideration if the building is to work efficiently for visitors and staff alike.

A museum's surroundings will have an important bearing on its function, and in many cases the museum's range of activities and services will be extended into its surroundings such as gardens, car-parks or open exhibition areas. The museum's requirements for collections storage and display should be well understood and provided for, and every precaution taken to ensure that services such as gas, water, heating or air-conditioning plants do not run through or affect sensitive areas, such as storage areas, and put collections at risk.

All countries have different forms of planning and building regulations, and the form and function of buildings will be affected by these. Where museums are located in important historic buildings, the MUSEUM MANAGER must bear in mind his/her professional responsibilities towards the building as a historic artefact in its own right. Balancing building regulations, with health and safety requirements, architects' 'solutions', aesthetic considerations and the museum's needs is no easy task. Whatever the scale, a conversion or a new-building are both complex matters.

The most successful museums are those which match their needs to the space(s) available. A rough rule of thumb for space allocation is reception/visitor facilities – 25 per cent; collections storage – 25 per cent; displays/exhibitions – 25 per cent; and support services – 25 per cent. In small–medium sized museums, it is more effective to use limited display space for regularly changing exhibitions making use of the collections resource in a variety of different ways than to take up space needed for other functions with displays.

Museums are not just about exhibitions and displays – a common misconception with groups and individuals wishing to set up new museums. All museums are concerned with a range of interlocking functions, and the form of the museum building(s) must allow for an appropriate balance of functions.

UNIT 60   PLANNING NEW MUSEUM BUILDINGS

Related Units: 9, 59, 61–6

Developing new museums or new museum buildings should always stem from feasibility assessment. It is of no value to develop new museums if they are not viable in the long-term, if the collections which they house are of limited significance or if few people wish to visit them or use their services. Feasibility assessment is a critical first step to determine whether a museum *should* be developed. Feasibility assessment should be carried out by consultants, not by the organisation or individual wishing to establish the museum. Specialist consultants can provide an objective assessment of your proposal.

The findings of a feasibility assessment can be used to build a case-for-support to funding agencies. The case is not simply being made on the basis of enthusiasm unsupported by objectivity.

A feasibility study for a new museum building will contain a number of elements and include:

1. The *market* within which the museum will operate. The study will look at the size and nature of the potential market; its demographic make-up; and the travel distances/methods to the proposed loca-

tion(s); the appeal of the museum in terms of its theme(s), collections, facilities and services; the quality of services visitors are likely to expect; competition from other museums and visitor attractions; and the ways in which the museum needs to be marketed, managed and financed.

2. The *numbers and type* of visitors which the museum can expect to attract over a period of years, their attitudes to museums and the range of services and facilities required for those visitors.

3. The *concept* of the museum and the sorts of themes it will interpret through its *collections* to meet the needs and interests of the market.

4. What necessary *research* will be undertaken to support the chosen themes and the availability of collections to illustrate them.

5. What form of *presentation* and *interpretation* will be required.

6. What range of *services and activities* the museum can provide for visitors and users (see Unit 59).

7. What range of *buildings* are required to accommodate the museum's functions and services and whether these are readily available, for example by adapting or reusing existing buildings, or whether it will need to be newly built.

8. What are the likely capital and operating *costs* (see Unit 71).

9. What *cultural or economic benefits* are to be gained from the new museum development, and what other local organisations will benefit from its establishment.

10. What will be its *relationship* with other museums or heritage facilities.

11. What type of *staffing and management* are required to run the museum and what will be its legal status.

12. Over what *timescale* the development is to take place.

13. What type of *fund-raising* is required and what organisations are likely to support the project.

14. What are the *income and expenditure projections* for the range of tasks and activities to be carried out.

15. Whether the project is *feasible*.

For organisations wishing to establish small museums, it is often helpful to assess feasibility by setting up a temporary museum programme to help gauge visitor interest. This does not preclude the need to carry out a formal feasibility exercise, but it does help to inform it.

It has the advantage of testing out skills and approaches in all the activities which the organisation will need to engage in later if a museum is established. It helps to train the organisation in necessary tasks, test ideas and ensures that money is not wasted on a large-scale project or permanent facility for which people are not equipped.

If the feasibility study is positive, then a development plan needs to be established to ensure that the museum project can be completed in the timescale required. It is essential to ensure that there are clear objectives agreed and established from the outset, financial ceilings and targets are identified and agreed, and that there is sufficient time available to prepare an initial, and later a full, brief for architects and designers (see Unit 62). A very substantial commitment of time will be required for research, and the definition of requirements for the range of services and functions chosen (see Unit 59). The steps following on from feasibility assessment are outlined here.

Client	Architect
Stage 1 – Objectives	
Mission defined	Architect selected
Objectives defined	
Capital and operating budget ceilings set	
Locational requirements defined	
Functional requirements defined	
Spatial requirements defined	
Administration/management of programme defined	
Stage 2 – Development	
Location or building selection	Site assessment
Land or building purchase	Building assessment
Planning regulations	Services assessment
Technical needs	Space specifications
Preliminary assessment	
Options	
Financial assessment	Preliminary assessment
Stage 3 – Implementation	
Preferred option	Outline proposals
Detailed specifications	Planning applications
Detailed costings	

Funding	Sketch designs
Scheduling	Costings

Stage 4 – Completion

Detailed timetable	Design development
Agreement to proceed	Detailed specifications
	Working plans/drawings
	Tendering
	Contracts let
	Building work
	Completion
	Handover/operation

The amount of time for each of the tasks outlined above will vary depending on circumstances such as planning requirements, or availability of materials. The order of the tasks may also vary. It is important, however, that the museum client is fully aware of the briefing and development schedule required for a museum development project, leaves adequate time for all of the tasks involved and complies with legislative and professional requirements (see Unit 6). Time costs money, and it is essential that a building or development schedule is planned and adhered to. Deviations will mean that additional costs are incurred.

A successful new museum or building project is one which is based on mutual understanding and agreement between the client museum and its architect.

UNIT 61   WORKING WITH ARCHITECTS

Related Units: 59, 60, 62–6

A good working relationship with the museum's architect(s) is essential for success. The working relationship will depend on three main factors:

– a detailed explanation of the objectives and requirements of the museum;
– a clear understanding of respective roles and responsibilities;
– a comprehensive and well-researched brief, together with an agreed schedule for the building project.

The outline stages given at Unit 60 identify four broad stages of planning and development through which the client and architect proceed. On the client's side, it is the first three stages of the project which are particularly important, as these reflect the client's briefing of the architect – a process which goes progressively from the general to the specific.

On the architect's side, it is the last three stages which are important. Here the architect develops his/her solutions to the brief provided by the client and specifies requirements to the building contractor and a range of sub-contractors who will carry out the building or building refurbishment through to completion. Working with an architect is a creative process, and one which requires detailed discussion and understanding. The client should thus be prepared to provide detailed answers to detailed questions.

UNIT 62   PREPARING BRIEFS FOR ARCHITECTS

Related Units: 59–61, 63–6

The first stage (objectives) in preparing briefs for an architect is a clarification and explanation of the museum's mission, objectives and requirements – *an outline brief*. An outline brief deserves a great deal of attention and provides a valuable checklist for the architect to respond to in developing ideas and solutions. Everyone involved in the operation of the museum – in particular conservation staff – should be involved in providing ideas and suggestions as to how the museum can operate efficiently and effectively for the future. The outline brief should include sections on:

☐ *Function* – defining the type of museum and the organisation to which the MUSEUM MANAGER reports; the general aims and objectives of the museum; the purpose of the museum and the range of facilities and collections which will be housed; the style and personality of the museum (see Unit 3); and its strength to combat disasters.

☐ *Collections* – explaining the range and type of collections; the value of the collections; the need for change and development; spatial requirements for collections; collections management, conservation and security needs; storage and display needs; relationships between collections areas, visitor areas and museum management and service areas (see Unit 34).

☐ *Users* – describing types of user, including users with special needs;

patterns of use; and special facilities including educational facilities, reception areas, rest areas, catering and retail areas and seating (see Units 5–7, 13–16).

□ *Museum staff* – identifying accommodation needs for different staff, administrative, curatorial, conservation, etc., and staff facilities.

□ *Space requirements* – specifying priorities, flexibility, relationships of spaces, conservation needs, visitor flow patterns, security, later development/additions.

□ *Displays* – quantifying the relationship of spaces to display/exhibition design; finishes to walls, ceilings, floors; services; signage; conservation and security needs (see Units 17–29).

□ *Services* – indicating the location of technical services and relationship to other spaces; supplies delivery and storage; maintenance needs.

□ *Site/location* – explaining servicing requirements; planning permission; legal agreements; expansion opportunities.

□ *Operational costs* – detailing maintenance requirements; revenue income needs; cost limits/ceilings; cash flow; fundraising schedule; insurance.

□ *Scheduling* – defining the overall scheduling of the programme; phasing and payment schedule; appointment of specialists/consultants.

In producing the brief, the client will need to pay a considerable amount of attention to detail. Much of this may be readily available, but there may well be a need, for example, to confirm policy in certain areas, or to carry out collections audits and research programmes or to engage in additional field collecting programmes in preparation for formal briefing. It is important therefore not to begin the formal briefing procedure until additional information has been or can be readily available, otherwise delays can ensue to everyone's frustration.

The second stage (development) includes the process of identifying buildings or locations to meet the requirements of the MUSEUM MANAGER and his/her committee, as laid down in the outline brief. The brief should also be further developed at this stage and technical and space specifications more closely defined. The architect will be assessing the site/building through a series of separate specialist studies examining different site factors, such as geology, access, comparative cost data or structural quality.

Planning permission will have to be sought at this stage. The architect will present his/her findings and agreement will be sought on the preferred option for development.

The third stage (implementation) will examine a range of proposals or solutions to the client's preferred option for development in the light of the outline brief and the architect's information about the site/building. The client now needs to develop the brief in more detail as the proposals are progressively refined. The architect will now produce sketch designs to illustrate how particular requirements in the brief will be met and detail what the cost implications are.

Once agreement has been reached on the way ahead (stage 4 – completion), and a detailed schedule established, the architect will then further develop the design in consultation with the client until detailed specifications and working drawings can be produced. It is these that will form the basis for tendering and contracting builders to carry out the building or refurbishment programme.

Additional input, for example from conservation experts, or display and exhibition designers is essential at this stage to ensure that specifications and working drawings meet the museum's requirements. Adaptation at a later stage, for example to service ducting or wall finishes, lighting points or security features, can be expensive. It is essential to ensure that all details required by those operating the museum have been carefully and fully checked well in advance of the production of specification drawings. Once these have been finalised and the contracts let, it should not be necessary for the client to make any further alterations.

Where displays are being designed in parallel with the briefing/building programme, it is important that the designer is involved at an early stage in the programme. The designer's requirements as agreed with the client will form an important part of the briefing process for the architect.

Most countries will have professional associations of architects and they will employ standard procedures in working with clients of all types. The checklist above should therefore be used in conjunction with such procedures as a general guide.

UNIT 63   MUSEUM BUILDINGS SECURITY: MANAGEMENT AND MAINTENANCE

Related Units: 56, 57, 58

Security

Museums have a special responsibility to ensure that their buildings are secure, and that effective security systems and procedures (see Units 56–8), physical defences and appropriate levels of staffing are in place during the day and night. Each museum will vary in terms of the level of protection provided. Different types of collections will require different levels of protection, depending on their value or importance. Different types of buildings will require different levels of protection related to their use. All museums should review their buildings security in terms of the following checklist.

1. *Have you assessed the security risks?*

Museums should regularly, at least annually, assess their security risks in terms of their location, surroundings and buildings. Ask the following sort of questions:

- Is the museum in a busy or isolated area? Is there a record of crime in the area, and what is the pattern of crime? Is the museum visible at night? Are there buildings or trees which might provide entry routes to criminals nearby?

- Are the surroundings secure? Is there a fence or wall around the museum? What is its condition? Are gates securely locked? Does the perimeter need to be guarded?

- What form does the building take? Are there many windows, doors, skylights? Is the structure solidly built? What are the weak points? Do they need to be strengthened? Can the doors be rammed by vehicles?

Survey your building as if you were a thief or a vandal. Think how you might gain entry, avoid security alarms, make your escape. Wherever possible seek professional advice from police or security consultants. Security should be a key requirement in the brief for new buildings or alterations to existing buildings. Security against theft or fire needs to be built into new developments from the outset. Changes later will mean increased costs.

2. *Are the museum's surroundings secure?*

Review the museum's surroundings. If you have a wall or fence around the museum and its grounds, check its effectiveness against intrusion. Are all those gates actually needed and are they strong enough? Is the circuit high enough to deter attackers? They are a front line of defence. Improve them if possible.

3. *How secure are the museum buildings?*

Your next line of defence is the building itself. Assess its strengths and weaknesses. You may have a museum based in a building not originally designed for the purpose. There may be conflict between security, safety or architectural integrity. But the fewer openings in the building shell there are, the better your security. If you have the option, light the exterior of the building. It serves as a useful deterrent, and promotes your museum.

4. *Is the roof secure?*

The roof of a building can often be vulnerable to attack. Check that drainpipes and other furniture do not provide easy access to the roof. Trees, climbing plants, repair scaffolding, adjoining buildings, unlocked ladders are all danger points.

Check the construction and physical strength of the roof. Will it deter attack? Or can it be strengthened by reroofing or the addition of materials externally or internally? Many roofs have doors and rooflights built into them. They represent yet more weak points and require careful consideration in terms of window grilles/bars, locks and alarms.

5. *How strong are the walls?*

Strengths of walls vary depending on their construction and thickness. As part of your security assessment, review the museum's walls, and reinforce weak points, for example blocked up windows, or doors. Use buildings for appropriate purposes depending on their strengths.

6. *Are your windows weak points?*

Two main considerations should be borne in mind – the nature of window glazing and making windows secure. Windows are weak points in your defences. Use glass which is appropriate and check its resistance qualities with manufacturers and security advisers. Protect windows with bar or mesh grilles, security bars, lockable shutters, steel sheet panels and locks, as appropriate. Remember that upper floor windows are also vulnerable from attack from above or below.

7. Are doors secure?

Like windows, doors are vulnerable points on your circuit at all times. Check the strength and standard of the door itself, and its frame. Consider its location in terms of the building. Doors vary in design and thus their methods of fastening. Exterior and interior doors will vary in strength and type of manufacture. It is important to ensure that door hinges and frames, together with their locking systems, are strong enough to resist attack.

8. Are your locks the key to security?

There is a very wide variety of locking systems available for doors and windows, and professional advice should be sought on the most appropriate for your needs. External doors should be fitted with two locks at one-third and two-third heights, preferably the mortice-lock type which meets accepted security standards. It is important to recognise the strengths and weaknesses of different types of locks and bolts, and fasteners. Key systems and key procedures are an essential part of your defences (see Unit 58). Cheap door locks and fastenings are no insurance policy.

To summarise, physical security should be the result of detailed and regular security assessment. Wherever possible seek professional advice on security fittings and risk limitation. Physical security must be supported by effective security alarm systems and staff procedures (see Units 57–8).

Prevention and protection should be your watchwords.

Management and maintenance

Museums not only have to look after their collections, but they also have to manage and maintain the buildings in which they are housed. Museum buildings vary in size, form and construction from one country to another. Whatever type of building(s) your museum is housed in, there are four basic requirements in their management and maintenance. Museum managers should:

– have a detailed knowledge of their museum buildings(s);
– assess the museum's maintenance needs, with external assistance if required;

- develop a schedule of maintenance work to meet these needs;
- determine the costs of the maintenance schedule and budget for the work to be carried out in the context of the museum's operating budget and capital programme.

It is helpful to build up a series of files about the management and maintenance needs of the museum building(s). For example, these might include the following:

- details of building construction;
- floor plans and internal layout;
- location and construction methods of doors and windows;
- plumbing systems;
- electrical systems;
- heating/air conditioning systems;
- leases and insurance policies;
- information about electricians, joiners, glaziers, etc;
- information about previous maintenance costs for comparative purposes.

Maintenance needs have to be determined through inspection procedures. Inspection inside and outside the building has to be carried out on a regular basis if it is to rectify problems which have occurred, or prevent problems arising. It may be necessary to bring in specialists, such as professional roofers or electricians, to help carry out inspection procedures.

Maintenance needs will occur on a regular basis such as replacing light bulbs, cleaning, painting, clearing drains and gutters or on an irregular basis such as mending storm damage to roofs or reglazing broken windows. The museum should draw up a written maintenance schedule identifying timescales for regular inspection, and known maintenance requirements. Timescales will vary with different needs. Where necessary these requirements, for example costs of inspections or redecoration, can be costed into the museum's financial and forward planning.

Rather like conservation which can be thought of in preventive and remedial terms, inspection and maintenance schedules are useful in preventing problems developing and avoiding expensive repairs through serious deterioration. For example, leaking roofs if ignored can create damage which may cost a substantial amount to put right, and they may also adversely affect museum collections in store or on display.

Maintenance is not only necessary to prevent problems escalating. It is also important in maintaining a pleasant and safe environment for museum staff and visitors. The museum may have legal responsibilities to comply with in this latter respect. While this unit focuses on buildings management and maintenance, it is also important to note the need for regular maintenance and servicing schedules to be drawn up for equipment (for example computers, photocopiers, typewriters, power tools), furnishings and vehicles as well as displays and exhibitions.

Regular maintenance will help to ensure the efficient operation of the museum and in the long term will help to save money. Museum buildings which are well maintained and in good repair reflect efficient management and a concern to care for one of the museum's most important assets.

This checklist provides an indication of some regular maintenance needs.

☐ *External*

– Gutters and drainpipes
– Drains
– Paintwork to doors, windows
– Stonework
– Roof furniture, for example weather-vanes
– Fences
– Paths

☐ *Internal*

– Window cleaning
– Electrical fittings, light bulbs
– Paintwork to walls, ceilings, woodwork
– Heating/air conditioning systems
– Cleaning and displays, exhibitions

UNIT 64   ACCESS AND ACCESSIBILITY

Related Units: 28, 29, 66

There are many ways in which museums prevent people from visiting them. This unit looks at some of the barriers museums unconsciously erect against visitors, and at ways we can knock them down again.

'It's not for people like us.'

One of the main reasons that people do not visit museums is that they think they will not feel comfortable there. Sometimes, indeed, the idea of visiting a museum may not even have occurred to them. In almost every country, museum-going tends to be an activity of the better-educated and better-off.

Too often, museums seem to make special efforts to make ordinary working people feel uncomfortable. Many earlier museums were designed to look like palaces, and though they may be *meant* to be 'palaces of the people', in fact they are easily associated in people's minds with the elite.

Many of the most famous museums, too, attract a very large number of foreign tourists. As a result local people feel that they are 'not for us'. Like the big tourist hotels, they may make people feel like strangers in their own country.

What can we do to counter this alienation, to make ordinary local people feel that their museums belong to them?

The first step is to recognise and understand the problem. A market survey (see Unit 6) will reveal what people think about the museum, but many lessons can be learned simply by visiting the museum and trying to see it with the eyes of a modest person who has never been to a museum before. Or perhaps you might invite representatives of different ages or ethnic groups to visit the museum with you and discuss their visit in detail with them.

Can the outside of the museum be made to seem more friendly, perhaps by flags and banners, by 'welcome' signs, by pictures showing what is to be found inside, etc?

Can special marketing campaigns be aimed at sections of the community who do not visit? If you can discover what it is that discourages them, perhaps appropriately designed leaflets, posters, radio and TV can be used to reassure them.

Could special openings and events be arranged for special groups? Rather than trying to attract individuals or families, it may be easier to arrange special visits for existing groups, for example women's groups, religious groups, shared-interest groups, etc. Not only will the group members feel more secure and comfortable among people of their own kind, and whom they already know, but the museum may be able to arrange special talks or other activities suited to their interests (see Unit 12).

The museum reception and security staff must be trained to be equally welcoming to all sorts and conditions of people. In some countries museum security staff are traditionally drawn from one particular minority group: this may be off-putting to visitors from other groups.

What about the café? Is the food it sells acceptable and familiar to local people? Are toilets available? If the local custom is to sit on the floor rather than on chairs, is that comfortably possible? In general, is there anything else that can be done to make the ordinary person feel at home in your museum?

'It's never open.'

Too often museums seem to have opening hours to suit the convenience of museum staff rather than that of visitors. It is of the greatest importance to find out when your potential visitors could come to the museum. If the local custom is for such visits to be made in family groups, led perhaps by father or grandfather, then it is clearly essential for the museum to be open when he is not working: that may be in the evenings or at weekends, or at certain seasons of the year.

'It's too tiring.'

It's easy to get tired in museums; old people and children may tire particularly quickly. Not only should the displays be designed to counter the 'museum effect' through changes of atmosphere and pace (see Unit 65), but plenty of seating should be provided throughout the museum, with refreshments – if only water – readily available.

'But I can't take the children.'

Is the museum designed with children in mind? Are there places where they can run around and let off steam? Is there a special children's section? Is there a creche where small children can be safely left while their parents explore the displays? Are there special guidebooks and worksheets designed for children? Is there somewhere where babies' nappies (diapers) can be changed? Are the stairs safe for small children? Are push-chairs and baby buggies welcome?

Few museums will have all these things, but the more the museum is welcoming to children, the more their families will come too. This is important because the majority of visits to museums take place in family or social groups.

'How can I get there?'

Where is the museum located? Many museums are in the richer parts of town, well away from the areas where most people live. Many others are designed to be convenient for car-drivers. Yet even in the richest industrialised societies of the West, perhaps 50 per cent of the population may not have daily access to a car. We should remember this, and try to find ways of helping people get to the museum.

It may be possible to persuade the bus company to run buses to the museum. It may be possible for the museum to run its own bus or transport service from the town centre, perhaps offering a cheap, combined ticket.

'I can't afford it.'

How much are visitors paying to come to the museum? They will have to pay for the transport to get there, the admission charge, refreshments and perhaps some small souvenirs for the children, and transport home again. For a family party this may add up to quite a large sum. What is the average weekly income of the sort of family we want to attract to the museum? *Can* they afford it? Does the museum provide free admission on certain days for the local community? Are there special admission rates for families and regular visitors?

'I can't manage the stairs.'

Many of the museum's potential visitors will have impaired mobility. Some will be in wheelchairs, but more will simply walk slowly and painfully, will use a stick or just find stairs difficult (see Unit 8).

Every museum should ensure that it is as accessible as it possibly can be to visitors who find it difficult or impossible to walk. All doors and displays must be wide enough for wheelchairs, stairs and steps should be as few as possible and always matched by lifts, escalators or ramps (see Unit 8).

'My eyes aren't good enough these days.'

Many of the museum's potential visitors will have impaired eyesight. No curator who has watched the concentration and joy on a blind child's face as he or she feels museum objects will need persuading of the value of arranging handling sessions and 'to-be-touched' displays.

Many more visitors simply have poor eyesight, and for them it is important to remember:

- to keep light levels as high as is compatible with conservation (see Unit 47);
- to provide good lighting on stairs;
- to provide handrails wherever possible;
- to provide large lettering on labels (see Unit 26);
- to train staff to understand and watch out for visitors' difficulties, and to offer discreet and tactful help when necessary.

UNIT 65   ATMOSPHERE, PACE AND FLOW

Related Units: 8, 63, 64, 66

In this unit we consider how visitors use the museum, and what museum managers, curators and designers can do to make their experience more enjoyable and inspiring.

Atmosphere

Atmosphere – ambiance – is the most difficult of all aspects of a museum to define, but in many ways it is the most important aspect of all. Why do *you* like some museums much more than others? Is it just the quality of their exhibits and the standards of their displays? Very often it is neither; some museums just seem to have a special atmosphere that makes them more memorable.

A few of the things that contribute to a special atmosphere can be identified. The first is a personal welcome. *Every* visitor in every museum – except perhaps the very largest – should be greeted personally with a smile and a 'welcome'.

The most welcoming museums are like the most welcoming houses; they may not be rich, but they are clean and neat, and give the visitor the impression that someone cares about them very much.

One way of helping to create a good atmosphere is to use some of the furnishings and decorations traditional in your country. For example, mosques and houses in the Middle East have floors covered with rugs which help make them feel much more welcoming than museums with cold hard floors. In cold countries, an open fire or traditional stove will instantly make a room seem welcoming; though there may be strong conservation reasons against them! In many countries the display of flowers or plants is customary in both private house, shops and offices; they too make a museum seem more homely.

Sound is also an important aspect of atmosphere. The sound of a fountain playing, or of quiet music may help enormously.

Pacing

A typical feature film consists of a series of different *moods* and *pace*. A slow conversation will be followed by a furious fight between hero and villain. A tense, quiet sequence will be followed by a noisy battle. There will be constant changes of mood: long sequences with sad music as the camera pans across the landscape, changing to love scenes, or short sequences of jokes and comedy, even dance routines. In all these ways the film director keeps our interest by varying the pace of the film and by changing its moods.

In a similar way the museum designer keeps the visitor's interest by varying the pace of the museum.

Where visitors are shown around the museum by a guide, design is less important because the guide can vary the pace of the tour and can respond to the visitors' needs. Every good guide knows how to spot when their visitors are getting tired or bored. He or she might tell an amusing story, ask the visitors questions, speed up or slow down, draw attention to an unusual object or change his or her voice. Like a good teacher, a good guide knows how to keep the interest of his or her group.

But for visitors who are looking around a museum on their own, the displays themselves must awaken and keep the visitor's interest.

One important way the museum can prevent its visitors getting bored is by varying the appearance and 'feel' of the different rooms or different parts of the museum. Ceiling heights, floor surfaces, brightness or darkness, colour schemes, 'hardness' or 'softness' of the furnishings can all be varied to suit the exhibits and theme, and moving from one to another will keep the visitors alert!

The types of display should ideally be varied, too. Thus a visitor who moves from a gallery of paintings to an archaeological display to a science gallery with plenty of 'hands-on exhibits', will be invited to take a new interest each time. Some displays, too, might be inspirational, some didactic, some just fun.

Another way of keeping boredom or tiredness at bay is by providing plenty of 'escape hatches'. Even the most interested visitor needs a break from time to time. When there is somewhere to go to for a few minutes rest which is quite different in atmosphere from the museum gallery, it may allow the visitors to return refreshed to the displays. Catalogues and other books might be provided. If possible this rest or study area should be close to all of the galleries. In many ways the traditional museum laid out around a courtyard or central hall is best.

Every museum should have a place to eat – a café or restaurant or at the very least somewhere in the museum where the visitors can get tea or coffee, or simply a drink of water. And there should be plenty of seats and rest areas everywhere.

Flow

How do visitors actually use displays? How do they move around them and how long do they spend in which areas? 'Flow' – movement around the museum – refers to the way visitors flow through and around the museum displays; how long they spend in the various rooms; which direction they go in; and which displays they choose to look at first. In planning a new display or exhibition, it is crucially important to plan very carefully for the movement pattern or flow, based on your knowledge of the target audience, their characteristics, and forecast of the numbers likely to visit at various times. It is worthwhile observing how your visitors move around the museum. Plot movement by different types of visitors on a plan of the museum. You may be surprised how visitors bypass a particular display or object! Their movement pattern can help in evaluating the success or failure of an exhibition or display.

BOX 1

Museum fatigue

'Museum feet' is the nickname for *museum fatigue*, the special sort of tiredness that museum visitors can suffer from. What causes it?

- learning on your feet – only in museums are people expected to do this.
- disorientation – not knowing where you are or what you are looking at.
- looking, but not using other senses of touch, hearing or smell, for a long period.
- looking for long periods at similar-looking but different things.
- lack of contrast, sameness of surroundings.
- crowds of people.
- excessive heat.

Minimising fatigue on the part of your visitors is a challenge to be met by the museum.

BOX 2

To work out how much space will be needed in a new gallery or exhibition ask the following questions:

- how many people are in the museum at the busiest time?
- how many extra are likely to be attracted to a new display?
- how many of them are likely to be in the gallery at any one time?
- and then allow roughly 5m^2 space per person.

Remember about 80 per cent of the gallery space will be used for circulation and about 20 per cent for the displays themselves.

UNIT 66   ORIENTATION

Related Units: 8, 60–2, 63–5

Orientation means showing people where they are and where they could go. If visitors to museums are to get the most out of their visit, they need to know both what they are going to see (intellectual orientation) and where things are (physical orientation).

Physical orientation

Every visitor – except perhaps in the largest museums – should be welcomed personally. In some museums, especially where visitors speak many different languages, it may be possible only to say 'good morning, welcome to the Smalltown Museum'. But the visitor's arrival is an opportunity to give some information as well. For example:

> Good morning; welcome to Smalltown Museum. Is this your first visit? Would you like to know what there is to see? If you go that way, you will find the archaeology galleries – you may have heard of our famous Smalltown Bronze Hoard. The other way are the natural history galleries, and we've got a special exhibition of local paintings this month. If you want to see everything, it would take you probably two hours, so you might like to choose.
> There's a cloakroom to leave coats in over there, and a restaurant if you need a cup of tea. We close at 5 o'clock. Please ask if you need anything. I hope you enjoy your visit.

It is a good idea to give every visitor a leaflet containing a plan of the museum, and perhaps pictures of some of the principal exhibits. This is particularly important in a museum which charges for admission; visitors must get something for their money that they can take away. This leaflet could perhaps contain a voucher for use in the shop, which would encourage visitors to buy something. It might include information on the museum's events and activities programme (see Unit 12), and information about other services.

The entrance area should contain a plan of the museum, but remember that not all visitors will be able to understand plans. An alternative might be a drawing or painting of the galleries, or a model.

There should be a well-designed and carefully-planned system of signs throughout the museum. The toilets, restaurant and exit (including emergency exits) should be well-signposted!

Above all, there should be people to answer visitors' questions. *All* staff should be able to answer the ten most common questions (do you know what they are?) in the language spoken by the majority of visitors. And someone in the entrance hall should be able to answer the fifty most common questions: that may be the ticket-seller, the custodian or someone at a special information desk.

A manual detailing common questions and appropriate answers is a useful way of ensuring consistency between staff and continuity when the museum employs new staff. It can be updated on a regular basis and used as part of the museum's training and induction programmes (see Unit 80).

Intellectual orientation

Explaining to visitors what there is to see is an important – but often neglected – part of the museum's service to visitors. Intellectual orientation is, of course, closely related to physical orientation (see above) and to the museum's programme of interpretation (see Unit 17). The following are some of the techniques.

THE WELCOME

The welcome described above gives the visitor a first idea of what there is to see, and an opportunity to ask questions. The welcome should be in the main languages of the museum's visitors.

THE LEAFLET

The visitor's leaflet described above gives a little more information.

GUIDES

Where the museum employs guides, or where guides from outside are permitted to work in the museum, intellectual orientation will be easy. A good guide can readily explain what there is to see and why the visitor might find it interesting. He or she can give as much or as little information as the visitor seems to want, and can adapt it to the visitor's interests and background. But it is crucially important that the guide actually knows a lot about the museum and its displays, as well as being a good teacher; training is essential (see Unit 21).

Unit 66   Orientation

Some museums have experimented with Orientation Galleries. An Orientation Gallery tries to tell the visitor what he or she is going to see, and also to suggest how to look at it – what aspects to look at and what question to ask. For example, an exhibition of Coptic icons could be looked at from different points of view: How were they made? Who were the saints depicted? How were they used by worshippers? How did the artistic style change over the centuries? An Orientation Gallery could encourage the visitor to look at the exhibition from one or other points of view. By changing the Orientation Gallery, it is to some extent possible to change the visitor's experience of the displays.

STUDY GALLERY

In some museums, computerised information is now being made available in special information or study galleries. Here the visitor can explore the collection on inter-active computer screens and either support or plan a visit. While such systems are unlikely to be within reach of many small museums, the principle can be developed using study materials of different types linked to illustrated catalogues and indexes of the collections provided in traditional formats. Such resource or study centres are a valuable opportunity to invite visitors to add to the museum's information resource and thus encourage greater participation in the museum's work.

Section V
The museum and its management

UNIT 67   LEGAL STATUS AND MANAGEMENT STRUCTURES

Related Units: 68–82

Every museum worker should understand the legal basis on which his or her museum operates. The laws of different countries vary so greatly that it is often difficult to know how their different museums are established. Within countries, too, the legal basis on which different museums are established varies greatly. Of three museums which seem to the visitor very similar in size and type, one may be set up by a special decree of the state authorities, one may be run by a government department as part of their general activities, while the third may be run by the Board of Trustees operating under laws which govern voluntary associations.

Do these differences matter? They do matter because they affect what the museum is allowed to do, and especially because they affect the options open to the museum when it is considering how it will develop in the future. For example, a museum run by a Board of Trustees may not be able to develop a close relationship with the Local Schools Service, while a museum run by a government department may not be free to develop a museum shop.

It is not only its legal basis that determines the character of a museum, but the actual management structure. It may seem, for example, that the MUSEUM MANAGER runs the museum, but his or her ability to take decisions may be very severely constrained. The MUSEUM MANAGER may, for example, be responsible to a senior bureaucrat who has no time to attend to the museum, but without whose approval no decisions can be made.

Finally, the character of the museum will be determined by the actual people who are in control. The museum may be run by a Board of Trustees who treat the museum as a private club, and have no interest in the public. Or it may have been set up by a politician whose successor has no interest. Or there may be someone in a key position in the wider organisation whose support may permit the museum a period of lively growth.

There is no doubt, though, that in the best system there are two levels of management: the Governing Body, which decides on the policy of the museum, and the MUSEUM MANAGER and his or her staff, who both advise the Governing Body and who put its policy into practice.

The Governing Body may itself be responsible to a central or local government agency, to a University Council, to a military authority or to a commercial company. Or it may be an independent Trust. Every museum, though, should have a Governing Body responsible for deciding the overall policy of the museum (see Appendix, Section 2, pp. 297–300).

The ways in which the Governing Body will decide the museum's policy, especially through its Forward Plan (see Units 68–9), are described in the next two units.

The first reponsibility of the MUSEUM MANAGER is to advise the Governing Body on the museum's policy. First, he or she must ensure that the members of the Governing Body know the museum and its work well. They should visit the museum regularly, and the MUSEUM MANAGER should take every opportunity to keep them in touch with the wider world of museums both nationally and internationally. When new members are appointed to the Governing Body the museum should try to provide at least a one-day training session, to help them to learn their new responsibilities, and to introduce them to the museum and its work. A number of museums have devised a Manual for the members of their Governing Body which explains the mission and objectives of the museum, its policies and the role and responsibilities of the Governing Body.

The second responsibility of the MUSEUM MANAGER is to implement the Governing Body's policy. Museums vary greatly in the amount of responsibility the MUSEUM MANAGER is given: what matters most is that everyone concerned is clear who is responsible for what. That is the fundamental purpose of the museum's management plan, which is described in the next unit.

KEY WORD

GOVERNING BODY – the formal body of men and women responsible for deciding the overall policy of the museum and ensuring that it is carried out by the MUSEUM MANAGER and his/her staff.

BOX

Everyone associated with a museum should be able to answer these basic questions about the power-structure behind the museum:

— what is the legal basis on which the museum operates?
— what is the chain of command leading to the MUSEUM MANAGER?
— at what level are key policy decisions taken?
— who are the people involved, what is their background and how effective are they?

UNIT 68   MANAGEMENT PLANNING AND POLICY DEVELOPMENT

Related Units: 67, 69, 70, 73

Every museum should have a clearly written and agreed management or forward plan. The plan is an expression of how the museum's policy agreed by its governing body will be put into action over a defined period of time. A management plan essentially describes the museum's purpose, its objectives and its programme of action, explains how its resources will be used to implement the programme and defines the steps which will be used to monitor progress and evaluate the impact of the museum's work (see Unit 69).

The management plan must, however, derive from policy agreed by the museum's governing body. It can help to clarify and develop policy. Museum managers therefore have to work with their governing bodies first to establish a policy framework within which they can carry out the museum's work. Policy development requires a great deal of time and consideration, reference to existing professional codes of conduct and standards and comparison with other museums. It must cover all aspects of the museum's activities in the broadest sense.

The museum's policy must follow from the museum's formal constitution which identifies its legal status, not-for-profit nature and objectives. The constitution must be drawn up in accordance with the appropriate national laws relating to museums, the cultural and natural heritage and not-for-profit institutions. The governing body must publish a clear statement of:

- the museum's purpose, policies and objectives;
- the role and composition of the governing body itself.

It should confirm that it recognises its professional obligations to:

- its collections, in terms of their safeguarding and safekeeping;
- its buildings, in terms of their care and maintenance;
- its staff, in terms of their well-being and development; and to
- its users, in terms of their education and safety.

Reference should be made to its recognition of existing professional codes of conduct at national or international level (see Appendix).

Policy development should therefore cover the following key areas of the museum's operation:

- the purpose of the museum – many museums define their role through a 'mission statement', a succinct expression of their primary purpose.
- collecting and disposal of collections – with due reference to professional and legal requirements.
- care and security of collections.
- research – collections research and fieldwork.
- communications – including all forms of communication with the public – exhibitions, displays, enquiries, educational services, marketing.
- access and accessibility.
- finance and accounting procedures.
- staffing and staff training and development.
- housing the museum – buildings care and maintenance.
- conformity with relevant national and international laws.

Developing a general policy statement or a number of linked statements, covering these areas, helps to clarify objectives and ensures that the governing body meets its responsibilities for policy development and its maintenance. A general policy statement of this type should be formally reviewed every three or every five years. The museum should, however, maintain a policy manual so that in the intervening period any new policy decisions by the governing body can be duly recorded and used to update the formal statement later.

The policy statement can then be used as a basis from which a set of objectives can be drawn. These are simple working statements of the museum's policy objectives, and encompass the definition of a museum as an 'institution which collects, documents, preserves, exhibits, and interprets material evidence and associated information for the public benefit' (see Unit 2).

Here is a mission statement and set of objectives for a local government museum as an example.

The purpose of the museum is to provide a range of high-quality services for the benefit of the collections in our care and for the education and enjoyment of all our users.

The objectives listed below are together designed to meet this purpose and fulfil the policy requirements of the governing body.

— to provide a high standard of care and management for collections in order to ensure their long-term well-being;
— to develop new collections and associated information within an agreed collecting policy in order to reflect the cultural and natural history of the museum's area;
— to provide displays and exhibitions interpreting collections of a recognised standard of excellence for the education and enjoyment of the museum's users;
— to undertake and commission research on collections in order to ensure that up-to-date and accurate information is available for use by museum staff and the museum's users;
— to undertake and commission scientific recording programmes in order to support the work of the museum;
— to provide identification and enquiry services relating to items held by the public;
— to provide educational services to formal education groups in order to maximise the educational potential of the museum's collections;
— to organise informal learning opportunities through events and activities programmes in order to encourage public interest in and support of the museum;
— to provide high-quality retail services for the public in order to enhance their enjoyment of the galleries and other facilities within the museum;
— to market the museum effectively to the public in order to maintain existing audiences and to develop new audiences for the museum;
— to generate funding support from a plurality of sources to assist in the development of the museum's work;
— and to ensure that the museum at all times provides for efficiency, effectiveness and economy in its financial management.

Translating these requirements into an action plan is the subject of Unit 69.

UNIT 69   MAKING A FORWARD PLAN

Related Units: 67, 68, 70

The process of writing a 'forward' or 'management' plan for your museum will provide valuable insights into the ways in which the museum can carry out its overall objectives. However large or small the museum is, the preparation of a plan is something which covers all aspects of a museum's work and every level of staff, professional or volunteer, as well as the governing body.

It is a method of bringing all those working for the museum together with a common purpose and provides a framework for a programme of action to drive the museum forward. As we have seen in Unit 68, a forward plan must derive from the museum's policy. It describes the purpose of the museum, something of its historical development, its current context, its functional objectives, its programme(s) of action, its resources and their use and the methods by which it will monitor progress and evaluate the impact of its work.

A forward plan can help you to:

- identify those areas of your museum's operation which require improved management or increased resources;
- assess the strengths and weaknesses of the museum in an objective way;
- provide a mechanism which allows staff and others to see what directions the museum is moving in;
- induce management to develop a future strategy for the museum;
- improve the quality of decision-making by means of performance indicators and management information systems;
- pinpoint areas of development and innovation which require new resources or expertise;
- demonstrate to funding bodies and patrons of all types the professionalism of the museum and its management.

The purpose of a forward plan is to provide the museum and its staff with a sense of purpose, a sense of direction and a sense of achievement.

The steps to take in drawing up a forward plan can be simply described as:

1. Assessment and appraisal;
2. Discussion and drafting;
3. Agreement and implementation;
4. Evaluation and updating.

Within these the museum should cover the points listed in the checklist here.

☐ *Collections management*

– Acquisition and disposals policy
– Documentation
– Storage
– Preventive conservation measures
– Remedial conservation services
– Research programmes
– Databases
– Collections security

☐ *User services*

– Displays
– Education services
– Outreach/extension services
– Temporary exhibitions
– Retail services – catering and shops/sales points
– Publications
– Events and activities programmes
– Marketing
– User facilities – cloakrooms, toilets, etc.

☐ *Management*

– Staffing structures
– Friends/volunteers
– Training programmes
– Security
– Communications systems
– Public relations
– Buildings – space allocation

BOX 1

'SWOT analysis'

One useful method of analysing the position of the museum in step one above is by SWOT analysis. SWOT stands for Strengths, Weaknesses, Opportunities and Threats. Try analysing each of the points covered in the checklist by this method, or analyse the museum as a whole using this approach. By involving staff and outside observers, you can build up valuable understanding of what will need to be done in the museum through your forward plan in steps two to four.

BOX 2

Annual reports

An annual report is a useful way of demonstrating how well the museum has achieved the planning objectives it set itself over the previous year. It can be structured in a variety of ways and can be produced in a variety of different styles. Length and design style (illustrated, typeset, etc.) will be conditioned by available resources for production. The costs of distribution will depend on size and weight, and the length of the distribution list. Whatever style you choose, target the annual report at all those whose support the museum is concerned to maintain or attract. It can be a valuable tool in helping the museum to build its reputation (see Unit 32).

- Buildings – condition
- Buildings – maintenance programme
- Finances – capital
- Finances – operating
- Income generation/fundraising
- Performance indicators/measurement
- Standards

The first step is the *assessment and appraisal* of your current position (see Unit 68). Is the museum's constitution and legal status appropriate?

What policies does the museum have at present? What are its stated objectives? What market is the museum operating in? What standards of collections management are being pursued? What range of services for its users are being provided? Is its staffing or staffing structure adequate? What is security of collections/buildings/staff like?

What condition are its building(s) in? What sources of finance does it have? How is it monitoring and measuring progress? What standards of comparison are being used for all its operations? All of these questions follow on from the checklist and there will be many more. They are designed to generate discussion amongst the museum's management and staff, instigate comparative research and help management and staff look objectively at *where they are now, how they have got there and what they are there to do.*

The second step is *discussion and drafting*. The key question posed here is where do we want to get to and how are we going to get there? As we have seen, it follows that the process of assessment and appraisal provides a draft management plan which covers the following points:

- purpose or 'mission' and objectives (see Unit 68);
- historical development – a brief perspective on the historical development of the museum to date;
- contemporary context – an examination of the market context within which the museum is operating (see Units 5–6);
- a series of *programme areas* (see checklist, above);
- a series of *programme objectives* within these areas – that is, specific tasks to be carried out;
- a timescale against which these objectives need to be carried out – for example a three-year period. Some aspects of the museum's work may of course need a longer timescale;
- and an assessment of how to deploy existing resources and what additional resources are required to carry through everything that needs to be done.

The programme objectives or tasks then have to be allocated to staff on an individual or team basis to carry out. These have to be built into their personal work programmes. Performance indicators help to monitor progress on these tasks and how well they are being met.

The third step is to reach *agreement* over the draft proposals with staff and then present the finalised draft to the governing body for scrutiny and final agreement. The plan can then be circulated in a final version, a resumé prepared for publication and fundraising purposes, and regularly referred to. Remember to build in sufficient flexibility to allow for change and those unsuspected developments!

The fourth and final step is *evaluation and updating*. It is the task of management to monitor progress and evaluate the impact and success of the action programme. Regular reviews and reports of progress need to take place for staff and governors. The plan also needs to be revised and 'rolled forward' on an annual basis to maintain currency and to mesh with the preparation of the following year's operational and capital estimates.

The museum is therefore always working within the framework of a management/forward plan and can always demonstrate what it has to do. The plan should go hand in hand with the museum's annual report which provides a convenient written and illustrated summary of achievement against planning objectives.

The museum should use its forward plan to plan for success and its annual report to demonstrate success.

UNIT 70   PERFORMANCE MEASUREMENT FOR MUSEUMS

Related Units: 67–9, 71, 73, 79

Measuring performance in museums is becoming of increasing importance. Museum managers have to monitor how well their museum is doing in terms of the museum's mission and the objectives set out in their forward planning. A system of *performance measurement* can be developed to help managers understand and communicate how well the museum is meeting its objectives over time. A system of performance measurement can help to lead to greater accountability and efficiency, and an improved sense of corporate purpose.

Museum managers are accountable for the effective use of the resources for which they are responsible, whether these are people, collections, equipment, buildings, money or time. Museum managers are also responsible for how well the museum performs. How then can museum managers working with their staff develop a system of mutually acceptable and meaningful performance measures to assist in their work?

Performance measurement can be related to the museum itself as an organisation; to the personal performance of members of staff (see Unit 78); and to the financial efficiency of the museum (see Unit 71). Performance can be measured in *qualitative* and *quantitative* terms.

Qualitative performance tends to be more difficult to measure. Where possible, qualitative performance should be measured against agreed standards, whether these are set internally by the museum, or devised externally. Performance can thus be measured as the attainment of a specified standard, where these have been produced.

A museum may reach a defined standard, for example in terms of the quality of care or storage for its archaeological collections, or a member of staff may be able to demonstrate a level of competence within an overall standard in terms of documenting an archaeological collection. Another example might be a museum or member of staff winning an award in a national or regional competition, because they have achieved a particular standard set by the competition.

Quantitative performance can be measured in different ways at different levels of complexity. Simple performance indicators might be represented through the measurement of numbers, for example numbers of items conserved in one month, one year, etc. More complex indicators might be based on comparisons or percentages, for example what percentage of the items in the museum collection are waiting for conservation treatment? Lastly, the measurement of *input* and *output* provides a method of determining efficiency or value-for-money, for example how many hours of staff time – and therefore cost – have been put into the accession of a new item for the collection? Can this be improved for the future?

Museums should develop a range of performance measures in a number of key areas of their work. The indicators chosen will vary from one museum to another, depending on circumstances and priorities. The number of performance indicators used needs to be manageable in terms of time. Managers need to remember that there is a cost implication for every indicator used in terms of staff time spent on monitoring performance.

While qualitative measurement against standards can often provide an immediate picture of performance, the benefit of quantitative measurement will only be effectively realised through the analysis of trends in terms of year on year comparison of performance in the museum. Performance indicators used in performance measurement are only a means towards an end. They should be used to complement the professional judgement and experience of the MUSEUM

MANAGER, and support the museum's management information system. The principal focus of museum management should be on its mission, not on the performance system.

Performance measurement should be concerned with three main areas of a museum's work – collections management, user services and museum management or operation. Each area can be broken down into a number of sub-sections. For example, collections management may include acquisition, disposal, preventive conservation, storage, remedial conservation, research, documentation and collections security (see Unit 69).

These areas will all relate to the museum's forward plan. Within these sub-sections, museums may wish to define a series of performance indicators of value in helping the museum measure its performance against its functional and planning objectives (see Unit 69). Some examples are given below:

– *Documentation*
– *Performance measurement*
– Numbers of items documented
– Numbers of items not documented
– Percentage of collections documented
– Percentage of collections not documented
– Change in percentage documented on an annual basis over three years
– Cost of documentation per item
– Quality of documentation against agreed standard
– Hours of work/staff cost spent on each new object
– Use of documentation by staff and/or members of the public
– Percentage of records available to the public

Another example taken from a sub-section within the user services area might include:

– *Education*
– *Performance measurement*
– Number of school class visits to museum
– Number of children visiting museum
– Use of school's loan service
– Percentage of schools in museum's catchment area serviced
– Production of education packs
– Cost per child of museum visit

By measuring performance against objectives in a coherent way and on a regular basis, museum managers and their staff can monitor performance over periods of time within their forward planning. Many aspects of performance need to be measured over a long period of time, and trends identified and understood. Performance measurement helps museum managers take informed decisions, builds team spirit in the workforce and forms an important part of the museum's management information system.

Performance measurement also provides added information of value for Governing Bodies, Annual Reports and for the public presentation of the museum's work (see Unit 69). Measuring performance on a regular basis provides much of the information needed to present the museum's achievements internally and externally.

UNIT 71   FINANCIAL MANAGEMENT

Related Units: 67–70, 72

The money which a museum needs to carry out its operation can be described under two headings – *operating* and *capital*.

Operating budgets

An *operating budget* is concerned with the day-to-day finances of the museum. It defines the relationship between operating income and expenditure. Operating income is the money which a maintained museum receives from its funding body and what it earns, for example through retailing/catering activities and fundraising. If it is an independent museum without a main funding body, its operating income will depend on money earned through, for example, admission charges and retailing, together with any grants, donations, etc. it raises from fundraising. Operating expenditure is the money which a museum pays for staffing costs, collections management requirements, marketing, energy costs, etc. (see budget breakdown below). The balance between income and expenditure represents profit and loss.

The museum's management are responsible for ensuring that the museum's finances are soundly managed and that deficits do not occur.

Museum managers should seek external professional advice wherever required from qualified accountants who will help to draw up guidance and financial procedures for managing finances. They will also provide help over record-keeping and taxation. Laws on finance and tax vary from country to country. The museum may be required under law to submit financial returns and it is therefore of critical importance that scrupulous records are kept of the day-to-day earnings and outgoings of the museum.

Within the museum, financial matters should be controlled by one individual who reports to the Governing Body on a regular basis. The Governing Body should ensure that monitoring procedures are established so that monthly statements of actual expenditure are provided against the estimated expenditure of the museum. This helps managers and staff with day-to-day responsibility for income/expenditure to know precisely how well the museum's finances are doing. If necessary, action can be taken to reduce expenditure if income is not as great as anticipated, or to generate more earnings.

The museum should draw up a *cash-flow projection* for the coming year. This will show on a monthly or weekly basis how income and expenditure is expected to fluctuate during the year. The projection will include fixed costs like salaries, energy costs, etc. as well as variable costs like equipment costs.

A clear understanding of the pattern of your cash-flow is important for effective financial planning. Many museums are dependent on seasonal fluctuations in visitors and therefore income. Such anticipated fluctuations need to be built into your projections. Many bills are paid at set times of the year. This needs to be taken into account when planning income forecasts.

In summary, seek professional advice where required. Ensure that income and expenditure projections are drawn up in the light of your and others' experience. Monitor progress on a monthly or weekly basis and ensure close financial controls are kept over cash-handling and records. Report regularly to the Governing Body who are ultimately responsible for ensuring the museum is financially healthy. Ensure that your annual report includes an audited statement of the museum's finances for the year.

Capital budgets

Capital is money which is used for purchases or developments, such as new equipment, buildings or major refurbishment programmes. It does not appear in the operating budget because it is additional expenditure to the day-to-day finances of the museum.

Capital expenditure may have implications for operating budgets, however. For example, a new museum building may require significant amounts of capital secured from endowment funds, appeals, government grants, borrowing, etc. to cover building costs. However, when the building work is completed and the building comes into use, there will be recurrent costs such as interest charges, heating, lighting, staffing and furnishing which have to be covered in your revenue budget. Capital programmes therefore should only be entered into with these running costs established.

Capital projects need to be very carefully managed, and strict controls and monitoring should be put in place in advance. Detailed briefs and clear contracts need to be drawn up for architects, designers and contractors, where building work takes place for example.

Where the museum is making a major purchase of an item for the collections or for a piece of equipment through its capital expenditure programme, financial managers should require formal procedures to be adhered to and appropriate insurance cover provided. Managing capital programmes can be very complex and professional advice and careful forward planning can provide significant benefits.

A museum's reputation will depend on how well its finances are managed. Efficient day-to-day operation is dependent on efficient financial management. Without effective financial management, the museum's collections will undoubtedly suffer and the museum's responsibilities will not be met.

OPERATING BUDGET CHECKLIST

Operating expenditure	Operating income
Museum management	Admissions to museum
Staff costs	Grants
Travel and subsistence expenses	Donations/bequests
Building maintenance	Museum shop
Energy costs – water, electricity	Museum catering
Insurance	Events programme
Cleaning	Services
Security	Sponsorship
Telephone	Loans
Postage/stationery	Membership subscriptions
Office equipment	
Depreciation	

Interest charges
Specialist services, such as auditors

Collections management
Staff costs
Travel and subsistence expenses
Conservation – materials and equipment
Documentation – materials and equipment
Storage – materials and equipment
Insurance
Purchase funds for collections
Collections security

Museum services
Staff costs
Travel and subsistence
Displays
Exhibitions
Shop stock
Catering
Publications
Education materials
Events programmes

UNIT 72   FUNDRAISING

Related Units: 67–71

The need for fundraising for project development, for special events and activities, for publications and for the many activities associated with museums varies from museum to museum. Generally speaking, museums are seeking to raise funds for projects of one sort or another which they would not otherwise be able to fund from their normal revenue budget. Funds may be raised from public or private sector sources – central government or international agencies, charitable trusts, local government on the one hand or commercial companies, local businesses or individual patrons on the other hand.

Basic questions

Whatever organisation your museum is seeking funding from, the first basic question to ask is what are we fundraising for? The answer to this question will largely determine what sources of funding are to be approached.

For example, if the museum is seeking funding for a special exhibition, then commercial sponsorship may be the answer. If the museum is seeking to extend a building or provide new facilities for the disabled, then a government agency or a charitable trust which will fund capital projects is likely to be the source. If the museum needs equipment then a gift-in-kind rather than in cash may be obtainable from a private sector source. If the museum is seeking special skills then an attachment or a recently retired business person may be available at reduced or nil cost.

The second question to ask is who will be carrying out the fundraising? Fundraising has its own techniques and rules, it is never easy, and has to be carried out by somebody capable of keeping accurate records, carefully researching possible sources, producing well-constructed and well-written 'cases-for-support' and arguing the case persuasively. He/she has to ensure all the necessary follow-up is carried out, conditions of help are met, the relevant people are thanked, progress reports on the project are provided and appropriate acknowledgement is given to the funding body. Above all the fundraiser – whether a museum employee or a professional consultant on contract to the museum – needs tact, persistence, optimism and energy. It is best for somebody with the right skills and professionalism to raise funds rather than to get the MUSEUM MANAGER, who will have plenty of other things to do already, to add this responsibility to his/her workload.

The third question is what sort of return will the funding body want? In the case of government agencies or charitable trusts, requirements will vary, but accounting officers will expect to see formal receipts, audited accounts and evidence that their money has been spent well and wisely. Your case-for-support will need to include what other sources of funding are being used to support the project.

Commercial sponsorship

With commercial sponsors fundraising is in many ways more complex. Commercial companies are looking for specific returns from sponsorship and sponsorship is a business relationship. The museum should enter the relationship knowing the basis on which an agreement will be struck. The museum therefore has to decide what it can offer in terms of publicity, acknowledgements and services such as letting the museum be used for corporate entertainment.

Companies look for the following in sponsorship deals:

- projects which will appeal to their target markets;
- professionalism on the part of the museum;
- the opportunity to mix sponsorship with their other activities;
- value for their money; the benefits package must be worth the investment from the sponsor;
- media and publicity potential;
- opportunities and the right facilities to provide client entertainment/ hospitality;
- a detailed contract of what is and what is not included in the sponsorship agreement;
- a list of responsibilities for action;
- a timescale and schedule for meetings.

Hence the need for the case-for-support to set the scene, make the funding proposal, identify and list the benefits and demonstrate track record for previous sponsored projects. Writing up projects which have been sponsored into case study material for later use with cases-for-support can be particularly helpful in demonstrating track record. Press coverage, video, films, photographs and testimonials are all helpful.

If a museum is involved or going to be involved with commercial sponsorship, it is essential to look after your sponsors. Maintain contact throughout a sponsorship deal, and afterwards. Successful fundraising in the commercial sector is about retaining sponsors and increasing their investment.

The museum should however be realistic – it is pointless asking for sums of money that are unrealistic. Museums have to recognise that commercial sponsorship is a two-way process. More and more companies now base sponsorship deals on a contractual basis to ensure that the museum delivers the benefits which the company is buying. Marketing and public relations departments have to justify what they are buying to their Boards – they are looking for value-for-money.

A good fundraising project will always attract support if fundraising is handled with tact, professionalism and care. The fundraiser does not necessarily need glossy brochures and expensively designed information packs to beat the competition. You must consider your needs and objectives carefully before you type a letter, pick up the telephone or send off a case-for-support. Inadequate research, preparation and carry-through can waste a lot of people a lot of time and money!

UNIT 73   INTERNAL COMMUNICATIONS AND PROCEDURES

Related Units: 67–70

We have noted elsewhere (see Unit 17) the need for museums to have a communications policy so that external communication with their public can be carried through effectively. It is equally important for the museum to have internal communications and procedures so that governing bodies, management and staff are informed of the progress and the achievements of the museum. Information flow through the organisation needs to happen in a variety of ways, and we look at some of the communications procedures which museums can use below.

Of crucial importance, however, is to ensure that all individuals within an organisation have access to the information they need to carry out their jobs effectively, to maintain and develop interest in their work, see how their work is contributing to meeting the museum's objectives and understand in a more general sense the progress of the museum. No one person can or should know everything! All people working for the organisation should be served by the museum's communications procedures. Procedures should be in place to ensure the appropriate direction and level of information flow.

Governing bodies

What does the governing body of the museum need to know, how do they know and who or what provides them with information? In the first instance, governors have a responsibility to ensure that the museum is operating within a policy framework which they have formally agreed and is working to meet its defined objectives (see Unit 68).

The museum's forward plan is the management mechanism which translates the museum's policy and objectives into a plan of action.

Governors therefore need to know and agree both how their policy and general objectives are going to be carried out, and receive regular reports on progress in the different programme areas in which the plan is structured. They therefore need to see and agree the forward plan prepared for them by the MUSEUM MANAGER, and receive reports from management on an agreed schedule.

Governors will also have to respond to new requirements, new opportunities and new difficulties which appear from time to time and have an effect on the overall performance of the museum and forward plan. They therefore need to meet regularly, between four and twelve times per year as appropriate – governors of smaller museums should meet more regularly than those with professional staffing – to receive written and oral reports on progress.

These reports come from the MUSEUM MANAGER and his/her staff and allow governors to monitor progress against their planning objectives and take any further policy decisions required. Where more specific attention needs to be paid to particular areas, governors may wish to establish committees from their membership, and perhaps external advisers, or advisory panels of external advisers.

Their meetings will also need to be informed by management and relate to the cycle/schedule of governors' meetings to which they report formally. All formal meetings of governors, or committees/advisory panels should be minuted in writing, typed up with copies sent to all members and agreed as a correct record at the subsequent meeting. Necessary steps to implement decisions should be described in an action checklist/memorandum for implementation sent to all relevant staff, with a timetable for the action to be taken and subsequently reported on. In these ways, governors who are ultimately responsible for the well-being of the museum can be kept informed of progress and take decisions within their agreed policy and forward planning.

Managers

Museum managers have to ensure that progress within the museum's forward planning is communicated to staff, and they also have to ensure that staff communicate progress in the workplace to them. Managers have a responsibility to communicate understanding of those matters that affect people's work. Staff do not have to agree in order to cooperate with a decision, but they must understand how and why it has been made.

No matter how large or small the workforce, formal systems need to be established for efficient information flow. In small museums especially it is possible to think that someone knows something, but because they have not been informed within a set procedure the opposite may all too easily be the case!

Museum managers have to ensure that the museum staff receive accurate and correct information, and take every step to discourage and correct, if necessary, rumour and distortion. Reporting mechanisms need to be established so that information, and critically ideas and suggestions from staff at all levels can be fed into the communications system.

Team briefing

One method of communicating with the workforce is through 'team briefing'.

Briefing can be conceived of in four sections:

- progress and forward planning – achievements/progress made since the last briefing against planning objectives and work planned for the month ahead. This information can be written down and circulated in advance of the meetings;
- policy – new policy decisions taken or initiatives under development;
- people – new appointments, people leaving, qualifications gained by individuals;
- points for action – specific action points, reminders of dates/events, 'housekeeping' points.

Briefing should take about half an hour on an appropriate timescale. This may be weekly, fortnightly or monthly depending on the needs of the museum. Questions and clarification of points should be sought and answered, if necessary later, following reference to senior management. This ensures that essential core information is transmitted quickly and accurately through the organisation.

Such a briefing procedure needs to be informed through progress reports from each member or unit of staff to line managers on a regular basis to mesh with the team briefing cycle.

Other forms of communication

There is a wide range of other forms of communication within the museum – some will be more or less appropriate depending on local circumstances. The checklist below provides some guidance:

- news/information in written format circulated on an internal post system to designated staff;
- current awareness circulars including copies of press coverage;
- noticeboards – but make certain these are the responsibility of a designated individual to manage, and ensure that all notices are signed to identify source;
- manager's newsletter;
- employees' and governors' handbooks or information packs – essential to keep updated, but invaluable for reference purposes and ensuring consistency of communication;
- project presentations, by project leaders;
- annual reports for employees.

Staff

All staff have an important part to play in information and communications procedures. It is essential that all staff are encouraged to recognise, record and transmit information which will be of value to colleagues or the museum as a whole. An organisation which is well informed and can communicate news, tasks and requirements effectively internally will be a more efficient and successful organisation. It is therefore vital for all staff to communicate effectively with each other at all times and to participate in the communications procedures fully.

UNIT 74   STAFF STRUCTURES

Related Units: 67–9, 75–80

Every museum has staff, even a private museum run as a hobby by one person. As soon as two people are involved, even if they only meet at weekends, the museum has a staff 'structure'.

The staff structure describes the relationship between the people who work for the museum: who can tell whom what to do, who does what part of the work, who needs to give information to whom. Normally one person is in charge and must learn to manage, to delegate and to inform, while the others must learn to advise, to report and to carry out instructions. Even if the museum is run by a cooperative in which everyone is equal, there is still a need to have formal arrangements for decision-taking, the division of the work and the exchange of information (see Unit 73).

A great deal of thought should be given to the best staff structure in a new museum: an old museum, too, will benefit from a fresh look at its staff structure every few years.

The staff the museum needs, and their relationships, should reflect the nature and purpose of the museum. If it is a university museum, teaching and research may have high priority and early appointments may be a lecturer and a researcher. If it is an educational museum an education specialist may be one of the first people appointed. A small community museum deciding to concentrate on lively temporary exhibitions may decide that a designer is the most important post.

In the same way, as the museum grows the staff structure should reflect the priorities of the museum. The staff structure should also reflect the work that actually needs to be done in the museum. The museum managers should measure the work that needs to be done and ensure that it is clearly someone's responsibility. Otherwise vital work will go undone, or else more and more jobs will end up being done by one or two overworked people.

Areas of responsibility often forgotten in museums include administration, documentation, fieldwork and building maintenance. A well-thought-out staff structure will help the museum maintain its policies and achieve its objectives.

However, there is no perfect structure for the staff of a museum.

UNIT 75   VOLUNTEERS IN MUSEUMS

Related Units: 74, 76–80

Few museums could manage without the help of any volunteers at all, though the way in which volunteers are involved varies greatly from museum to museum and from country to country.

The key to getting the best out of volunteer help lies in treating volunteers as formally as you treat paid members of staff. Expect the same level of commitment from them, and accord them the same degree of respect.

DEFINING THE JOB

Just as with the appointment of paid staff, the first step must be to define the job that needs to be done. It may indeed be worth going through the same procedures as for a paid job, and drawing up a job description and even a person specification (see Unit 76).

RECRUITING VOLUNTEERS

Ways of recruiting will vary from country to country, but a museum's volunteers will be a valuable link with the community it serves. It is important, therefore, to try to make sure that the volunteers reflect the community, and do not come from just one group. Rather than rely simply on word-of-mouth to recruit volunteers, it is often worth advertising formally, or writing to organisations that might include potential volunteers.

SELECTING VOLUNTEERS

People applying to work as volunteers at the museum should be asked to apply formally and should be selected just as if they were applying for paid work. If acceptance as a volunteer is seen to be a privilege it will be valued the more.

Volunteers should be invited to apply formally, and should be formally interviewed before acceptance. They should be asked to promise to be available for a minimum number of hours each week or each month.

THE ATTITUDE OF THE STAFF

There are two reasons why paid staff sometimes object to a museum using volunteers. The first is that they fear that volunteers will replace them, and will end up doing their jobs for free. The second is that they will be expected to spend a lot of time training and supervising volunteers, who will prove more of a hindrance than a help.

The first worry will need to be handled very tactfully and sympathetically by museum management, who should make quite sure that volunteers are used only in a supporting role and never to replace paid staff. In some museums it may be necessary to negotiate the use of volunteers with the Trade Unions concerned.

The second worry will be lessened if staff see that the volunteers are willing to commit a substantial amount of time for a long period – that their commitment is serious.

A VOLUNTEERS' ORGANISATION

If the museum has more than a few volunteers, it is probably worth forming a formal organisation, perhaps itself run by a volunteer.

TRAINING VOLUNTEERS

The training of volunteers is as important as the training of professional staff. Every museum with more than one or two regular volunteers should have a formal training programme for them. The volunteer body should be trained by a volunteer trainer.

This will have three elements:

■ On-the-job training. Informal training will be the most important element, whether the volunteer is acting as a guide for visitors, sorting pottery, helping to build displays or fulfilling any other role.

■ Lectures. Formal lectures and gallery tours are essential, and should if possible be arranged especially for the volunteers, so that they feel special. They can cover all aspects of the work of the museum: their purpose is to make the volunteers' work richer by helping them to understand more of its context.

■ Discussion sessions. Discussion sessions are especially important in the training of guides, but all volunteers will benefit from a regular opportunity to discuss different aspects of their work with each other and with museum staff.

BENEFITS FOR VOLUNTEERS

If we expect volunteers freely to give their time to the museum, and to accept the discipline of regular work, we must make sure that they receive real rewards.

The first reward that every volunteer is seeking is the assurance that he or she is doing something valuable, that is of real benefit to society. It is therefore important that volunteers are properly thanked: the MUSEUM MANAGER should make a regular habit of speaking to volunteers, of paying tribute to their work and of introducing visiting dignitaries to them.

Many people volunteer because it gives them an opportunity to get to know like-minded people. The museum should ensure that there is a programme of social activities for them that will help to weld them into a team and that will help them identify with the museum.

Volunteers could be given free admission to the museum and its events and exhibitions.

Everyone likes to be allowed 'behind the scenes', and to be allowed to go where others cannot. Volunteers should be given a regular opportunity to see all aspects of the museum's work and to talk to museum staff about their work.

Some museums will find it helpful to give special titles — and perhaps badges or other insignia — to volunteers who have worked at the museum for a long time.

WORK DISCIPLINE

In a small museum where there are only two or three volunteers who are almost personal friends of the staff, arrangements will be comparatively informal, but in a larger museum volunteers must be willing to accept the same work discipline as the paid staff. That means, for example, that they must carry out the instructions of whoever is in charge of them, and must arrive for work on time.

The museum must carry out its side of the bargain, and must ensure that the volunteers understand to whom they are responsible and what their conditions of service are. It is worth considering providing them with a 'volunteers handbook' like the 'staff handbook' given to paid staff (see Unit 82).

Occasionally, it will be necessary for the museum to tell a volunteer that his or her help is no longer needed. This is always an extremely difficult situation, and a resentful volunteer who feels he or she has been unfairly 'sacked' can cause the museum a great deal of harm. There is no simple answer, though a formal relationship with the museum, and perhaps an agreed time-limit on the 'job', will help to make the parting less bitter.

For the most part, though, volunteers bring to the museum not only their time and their skills, but a fresh enthusiasm and links with the wider community that are invaluable to its mission.

Finally, it is worth remembering that volunteers are often the people who actually run museums. Throughout the world museums are set up and run by groups of volunteers or single enthusiasts, while the Governing Bodies of the world's greatest museums are composed largely of volunteers.

UNIT 76   RECRUITING MUSEUM STAFF

Related Units: 74, 75, 77–80

In many countries museums cannot recruit whom they want to join their staff. They may be obliged to take as curators the people sent by the government to work in the museum. They may be obliged to accept as security staff people rejected as unfit by the police. They may be obliged to accept as assistant curators people transferred from another part of the State Antiquities Service.

Fortunately, many museums *can* choose their staff. The staff is the most important aspect of any museum. Without good, well-trained staff it is impossible to create a good museum. Recruiting staff is therefore one of the most important things that the MUSEUM MANAGER does.

This unit outlines the steps the MUSEUM MANAGER must go through in recruiting staff for any position in the museum – from Deputy Director to ticket seller.

THE JOB DESCRIPTION

There should be a Job Description written for every job in the museum. When a job falls vacant, it should always be reviewed. Is this an opportunity to change the job, perhaps to change the whole structure of the museum, or of part of it? Or has the job changed slightly, so that the old Job Description is now out of date? A security guard's job may have become more to do with welcoming visitors or with interpretation, and less with security. A curator's job may have become more to do with archaeological fieldwork and less with care of collections.

The good MUSEUM MANAGER should be continually reviewing the jobs of his/her staff, and making sure that they contribute most effectively to the purpose of the museum. A new appointment is an extra opportunity to make changes.

THE PERSON SPECIFICATION

Having written the Job Description, the next step is to write a Person Specification to match it. Where the former describes what the job-holder is expected to *do*, the latter describes what sort of person he or she is expected to *be*.

What qualities and what skills are you looking for in the job-holder? Set them down on paper, and it will be easier to assess applicants for the post. Make sure that the qualities you decide on really are appropriate to the job, and not merely the result of your own prejudices!

ADVERTISEMENT

The usual way of attracting applications for museum jobs is by advertising the job in the newspapers or in a professional journal. It is important to think carefully about both where to advertise (which are the newspapers most likely to be read by good applicants?) and about the contents of the advertisement.

The advertisement should include:

– The name of the museum.
– A brief, accurate but attractive-sounding description of the job.
– The pay offered, with any other benefits.
– Where the job will be based.
– The hours worked, and other conditions.
– A brief description of the sort of person you are looking for, and the qualifications you require or would like the applicants to have.
– Where further details of the job can be obtained.
– Information on *how* to apply (by letter, or on an application form?), *where* to apply and *when* to apply.

Be very careful to make sure that the advertisement obeys the law, for example any laws forbidding discrimination on grounds of sex, age or race. The aim of the advertisement is to attract a sufficiently large pool of applicants from which to select.

FURTHER DETAILS

Information should be ready to send to enquirers. This information will probably include a description of the museum, a description of the

257

work of the section in which the job is based, a copy of the Job Description itself and an application form. A great deal of care should be put into preparing these 'further details': efficient, well-presented and helpful information will encourage the best people to want to work in your museum.

For the same reason, it is crucial to reply promptly and courteously to all enquirers and all applicants, even if they are likely to be quite unsuitable for the job.

SHORT-LISTING

The process known as 'short-listing' or 'screening' selects the best six or so applicants for further investigation.

The best way to do this is to use the Person Specification as a checklist, and tick off for each candidate those essential and desirable characteristics, experience and qualifications they seem to have. It is helpful to have three people carry out this process, and then to compare results.

Check, if you feel it is necessary, that the applicant has told the truth about his or her experience by writing to or telephoning the referees whose names are given. Did she really pass these exams? Was he really promoted to that post? Why did she leave that job so soon?

Write promptly to those applicants you have rejected, and thank them for their interest.

SELECTION

The interview is the traditional way of assessing and selecting people for jobs. It will probably always continue to be used, but research shows that it is a very bad way of choosing someone for a job. A good performance at an interview does not guarantee good performance in the job.

The effectiveness of the interview *can* be improved, though, and everyone who has to interview applicants for jobs should take every opportunity to acquire training. You may wish to have preliminary or secondary interviews to discuss candidates in greater detail.

A much more successful selection technique is the *work sample*. This simply means giving the applicants a sample of the work they will be doing in the job, and assessing how well they do it. If you are appointing a typist or a bricklayer, devising a sample will be easy, but it should be possible for any job, even a very varied one like a curator in a small museum.

Other selection techniques increasingly used in large organisations involve various types of psychological testing. These are very effective, but they should only be carried out by experts.

MAKING THE DECISION

The aim now is to choose the best candidate for the job – *not* the candidate you liked most! You now have a good deal of information about all the candidates – from their application forms, from their referees' comments, from the notes you took at their interviews and from the work samples and any other tests they may have been given.

Now look again at the Person Specification, and give each aspect a weighting out of ten. Then give the candidates marks out of ten for each aspect. Multiply the weighting for each aspect by each candidate's mark for that aspect. Then add up each candidate's now-weighted marks. This is as objective as possible a method of finding the best person for the job, but no method is perfect: we are dealing with human beings!

UNIT 77   CONDITIONS OF SERVICE

Related Units: 74–6, 78–80

Museum staff will work better and more happily if they know precisely what is expected of them, and on what conditions they are employed.

Different countries vary very greatly in the laws that govern employment. Different museums vary greatly, too, in the working conditions and practices of their staff. In this unit, therefore, we can only mention some of the points that every museum employer should consider.

Put it down on paper

Every employee should be given a document setting out the conditions of service under which he or she is employed, and his or her rights. In some cases this will be a formal legal contract; in others a less formal set of notes for the guidance of employee and employer. In either case

BOX

The staff handbook

An excellent idea for any museum with more than a very few staff is the staff handbook. A staff handbook is an excellent way of backing up their staff training.

The handbook should be designed for the individual needs of the museum, but the sort of things that might be included are:

■ *Background information about the museum*

- History of the museum
- Statement of the museum's purpose and objectives
- List of staff and their responsibilities

■ *General advice and information on working at the museum*

- Working hours
- Rules on punctuality, uniform, dress and behaviour
- Security arrangements and responsibilities
- Health & Safety arrangements and responsibilities
- Disciplinary & Grievance procedures
- Summary of conditions of service
- Sickness arrangements
- Staff privileges
- Team Briefing timetable

■ *Guidance on helping visitors*

- Answers to the ten most common questions visitors ask
- Notes on location of toilets, café, cloakroom, etc.
- What to do in the event of fire
- What to do in the event of theft
- What to do with lost children
- First Aid arrangements

A looseleaf handbook allows the easy addition of new information, new rules, details of exhibitions and events and different sections appropriate to different members of staff.

a great deal of trouble should be taken in drawing up the document, which will normally be given to the employee before or immediately on starting work. It could include the following points:

— The names of the employer and the employee.
— The employee's job-title.
— The date on which the job will start.
— The date on which the job will end, if it is for a fixed term.
— Normal working hours and any other rules about working hours, such as overtime payment or time-off instead of overtime payment.
— The rate of pay.
— Holidays, including public holidays, and rates of holiday pay. Rules of sickness or injury absence, and sick pay.
— Rules of maternity and paternity absence.
— Pension arrangements.
— Notice to be given, on either side, to end the contract.
— Rights to belong to and be represented by a Trade Union.
— Arrangements for meals, e.g. staff canteen or lower rates in the muscum café.
— Rules of dress or uniform.
— Grievance procedure; if the employee has a grievance, whom should he or she discuss it with first, and who afterwards, if not satisfied?
— Disciplinary procedure: a good employer has a formal disciplinary procedure which is set out in every employee's Contract or Conditions of Service document.

UNIT 78   PERFORMANCE STANDARDS FOR THE INDIVIDUAL

Related Units: 74–7, 79

All staff working in the museum environment need to be able to measure their performance against defined standards. Without standards staff and management cannot judge performance objectively. Standards can be developed internally by management working in conjunction with their staff, or the museum can adopt standards which have been developed externally by professional bodies which establish standards for the different types of work undertaken in museums.

A standard is a means both to define and measure performance, and this is important both for the employer and the employee. Standards are equally applicable in public as in private sector museums.

By measuring an individual's performance against a set of objective standards, it is possible to determine how effectively the individual is meeting the identified requirements of his/her post. If performance is below the requisite level, then training may be required. The outcome will be better job satisfaction for the individual, better service for the public, improved efficiency and effectiveness for the museum and for the individual, and enhanced career opportunities for the individual.

If a member of staff cannot meet a requisite level of performance other steps may need to be taken to relocate him/her.

Standards also provide an opportunity for the employer to clarify precisely what has to be done in a particular job, what skills and qualifications are required on the part of staff and how the tasks should be carried out.

Performance standards should be set at a level which the individual can or has been trained to achieve. It is pointless establishing performance standards which are too difficult to reach, are beyond the level of competence of staff or so difficult as to create anxiety and worry on the part of the individual.

They should be set in conjunction with the individual so that he/she can feel 'a sense of ownership' of the performance standards which he/she will be working to. Where a museum is establishing its own sets of standards for staff posts, reference should be made to other museums and the standards under which they are working for comparative purposes.

The relationship between performance standards for the individual and performance measurement for the museum is a close one. The range of tasks which any one individual carries out within the museum should be related to the objectives of the museum (see Unit 69) and its forward planning. For example, one of the objectives of the museum might be 'to provide high quality educational services to the formal education sector in order to maximise the educational potential of the museum's collections'.

In this case, the member or members of staff who will have responsibility for ensuring that the objective is met, will need precise descriptions of what they must do. By analysing the tasks to be carried out to meet that objective, standards of performance can be set.

For an education specialist, these might include for example:

■ TEACHER TRAINING
- *Standard*: Ensuring that six in-service training days are organised for primary school teachers in schools in a specified area.

■ MUSEUM TEACHING
- *Standard*: Providing five museum lessons per week from x month to y month for primary school children from schools in a specified area.

■ INFORMATION DEVELOPMENT/PROVISION
- *Standard*: Developing four information packs on key syllabus topics in one year.

■ ADMINISTRATION
- *Standard*: Responding to enquiries from school teachers within five working days,

and so on. The number of standards under each of these four main headings will be determined by time available and other constraints such as resources and staff.

Each museum would approach that particular objective, if included in their functional objectives, in a different way depending on their resources. The museum would, however, be able to demonstrate:

- how that objective was broken down into component tasks;
- how, given staffing and other resources, staff would meet those tasks;
- what measurable standard of performance they would be working to. Note the quantified measure in each standard set.

Further refinements can be made. For example, standards can be developed for each in-service training day to ensure that training is carried out in a consistent and systematic way; or standards can be set for each information pack to provide quality assurance.

It is the task of the MUSEUM MANAGER to agree standards of performance for each staff post, to monitor performance on a regular basis against standards and to provide support and training to help staff meet standards.

UNIT 79   JOB APPRAISAL AND PERFORMANCE MEASUREMENT

Related Units: 74–8, 80

It is a principal task of museum managers to ensure that the museum's forward plan is implemented successfully. In order for this to happen, staff working in museums will need to carry out a range of projects in addition to their day-to-day work. The success of the museum is dependent upon the success of staff in meeting planning objectives and in carrying out their routine work. The museum's reputation and standing is therefore dependent on all members of staff carrying out their jobs efficiently and effectively.

Managers have therefore to monitor on a regular basis how well staff are carrying out their duties or meeting specific project targets which have been set. As we have noted in Unit 78 this process is made substantially easier if specific performance standards for routine tasks have already been established. The ways in which monitoring is carried out will vary from museum to museum depending on staffing strengths.

In some museums, formal weekly progress reports from members of staff to their managers will be made, in others monthly written progress reports might be provided. In addition to written reports, group or individual meetings may take place where specific projects are being developed or carried through. While it is not necessary to go into overmuch detail, managers should essentially be tracking progress against forward planning requirements and keeping an eye on the success of members of staff in carrying out their duties to the required standard on a regular basis. All museums should devise their own reporting procedures (see Unit 73).

Regular progress reports should be written, preferably typed and filed for later reference. Managers, however, should note any points of concern over individual performance in writing and discuss these with staff at an appropriate time.

We suggest that an annual job appraisal or performance review should be carried out on a routine basis for all members of staff. These should be conducted by the member of staff's line manager, and should examine achievement (or failure) over the year, explore any areas of difficulty or complication, seek genuine feedback on the manager/ employee relationship and identify training needs and training provision to meet these. The individual member of staff should be provided with a structured checklist of questions to record any significant points/concerns for later discussion.

The line manager should undertake an interview on the basis of the completed checklist with the member of staff. The interview should be written up and agreed and signed by both the line manager and member of staff, and passed to senior management for noting. Any action points, improvements, changes to standards in the light of experience, or training provision should be implemented as appropriate.

The performance standards which were discussed in Unit 78 were all quantitative. In measuring performance, however, qualitative standards and assessment should also be developed. These are more difficult to develop, but should be taken into consideration in job appraisal and formal performance measurement.

It is one thing to run in-service training courses for teachers, but another thing to ensure that each teacher is pleased with the course arrangements, has benefited from the course and will continue to attend training events organised by the museum. In this situation, questionnaires can be devised for completion by those attending a course asking for feedback and how the course has been perceived. The information from these can be used to assess achievement.

In job appraisal therefore, line managers should seek to comment on the quality, as well as the quantity of work, carried out and to assess the quality of achievements which have taken place during the year.

The key benefits of job appraisal are that a member of staff gains improved job satisfaction through knowing that their work in terms of quantity and quality has been duly recognised, acknowledged and valued. Weaknesses can be identified and strengthened through training, or readjustment of work programmes. Managers are able to report to their governing bodies on the effectiveness and efficiency of their staff in terms of their performance within the forward planning framework.

UNIT 80   STAFF TRAINING

Related Units: 74–9

Staff development through in-service training programmes is an important responsibility of all those managing museums or in management positions in museums. The MUSEUM MANAGER should ensure that the museum has a training policy and a training programme for all staff. Those individuals working for the museum will have experience and/or qualifications of different types, but as we have seen in Unit 79, it is up to managers to identify where additional in-service training is needed through regular job/performance appraisal. The benefits of training in whatever form it takes will be experienced by the museum's users, by the museum's staff and by the museum's collections.

It is necessary for museum governing bodies to 'recognize the need for, and value of, a properly qualified and trained staff, and offer adequate opportunities for further training and retraining in order to maintain an adequate and effective workforce' (ICOM, *Code of Professional Ethics*).

Because so many different skills are required in museum work, and so many different disciplines and professions are represented, it is not surprising that a correspondingly wide range of training provision is required. Each museum will have different opportunities to gain access to training in different areas of museum work because provision in different countries varies so greatly. Museum training needs cannot always be provided locally.

There are, too, different types and levels of training. Some training programmes can lead to vocational training qualifications. Some training programmes are not qualifications-based and are provided on a more informal basis, such as ICOM workshops. Some are residential programmes, some are through distance-learning methods and some are built up in-house through local resources.

Wherever possible the organisation and use of training courses should be based on institutions with recognised standards, appropriate curricula and a good reputation in museum education and training. It is worthwhile discussing training provision with professional associations, colleagues and staff in other museums, and seeking advice and information through national documentation centres where these exist.

Training programmes devised in-house might include guided reading, visits to other museums, discussion groups, seminars, project work and dedicated study and reading time. Distance-learning programmes are becoming more widely available on an international basis, and some of these are qualifications-based. Information on training programmes and materials is available through national, international and specialist journals and periodicals including ICOM *News* and ICTOP's training bulletin (IT) (see Unit 84). Training resources acquired by the museum – publications, videos, information sheets, films, audio-tapes – should be up-to-date.

The success of your museum depends very largely on the quality of staff in all aspects of the museum's work, on their skills and abilities, knowledge and understanding. Every effort should be made to define training needs in terms of regular job appraisal and meet them through whatever form(s) of provision are available and of course affordable.

Museums should allocate at least 2 per cent of their annual operating budgets for training, and every museum should develop and maintain a training policy for its staff. Training should be designed to help people become more flexible, adaptable and versatile in their work. Training should be related to people's needs either in their current posts, or for their career development.

Career guidance should be provided to all staff as appropriate. Training provides increased job interest, and commitment, as well as giving staff more incentives for achievement. Qualifications provide recognition and credit for skills and knowledge gained through training programmes.

Where training provision is limited and resources are scarce, it is important to spend hard-earned money wisely. Seek advice on developing a selected range of up-to-date text books, training resources and journals in key subject areas   collections management, user services and museum management – and develop your own information manuals through acquiring information sheets, photocopies and notes in those areas of museum work relevant to you.

Training is about learning, and learning from other's experience and knowledge through different media. Gaining access to that experience and knowledge can only prove beneficial. Keeping up-to-date is essential.

UNIT 81   HEALTH AND SAFETY

Related Units: 67–80, 82

Every museum has a responsibility to protect the health and safety of its employees, volunteers and visitors, as well as of the public generally.

Because so many different activities take place in museums there is a great variety of potential hazards. How can the museum reduce the risk of danger to people?

THE SAFETY REPRESENTATIVE

The first and most important step must be to make one person responsible for maintaining Health and Safety in the museum. This Safety Representative should ideally be someone who is trusted by everyone – staff and volunteers. Even in a museum with only two or three staff, one person should be the Safety Representative.

The Safety Representative should be the person who sees all the official literature about safety. He or she must have authority to go anywhere in the museum without special permission, and must be allowed time from their job to fulfil their Safety Representative responsibilities. They will need training, and should take advantage of any regular training that is available.

The Safety Representative should – except in a very small museum – probably not be also responsible for fire prevention (see Unit 56), because he/she may end up spending all available time on fire precautions at the expense of other dangers.

The work of the Safety Representative involves:

■ Regular inspection of every part of the museum. This is the Health & Safety Review (see Box 2), the aim of which is to identify potential risks.

■ Examining the cause of every accident and making sure that as far as possible the cause is removed for the future.

■ Providing information on health and safety to everyone working in the museum, and organising regular training for staff, for example on how to lift things safely, on dangerous chemicals or on first aid.

■ Liaison with the health authorities and other official bodies concerned with safety.

■ Ensuring that Health and Safety are taken into account during the planning of new exhibitions and special events. Extra care is needed when anything unusual is happening in the museum, such as the construction of new exhibitions or public events.

■ Making sure that everyone knows what to do in the event of an accident.

THE SAFETY REVIEW

'Safety Review' is the name given to regular inspection of all parts of the museum, to try to identify potential safety risks and health problems. It should be carried out regularly by the Safety Representative who should not only look for dangers him or herself, but should talk informally to other members of staff and encourage them to notice potential hazards. The Safety Representative should keep a book in which to record every Safety Review, and note every danger found and what was done to eliminate it.

The Safety Review will be looking at five different sorts of things:

– Safe practices. Are the ways in which people do things the safest ones?
– Authorised people. Are the right people doing things? For example, is everyone using a circular saw trained and authorised to do so?
– Equipment and clothing. Is all the necessary equipment available and in use? Are guards in place on cutting machinery? Is electrical gear safe? Is everyone wearing proper safety clothing?
– Notices and warnings. Are all the necessary warning signs and notices in place? Do staff read them?
– Staff awareness. What potentially dangerous things have happened? Are staff safety conscious? What training is needed?

THE SAFETY COMMITTEE

In some larger museums it will be helpful to set up a Safety Committee. This will consist of representatives of management and of workers, of all parts of the museum's staff. Health and Safety is in *everyone's* interest. The Safety Committee should meet regularly and should receive a regular report from the Safety Representative. Everyone working in the museum should know about its work and should be encouraged to make suggestions for improvements.

BOX 1

The Safety Review

Every Safety Representative will make their own list of things to check during the regular Safety Review.

The Safety Audit

SUBJECT	POINTS TO CHECK
Persons to be protected	
– Employees	How many, which work places, what duties, how much travel, special risks.
– Non-employees	How many volunteers, visitors on premises, contractors on premises, persons passing premises, special risks.
– Users of products	Customers of shops and cafés, recipients of loans, reproductions, etc.
Identification and control of dangers	
– Premises	Emergency evacuation, fire precautions, first aid, electrical safety, lifts, access to roofs, toilets and messrooms, house-keeping.
– Articles and substances	Poisions, fire hazards, gas cylinder, pesticides, laboratory materials, collection materials.
– Operations and processes	Workshop and laboratory activities, construction of displays, glass handling, electrical work, movement of objects, use of synthetic materials, model making, gardening, forestry, farming, excavation fieldwork, café, sales, warehousing.
– Environment	Heating, ventilation, lighting, noise, vibration dust, fumes, radiation, cleaning, plant maintenance.
– Jobs and work methods	Staff qualifications, training, supervision, working hours, workloads. Has training plan been implemented?
– Work systems	Staff responsibilities, standing orders, regulations, timetabling, monitoring, working conditions.
– Products and waste	Disposal of workshop or laboratory waste, taxidermy post-mortem materials, sewage, items sold or lent.

Monitoring and revision

— Safety inspections	Regular inspection of all premises. Checking of duties at all management levels. Are systems for introducing new equipment, substance processes effective? First aid, welfare and emergency procedures adequate.
— Accident, near miss and health records	Are accidents being reported and investigated? To whom are they notified? Are health records monitored? To whom are they notified?
— Safety representatives and workforce consultation	Which trade unions represent the workforce? Who represents non-unionists? Are workforce aware of consultation procedure. Is it effective?
— Formal audit and review	Senior management reviews. Health and Safety Executive involvement. Changes to safety policy.

BOX 2

There is a huge number of potential hazards in museums. These are just a few of the sorts of dangers for which all museum staff should be constantly on the lookout:

- lifting too heavy items
- carrying objects wrongly
- dangerous chemicals in laboratory or workshop
- unguarded machine tools
- dangerous wiring
- sharp tools in workshop and studio
- old and dangerous insecticides in reserve collections
- legionnaires disease bacilli in humidification and air-conditioning equipment
- lack of cleanliness in kitchen or staffroom
- steps and uneven floor levels
- cluttered stores, offices, etc.
- arsenic in old mounted specimens

BOX 3
The First Aid Box

In some countries there is a legal requirement to provide a First Aid Box, and what should be in it is laid down by law. For example, the following are required in Britain:

- A general guidance card on First Aid
- 20 individually wrapped sterile adhesive dressings (assorted sizes) appropriate for the work environment
- 2 sterile eye pads, with attachments
- 6 individually wrapped triangular bandages
- 6 safety pins
- 6 medium sized individually wrapped unmedicated wound dressings (approx. 10cm x 8cm)
- 2 large sterile ditto (approx. 13cm x 9cm)
- 3 extra large ditto (approx. 28cm x 17.5cm)

Where mains tap water is not readily available for eye irrigation, sterile water or sterile normal saline solution (0.9 per cent) in sealed disposable containers should be provided.

BOX 4
The First Aid Room

Every larger museum should have a separate First Aid Room, used for nothing else. Smaller museums should provide one, too, if at all possible, and should certainly have somewhere to take people – staff or visitors – who are taken ill.

The First Aid Room should contain:

- sink and running hot and cold water
- drinking water and disposable cups
- paper towels
- smooth-topped working surfaces
- First Aid Box
- chair
- couch with waterproof cover, pillow and blankets.
- soap
- clean protective garments
- refuse container with disposable plastic bags
- record book
- bowl

It should be the responsibility of the First Aiders to maintain the First Aid Room.

THE ACCIDENT BOOK

Whether or not it is required by law, as it is in some countries, every museum should have an Accident Book in which are written down not merely serious accidents, but small incidents and things which happen which might have harmed people.

FIRST AID ARRANGEMENTS

However careful we are, accidents will happen, so it is important to make sure that First Aid arrangements are adequate for visitors and staff. Planning in advance will ensure that in the case of accidents people know what to do.

Every workplace should have at least one person always present who is trained in First Aid, a 'First Aider'. Usually that will mean that two or three members of staff must be sent to regular refresher training courses – if more are trained, so much the better.

The First Aiders will ensure that the First Aid Box (see Box 3) is properly maintained and kept in the appointed place. The First Aiders will ensure that everyone knows how to call an ambulance or doctor in the event of more serious accidents.

In many countries there are laws prescribing arrangements for First Aid and for other aspects of Health and Safety. It is the job of the MUSEUM MANAGER to make sure that those laws are known and observed.

INSURANCE

The MUSEUM MANAGER must ensure that the museum is fully covered by insurance against any risks to members of the public or staff or volunteers. In many countries this is a legal requirement.

UNIT 82   ADMINISTRATIVE PROCEDURES

Related Units: 67–71, 73

Just as in any other organisation, so in museums: efficient administration is almost more important than anything else. Efficiency consists of:

- systems that achieve their aims with the least trouble and least paperwork;
- people understanding the systems and knowing who should do what;
- people doing their part of the work promptly and accurately;
- people doing their part of the work intelligently, making sure that the aims of the museum, and not the administrative systems themselves, are being served.

None of these things can be taught or described in a book. But there are some pieces of advice which may be helpful.

There are two main areas with which administration is concerned: finance and personnel. Units 71 and 77 describe some aspects of these. In many museums the administrative procedures will be laid down by others, with little possibility for the MUSEUM MANAGER to make changes. What he or she can do, though, is to ensure that the procedures are regularly reviewed, and that a report be prepared assessing their strengths and weaknesses, and recommending improvements. Such a review is best done not by the person in charge of administration, but by someone from outside the museum staff altogether, working closely with the *junior* staff of the museum – they are the people who know all the problems! Such an outside review is valuable even in a very small museum.

Administrative procedures tend to grow up haphazardly over the years, with only long-serving members of staff understanding them, and many procedures continuing long after they have ceased to be useful. One way to avoid this creeping bureaucracy is to ensure that all procedures are set down in an administrative handbook (see Box). Copies of the handbook should be given to every senior member of staff, and some sections of it will be included in the handbooks given to all staff and volunteers (see Unit 77).

Regular briefings of some sort are essential for all staff (see Unit 73). An important element of these staff briefings must be to assess whether the administrative procedures are working to support the museum's aims, and to assess whether museum staff are fulfilling their responsibilities. It is all too easy for bad feeling to develop between administrative staff, who accuse their colleagues of laziness and inefficiency, for example not completing time-sheets accurately or not recording expenditure properly, and curatorial and other staff who come to believe the administrators create useless procedures just to keep themselves in jobs. Such bad feeling can seriously damage the work of the museum; a regular opportunity to discuss difficulties will help to prevent its growth.

BOX

The Administrative Handbook

A handbook, available to all staff and containing an outline of all the procedures used in the museum, is a very helpful way of ensuring that everyone knows the procedures, and that they are kept up-to-date. In a small museum the Administrative Handbook may be combined with the staff handbook (see Unit 73). Their contents will certainly overlap.

What goes into the handbook will vary greatly from museum to museum, but the following will be found in most:

■ FINANCIAL ADMINISTRATION

- Accounting procedures
- Petty cash
- Staff travel arrangements

■ OFFICE PROCEDURES

- Filing
- Correspondence
- Answering the telephone

■ MATERIALS ADMINISTRATION

- Purchasing procedures
- Control of stores
- Fuel and light

■ PERSONNEL ADMINISTRATION

- Recruiting policies and procedures
- Induction
- Leave arrangements
- Sickness arrangements
- Grievance procedure
- Disciplinary procedure
- Briefing/reporting procedures
- Training arrangements

■ HEALTH & SAFETY

- Health and Safety arrangements (see Unit 81)

Section VI
Supporting resources and services

UNIT 83   GLOSSARY

We provide here a list of terms appearing in the text with comments on their usage. These have been selected on the basis that they may be unfamiliar terms to readers in some countries. In most cases they are introduced and defined within the most appropriate unit in greater detail – sometimes as 'keywords', and the unit reference is also given here for information.

Animatronics   Models of people or animals which move mechanically (see Unit 20).

Carers   People who look after children or adults on a voluntary or professional basis (see Unit 12).

Case-for-support   A written statement of need used for fundraising purposes (see Unit 72).

Dehumidifier   An item of equipment electrically operated designed to decrease the level of relative humidity where environmental conditions are too damp (see Unit 48).

Desk research   Information gathered from published and non-published sources (see Unit 6).

Diffuser panel   A panel of translucent plastic or other similar material used to diffuse or spread light from a light source. Diffuser panels are often used in display cases to obtain a more even light for display purposes (see Unit 47).

Diorama   A three-dimensional presentation technique consisting of scenes based on models in the foreground and painted backgrounds or surrounds (see Unit 19).

Disaster Control Plan   A written plan which sets out the steps a museum should take in preventing and reacting to disasters of all types (see Unit 56).

Display   The means by which museums present and interpret objects to their visitors, usually involving design, text and graphics. In the United States and Canada the equivalent term is **Exhibit**.

Exhibit   The term used in the United States and Canada for the means by which museums present and interpret objects to their visitors, usually involving design, text and graphics. In the United Kingdom the equivalent term is **Display**.

Exhibition   A temporary or short-term museum presentation.

Formative evaluation   The techniques associated with testing the effectiveness of displays and exhibitions in process of production (see Unit 29).

Forward plan   A written plan setting out the museum's functional and planning objectives to be met over a defined period of time (see Unit 69).

Friends' groups or Membership programmes   An organised group of people who support the museum and its work generally through fundraising activities of different types (see Unit 33).

Front end evaluation   The techniques associated with the testing of ideas and proposals for displays and exhibitions before production begins (see Unit 29).

Governing body/Governors   Those people with overall responsibility in law for conducting the policy and affairs of the museum, and to whom the museum staff are accountable (see Unit 67).

Heritage centre   A visitor facility providing interpretive displays on the cultural and/or natural history of a place or area. 'Heritage centres' which hold collections are functionally museums, although may be called heritage centres for marketing reasons (see Unit 19).

Humidifier   An item of equipment electrically operated designed to increase the level of relative humidity where environmental conditions are too dry (see Unit 48).

Hygrometer   An item of equipment used to measure relative humidity (see Unit 48).

Lux   A unit of illumination measured by a light meter (see Unit 47).

Market   The overall social and economic context within which a museum operates (see Unit 6).

Market analysis   Analysis carried out on the structure and composition of the market (see Unit 6).

Market intelligence   Information about the market, including composition and trends (see Unit 6).

Market place   The specific social and economic context within which a museum operates (see Unit 6).

Market research   The study of the different habits, attitudes and interests of the users making up the market for a museum (see Unit 6).

Market segment   An identifiable range of users or non-users within the market with shared characteristics (see Unit 6).

Market share   The extent to which the museum attracts users in the overall market (see Unit 6).

Market survey   A programme of investigation into the structure and nature of the market (see Unit 6).

Marketing   The techniques associated with developing and promoting the museum to meet the identified needs of the market (see Unit 7).

Marketing mix   A balance of factors – product, price, place and promotion – which museums can control in order to influence people's attitudes towards a museum (see Unit 7).

Micro-environment   A small space which can be controlled in terms of relative humidity and other environmental factors for special categories of material (see Unit 48).

museum manager (small letters)   Any member of staff with responsibility for managing resources – people, collections, finance, buildings or equipment. It is used in this book to show that many people in a museum contribute to its effective working.

MUSEUM MANAGER (with capitals)   The senior member of staff (sometimes called the Director or a similar title) with overall responsibility for the museum's operation who reports to the museum's governing body (see Unit 67).

Museum product   An amalgam of the quantifiable and non-quantifiable factors which go to make up the personality and identity of a museum in the mind of the user (see Unit 7).

Outreach   The methods by which a museum can take services out into the community which it serves through, for example, touring exhibitions or schools loan services (see Unit 12).

People mover   A vehicle in which users ride through display or presentation areas in museums (see Unit 19).

Pepper's Ghost   A presentation technique based on mirrors which allows one image to replace another (see Unit 20).

Performance measurement   Measuring a museum's or a person's performance against agreed objectives and standards (see Units 70 and 79).

Preventive conservation   The processes by which a museum's collections are stored, displayed, handled and maintained in ways which do not lead to deterioration (see Unit 46).

Public relations   The management of the relationship between the public and the museum (see Unit 32).

Recording thermohygrographs or electronic hygrometers   An item of equipment used for the continuous recording of temperature and relative humidity levels on a weekly or monthly chart (see Unit 48).

Relative humidity (RH)   Relative humidity is a ratio of water vapour in the air to the amount that it can hold if fully saturated, and is expressed as a percentage, for example 55 per cent RH (see Unit 48).

Remedial conservation   The processes involved in repairing damage or decay to collections, using techniques which are reversible (see Units 54 and 55).

Tableau   A presentation technique consisting of a reconstructed setting with life-size models of people or animals (see Unit 19).

Talking-head   A presentation technique consisting of a model face onto which a video film of someone talking is projected (see Unit 20).

U-V monitor   An item of equipment electrically operated which measures the proportion of ultra-violet light falling on an object or display/storage area (see Unit 47).

Volunteers' group   An organised group of people who provide practical support to museum staff on a voluntary basis (see Unit 75).

UNIT 84   SOURCES OF INFORMATION AND SUPPORT

We have discussed the importance of collections documentation in Unit 46, here we examine the other forms of information which museums use. Some of these are listed below. They include:

— information about other museum collections, for identification and research purposes;
— information about the museum's markets (see Units 5 and 6).
— information about organisations and individuals able to support or work with the museum.
— information about suppliers of services and goods.
— information about the theory and practice of museum work.
— information about other museums and their work.

Information for the museum manager may be available in the museum or from outside sources. Some information can be assembled systematically within the museum at limited cost, for example by compiling files relating to suppliers of services and goods for different aspects of the museum's operation. Other types of information may require regular financial outlay, for example through developing the museum's library by acquiring reference works.

Whatever balance of information is collected it should reflect the needs of the museum. In building up a reference library careful thought should be given to the most effective deployment of resources. The museum should establish clear policies for the development of its reference library. Maintaining the currency of information in a museum library is an important consideration. Keeping your library up-to-date means that staff can be kept up-to-date.

Different kinds of information require different collection methods. For example, in identifying objects, much information can be obtained about different classes of objects from illustrated examples in journals or other publications. But this may need to be complemented by museum staff visiting other museums/collections and examining their collections for comparative material. Recording this field information for future use should be carried out in a systematic way.

What sources of information outside the museum are available to you? Other museums can provide assistance in many ways, for example through advice over management issues or procedures, help with identifications and research, assistance with marketing intelligence, the loan of publications or information over suppliers or manufacturers of products. Building up networks of information at local, regional and national level plays an important part in museum work. Every effort should be made to stay in touch with colleagues in other museums.

Using information that is readily available in this way helps to avoid 'reinventing the wheel' and makes use of expertise and experience not otherwise available in your museum.

Second, museological information centres or museum studies training centres can be of enormous importance in finding the most reliable information or sources of information you may need. Wherever museums have access to such centres, they should make the most use of them.

Third, library networks are a valuable source of support. Availability of library services varies from one country to another. Wherever possible, use existing library provision rather than going to the expense of duplicating reference material which may not be needed regularly. Many libraries operate inter-library loan systems and access through these systems to material too expensive to buy may be a useful way of obtaining the publications which you want.

It is better to devote resources to standard reference works/publications rather than acquire material which will only be used very occasionally where budgets are limited. Take advice on which publications to buy or subscribe to from museum studies centres or information centres.

Remember also that joint purchase or subscriptions through groups of museums, specialist groups of curators or other museum workers may be an effective way of targeting resources.

There is a very wide range of publications about museum work now available internationally. Most museum organisations or associations will provide guidance on availability. Publishers will always provide information about their publication lists on request. Finally wherever possible, participate in training programmes. They provide a wealth of information and help to build up useful contacts. Training programmes allow for the free interchange of ideas and experience – learning from others is the most valuable source of information there is available.

CHECKLIST OF INFORMATION SOURCES

☐ *External*

– Other museums
– Reference libraries
– Museum Studies centres
– Museum associations
– Journals
– Reference books
– Documentation centres
– Professional colleagues
– Training programmes

☐ *Internal*

– Museum reference library
– Information files on suppliers/manufacturers
– Information files on other museum collections
– Village files (see Unit 39)
– Publishers' lists
– Examples of museum marketing materials

STUDY EXAMPLE

The curator of a small museum with a limited budget developed a series of 'topic files'. The files covered issues like conservation, design, display cases, education, and provided a ready source of information when the need arose. Copies of articles, suppliers' information, fact sheets from museum associations, references to publications, contact names and addresses all were included. Whenever a member of the museum's staff needed information the topic files were a useful first source of information. A system of this type needs to be kept up-to-date in a rigorous way if it is to be useful.

The curator had made the best use of available budgets to build up information which was regularly needed.

UNIT 85   FURTHER READING

Selected further reading is provided under each of the units listed here. Readers should be aware that references are to books, rather than periodicals. The majority of the publications cited should be readily available through libraries. ISBN numbers have been given, where relevant, to assist readers in identifying and acquiring books. There is, however, a very wide range of information available in periodicals and readers are encouraged to obtain information about their availability through the ICOM Information Centre or local or national museum information centres. The value of periodicals is that the reader can keep up-to-date with new information and ideas.

In building up a museum library it is recommended that the MUSEUM MANAGER identifies priority texts in those areas which will be of direct day-to-day assistance in the museum's work. For additional information see Unit 84, Sources of Information.

1   ABOUT MUSEUMS

Boylan, P. (ed.), *Museums 2000: Politics, People, Professionals and Profit* (London, 1992). ISBN 0415 05455 9.

Hooper-Greenhill, E., *Museums and the Shaping of Knowledge* (London, 1992). ISBN 0415 06145 8.

Hudson, K., *European Museum of the Year Awards, 1991* (1991).

Hudson, K., *1992, Prayer or Promise* (Norwich, 1990). ISBN 0 11 290504 8.

National Museums Taskforce, *Report and Recommendations of the Task Force Charged with Examining Federal Policy Concerning Museums* (Ottawa, 1986).

2   ABOUT THIS BOOK

Alexander, W. and Castell, L. (eds), *Museum Abstracts* (London). ISBN 0267 8594.

3   TYPES OF MUSEUMS

Danilov, V., *Science and Technology Centers* (London, 1982). ISBN 0 262 04068 9.

Hewison, R., *The Heritage Industry* (London, 1987). ISBN 0 413 16110 2.

Hudson, K., *Museums of Influence* (Cambridge, 1987). ISBN 0 521 305349.

Johnson, P. and Thomas, B., 'Museums and the Local Economy', in Kavanagh, G. (ed.), *The Museums Profession: Internal and*

External Relations (Leicester, 1991). ISBN 0 7185 1387 8.

Middleton, V., *New Visions for Independent Museums* (Association of Independent Museums, 1990). ISBN 0 907331 16 5.

Myerscough, J., *The Economic Importance of the Arts* (London, 1988). ISBN 0 85374 3541.

Scottish Museums Council, *Museums are for People* (Edinburgh, 1985). ISBN 0 11 4924309.

4   THE ROLE OF MUSEUMS

Horne, D., *The Great Museum. The Representation of History* (London, 1984). ISBN 0 86104 788 5.

Lowenthal, D., *The Past is a Foreign Country* (Cambridge, 1985). ISBN 0 521 29480 0.

Lumley. R. (ed.), *The Museum Time-Machine* (London, 1988). ISBN 0 415 00651 1.

Merriman, N., *Beyond the Glass Case: The Past, the Heritage and the Public in Britain* (Leicester, 1991). ISBN 0 7185 1349 5.

Walsh, K., *The Representation of the Past: Museums and Heritage in the Post-Modern World* (London, 1992). ISBN 0 415 05026 X.

5   MUSEUMS ARE FOR PEOPLE

Bradford, H., 'A New Framework for Museum Marketing', in Kavanagh, G. (ed.),

The Museums Profession: Internal and External Relations (Leicester, 1991). ISBN 0 7185 1387 8.

Merriman, N., *Beyond the Glass Case: The Past, the Heritage and the Public in Britain* (Leicester, 1991). ISBN 0 7185 1349 5.

Scottish Museums Council, *Museums are for People* (Edinburgh, 1985). ISBN 0 11 492430 9.

6   UNDERSTANDING YOUR MARKET

Middleton, V., 'The Future Demand for Museums 1990–2001', in Kavanagh, G. (ed.), *The Museums Profession: Internal and External Relations* (Leicester, 1991). ISBN 0 7185 1387 8.

7   MARKETING YOUR MUSEUM

Ames, P., 'Marketing in Museums: Means or Master of the Mission', *Curator* 32, (1989), 5–15.

Bitgood, S., Roper, J. and Benefield, A., *Visitor Studies – 1988 Theory, Research and Practice* (The Center for Social Design, 1988).

Bradford, H., 'A New Framework for Museum Marketing', in Kavanagh, G. (ed.), *The Museums Profession: Internal and External Relations* (Leicester, 1991). ISBN 0 7185 1387 8.

Diggle, K., *A Guide to Arts Marketing* (London, 1984). ISBN 0946890 01 3.

McDonald, M., *Marketing Plans* (Oxford, 1989). ISBN 0 434 91300 6.

Rodger, L., *Marketing the Visual Arts* (Edinburgh, 1987). ISBN 1 85119 021 X.

8   SPECIAL AUDIENCES: MUSEUMS AND DISABLED PEOPLE

Goldsmith, S., *Designing for the Disabled* (RIBA, 1984). ISBN 0 900630 50 7.

Groff, G. and Gardner, L., *What Museums Need to Know: Access for Blind and*

Visually Impaired Visitors (American Foundation for the Blind, 1989). ISBN 0 89128 158 4.

ICOM and Fondation de France, *Museums without Barriers* (London, 1991). ISBN 0 415 05454 0.

Majewski, J., *Part of Your General Public is Disabled; a Handbook for Guides in Museums, Zoos, and Historic Houses* (Washington, 1987). Video and book set.

9   THE MUSEUM VISIT

Finn, D., *How to Visit a Museum* (New York, 1985). ISBN 0 8109 2295 5.

Karp, I. and Lavine, S., *Exhibiting Cultures: the Poetics and Politics of Museum Display* (Washington, 1991). ISBN 1 56098 021 4.

Spalding, J., 'Is There Life in Museums?', in Kavanagh, G. (ed.), *The Museums Profession: Internal and External Relations* (Leicester, 1991). ISBN 0 7185 1387 8.

10   MUSEUM EDUCATION SERVICES. WITHIN THE MUSEUM

Ambrose, T. (ed.), *Education in Museums: Museums in Education* (Norwich, 1987). ISBN 0 11 493373 1.

Durbin, G., Morris, S. and Wilkinson, S., *A Teacher's Guide to Learning from Objects* (London, 1990). ISBN 1 85074 259 6.

Fairclough, J. and Redsell, P., *Living History, Reconstructing the Past with Children* (London, 1985). ISBN 1 85074 073 9.

Hooper-Greenhill, E. (ed.), *Initiatives in Museum Education* (Leicester, 1989). ISBN 0 9515005 0 3.

Hooper-Greenhill, E. *Museum and Gallery Education* (Leicester, 1991). ISBN 0 7185 1306 1.

Hooper-Greenhill, E. (ed.), *Writing a Museum Education Policy* (Leicester, 1991).

Unit 85 Further reading

11 MUSEUM EDUCATION SERVICES:
OUTSIDE THE MUSEUM

Hooper-Greenhill, E., *Museum and Gallery Education* (Leicester, 1991). ISBN 0 7185 1306 1.

Jay, H. and Jay, M., *Developing Library– Museum Partnerships to Serve Young People* (Library Professional Publications, 1984). ISBN 0 208 01941 3.

Nichols, S., *Museum Education Anthology 1973–1983* (Washington, 1984).

12 EVENTS AND ACTIVITIES: CREATING
PROGRAMMES

Collins, Z., *Museums, Adults and the Humanities – A Guide for Educational Programming* (American Association of Museums, 1981).

Stewart, D., *Building New Audiences for Museums* (Norwich, 1989). Video and booklet pack. ISBN 0 11 494087 8.

13 FACILITIES FOR VISITORS

Spencer, H. and Reynolds, L., *Directional Signing and Labelling in Libraries and Museums: a Review of Current Theory and Practice* (London, 1977).

14 PROVIDING SERVICES: SHOPS

Blume, H., *The Museum Trading Handbook* (Charities Advisory Trust, 1987). ISBN 0 907164 35 8.

15 PROVIDING SERVICES: FOOD AND
DRINK

Longden, J.P., 'Catering for the Tourist', in Burkart, A.J. and Medlik, S. (eds), *The Management of Tourism* (London, 1975). ISBN 434 90194 6.

16 IMPROVING FACILITIES FOR USERS

Scottish Museums Council, *Museums are for People* (Edinburgh, 1985). ISBN 0 11 492430 9.

17 INTRODUCING INTERPRETATION

Danilov, V., *America's Science Museums* (Greenwood, 1990). ISBN 0 313 25865 1.

Kavanagh, G. (ed.), *Museum Languages – Objects and Texts* (Leicester, 1991). ISBN 0 7185 1359 2.

Miles, R. S., *The Design of Education Exhibits* (London, 1988). ISBN 0 04 069 003 2.

Pearce, S. (ed.), *Museum Studies in Material Culture* (Leicester, 1989). ISBN 0 7185 1391 6.

Pearce, S. (ed.), *Objects of Knowledge. New Research in Museum Studies: An International Series*, vol. 1 (London, 1990). ISBN 0 485 90001 7.

Tilden, F., *Interpreting Our Heritage* (Chapel Hill, 1967). ISBN 0 8078 4016 5.

Zucker, B., *Children's Museums, Zoos and Discovery Rooms: An International Reference Guide* (Greenwood, 1987). ISBN 0 313 24538X.

18 PRESENTATION TECHNIQUES:
GRAPHICS

Belcher, M., *Exhibitions in Museums* (Leicester, 1991). ISBN 0 7185 1299 5.

Hall, M., *On Display* (Lund Humphries, 1987). ISBN 0 85331 4551.

Reeve, J. K., *The Art of Showing Art* (HCE Publications, 1986). ISBN 0 933 031 041.

19 PRESENTATION TECHNIQUES: THREE-
DIMENSIONAL

Belcher, M., *Exhibitions in Museums* (Leicester, 1991). ISBN 0 7185 1299 5.

Brawne, M., *The Museum Interior: Temporary and Permanent Display Techniques* (London, 1982).

Hall, M., *On Display* (London, 1987). ISBN 0 85331 455 1.

20   PRESENTATION TECHNIQUES: AUDIO-VISUAL/INTERACTIVE

Belcher, M., *Exhibitions in Museums* (Leicester, 1991). ISBN 0 7185 1299 5.

Hall, M., *On Display* (London, 1987). ISBN 0 85331 455 1.

21   PRESENTATION TECHNIQUES: USING PEOPLE

Grinder, A. L. and McCoy, E., *The Good Guide: A Sourcebook for Interpreters, Docents and Tour Guides* (Ironwood Publishing, 1985). ISBN 0 932541 00 3.

22   MUSEUM LIGHTING

Belcher, M., *Exhibitions in Museums* (Leicester, 1991). ISBN 0 7185 1299 5.

Hall, M., *On Display* (London, 1987). ISBN 0 85331 455 1.

23   MUSEUM SHOWCASES

Belcher, M., *Exhibitions in Museums* (Leicester, 1991). ISBN 0 7185 1299 5.

24   PLANNING A NEW DISPLAY

Bertram, B., *Display Technology for Small Museums* (Museums Association of Australia, 1982). ISBN 0 9596832 1 6.

Hall, M., *On Display* (London, 1987). ISBN 0 85331 455 1.

Klein, L., *Exhibits: Planning and Design* (New York, 1986). ISBN 0 942604 18 0.

Neal, A., *Help for the Small Museum. Handbook of Exhibit Ideas and Methods* (Colorado, 1969). ISBN 0 87108 138 5.

Witteborg, L., *Good Show! A Practical Guide for Temporary Exhibitions* (Smithsonian Institution Travelling Exhibition Service, 1991). ISBN 0 86528 007 X.

25   RESEARCH FOR DISPLAYS

Hall, M., *On Display* (London, 1987). ISBN 0 85331 455 1.

Miles, R. S., *The Design of Educational Exhibits* (London, 1982). ISBN 0 04 069 003 2.

Thompson, J. M. A. (ed.), *Manual of Curatorship* (London, 1984). ISBN 0 408 01411 3.

26   WRITING TEXT

The Brooklyn Children's Museum, *Doing it Right: A Workbook for Improving Exhibit Labels* (Brooklyn, 1989).

Harley, J., *Designing Instructional Text* (London, 1985). ISBN 0 89397 2185.

Kentley, E. and Negus, D., *Writing on the Wall* (London, 1989).

Miles, R. S., *The Design of Educational Exhibits* (London, 1982). ISBN 0 04 069 003 2.

Willis, E. and Bennington, S., *Handbook for Small Museums* (Perth, 1985).

27   BRIEFING A DESIGNER

Belcher, M., *Exhibitions in Museums* (Leicester, 1991). ISBN 0 7185 1299 5.

Miles, R. S., *The Design of Educational Exhibits* (London, 1982). ISBN 0 04 069 003 2.

28   EXHIBITION DESIGN AND PRODUCTION

Belcher, M., *Exhibitions in Museums* (Leicester, 1991). ISBN 0 7185 1299 5.

Hall, M., *On Display* (London, 1987). ISBN 0 85331 455 1.

Maclean, K., *Recent and Recommended: A Museum Exhibition Bibliography with Notes from the Field* (National Association for Museum Exhibition, 1991). ISBN 0 9629692 0 6.

Unit 85 Further reading

29 EVALUATING EXHIBITIONS

Griggs, S., 'Evaluating Exhibitions', in Thompson, J. M. A. (ed.), *Manual of Curatorship* (London, 1984). ISBN 0 408 01411 3.

McManus, P., 'Making Sense of Exhibits', in Kavanagh, G. (ed.), *Museum Languages: Objects and Texts* (Leicester, 1991). ISBN 0 7185 1359 2.

Miles, R. S., *The Design of Educational Exhibits* (London, 1982). ISBN 0 04 069002 4.

Prince, D., 'Approaches to Summative Evaluation', in Thompson, J. M. A. (ed.), *Manual of Curatorship* (London, 1984). ISBN 0 408 01411 3.

Tressell, G., *A Museum is to Touch* (Washington, 1984).

30 INFORMATION SERVICES

Clarke, D. T-D., 'Enquiries', in Thompson J. M. A. (ed.), *Manual of Curatorship*, (London, 1984). ISBN 0 408 01411 3.

31 PUBLICATIONS

Bann, D., *The Print Production Handbook* (London, 1986). ISBN 0 356 10788 4.

Kebabian, H. and Padgett, W., *Production of Museum Publications: a Step-by-step Guide* (New York, 1990).

32 PUBLIC RELATIONS AND THE MEDIA

Howard, W. (ed.), *The Practice of Public Relations* (Oxford, 1985). ISBN 0 434 90785 5.

International Council of Museums, *Public View: the ICOM Handbook of Museum Public Relations* (ICOM, 1986). ISBN 92 9012 107 6.

33 WORKING WITH OTHER ORGANISATIONS/SUPPORTERS' GROUPS

Ambrose, T. (ed.), *Working with Museums* (Norwich, 1988). ISBN 0 11 493437 1.

Museums & Galleries Commission, *Review of Area Museum Councils* (London, 1984). ISBN 0 11 290 430 0.

Paine, C., *Area Museum Councils – Museums Working Together* (Committee of Area Museum Councils, 1991).

34 TYPES OF COLLECTIONS

Burnham, B., *The Protection of Cultural Property. A Handbook of National Legislations* (ICOM, 1974).

Chamberlin, R., *Loot! The Heritage of Plunder* (London, 1983).

International Council of Museums, *ICOM Statutes and Code of Professional Ethics* (ICOM, 1990).

Lalive, P., *International Sales of Works of Art* (Geneva, 1985). ISBN 92 842 1051 8.

Messenger, P. (ed.), *Ethics of Collecting Cultural Property* (New Mexico, 1989). ISBN 0 8263 1167 9.

O'Keefe, P. J. and Prott, L. V., *Law and the Cultural Heritage vol. 1, Discovery and Excavation* (Abingdon, 1984). ISBN 0 86205 065 0.

Prott, L. and O'Keefe, P., *Handbook of National Regulations Concerning the Export of Cultural Property* (UNESCO, 1988).

Williams, S. A., *The International and National Protection of Movable Cultural Property. A Comparative Study* (New York, 1978). ISBN 0 379 20294 8.

35 POLICIES FOR COLLECTING

Lord, B., Lord, G. and Hicks, J., *The Cost of Collecting – Collection Management in UK Museums* (London, 1989). ISBN 0 11 290476 9.

Schroeder, F., *Twentieth Century Popular Culture in Museums and Libraries* (Ohio, 1981). ISBN 0 87972 162 6.

Sofka, V., *Originals and Substitutes in Museums* (ICOFOM Study series 9, ICOM, 1985).

UNESCO, *Convention on the Means of Prohibiting the Illicit Import, Export and Transfer of Ownership of Cultural Property* (UNESCO, 1970).

36   POLICIES FOR DISPOSAL

Greenfield, J., *The Return of Cultural Treasures* (Cambridge, 1990). ISBN 0 521 33319 9.

National Audit Office, *Management of the Collections of the English National Museums and Galleries* (Norwich, 1988).

37   DONATIONS, PURCHASES AND LOANS

Thompson, J. M. A. (ed.), *Manual of Curatorship* (London, 1984). ISBN 0 408 01411 3.

38   COLLECTING AND FIELD DOCUMENTATION

Kavanagh, G., *History Curatorship* (Leicester, 1990). ISBN 0 7185 1305 3.

Nystrom, B. and Cedrenius, G., *Spread the Responsibility for Museum Documentation: A Programme for Contemporary Documentation at Swedish Museums of Cultural History* (Stockholm, 1982). ISBN 91 7108 2113 1.

Pearce, S., *Archaeological Curatorship* (Leicester, 1990). ISBN 0 7185 1298 7.

39   FIELDWORK AND RECORD CENTRES

Pearce, S., *Archaeological Curatorship* (Leicester 1990). ISBN 0 7185 1298 7.

Sykes, M., *Manual on Systems of Inventorying Immovable Cultural Property* (UNESCO, 1984). ISBN 92 3 102080 3.

UNESCO, *Field Manual for Museums* (UNESCO, 1970).

40   PHOTOGRAPHY, FILM AND VIDEO

Thompson, J. M. A. (ed.), *Manual of Curatorship* (London, 1984). ISBN 0 408 01411 3.

41   ORAL HISTORY AND AUDIO RECORDING

Allen, B. and Montell, L., *From Memory to History – Using Oral Sources in Local Historical Research* (American Association for State and Local History, 1981). ISBN 0 910050 51 1.

Baum, W. K., *Transcribing and Editing Local History* (American Association for State and Local History, 1977). ISBN 0 910050 26 0.

Baum, W. K., *Oral History for the Local History Society* (American Association for State and Local History, 1987). ISBN 0 910050 87 2.

Kavanagh, G., *History Curatorship* (Leicester, 1990). ISBN 0 7185 1305 3.

Thompson, P., *The Voice of the Past: Oral History* (Oxford, 1988). ISBN 0 19 289216 9.

42   DOCUMENTATION SYSTEMS

Roberts, A. D. (ed.), *Collections Management for Museums* (Museum Documentation Association, 1988). ISBN 0 905963 61 X.

43   THE ROLE OF COLLECTIONS IN RESEARCH

Drysdale, L., *A World of Learning: University Collections in Scotland* (London, 1990). ISBN 0 11 49409 1.

Schlereth, T. J., *Artefacts and the American Past* (American Association for State and Local History, 1980). ISBN 0 910050 47 3.

Schlereth, T. J., *Material Culture Studies in America* (American Association for State and Local History, 1982). ISBN 0 910050 67 8.

44   CONSERVATION PLANNING

Ramer, B., *A Conservation Survey of Museum Collections in Scotland* (Norwich, 1989). ISBN 0 11 493 460 6.

Unit 85   Further reading

45 WORKING WITH CONSERVATORS

Museums & Galleries Commission,
Conservation Sourcebook (Norwich, 1991).
ISBN 0 11 290493 9.

46 PREVENTIVE CONSERVATION:
PRINCIPLES

American Association of Museums, *Caring
for Collections: Strategies for Conservation,
Maintenance and Documentation* (American
Association of Museums, 1984).

de Torres, A. (ed.), *Collections Care: A
Selected Bibliography* (National Institute for
the Conservation of Cultural Property,
1990).

Ellis, M. H., *The Care of Prints and
Drawings* (American Association of State
and Local History, 1987). ISBN 0 910050
79 1.

Sandwith, H. and Stainton, S., *The National
Trust Manual of Housekeeping*
(Harmondsworth, 1984). ISBN 0 7139
1598 6.

Stolow, N., *Conservation and Exhibitions*
(London, 1987). ISBN 0 408 01434 2.

UNESCO, *Conservation Standards for
Works of Art in Transit and on Exhibition*
(UNESCO, 1979). ISBN 92 3 101628 8.

47 ENVIRONMENTAL MONITORING AND
CONTROL: LIGHT

Thompson, J. M. A. (ed.), *Manual of
Curatorship* (London, 1984). ISBN 0 408
01411 3.

Thomson, G., *The Museum Environment*
(London, 1986). ISBN 0 408 01536 5.

48 ENVIRONMENTAL MONITORING AND
CONTROL: TEMPERATURE AND
HUMIDITY

Thompson, J. M. A. (ed.), *Manual of
Curatorship* (London, 1984). ISBN 0 408
01411 3.

Thomson, G., *The Museum Environment*
(London, 1986). ISBN 0 408 01536 5.

49 ENVIRONMENTAL MONITORING AND
CONTROL: AIR POLLUTION/INSECT AND
PEST ATTACK

Thompson, J. M. A. (ed.), *Manual of
Curatorship* (London, 1984). ISBN 0 408
01411 3.

Thomson, G., *The Museum Environment*
(London, 1986). ISBN 0 408 01536 5.

50 MATERIALS TESTING

Thompson, J. M. A. (ed.), *Manual of
Curatorship* (London, 1984). ISBN 0 408
01411 3.

51 STORAGE: LARGE AND HEAVY
OBJECTS

Thompson, J. M. A. (ed.), *Manual of
Curatorship* (London, 1984). ISBN 0 408
01411 3.

52 STORAGE: SMALL AND LIGHT
OBJECTS

Knell, S. and Taylor, M. A., *Geology and
the Local Museum* (HMSO/Museums &
Galleries Commission, 1989). ISBN 0 11
290459 9.

Thompson, J. M. A. (ed.), *Manual of
Curatorship* (London, 1984). ISBN 0 408
01411 3.

53 HANDLING AND PACKING

Thompson, J. M. A. (ed.), *Manual of
Curatorship* (London, 1984). ISBN 0 408
01411 3.

54 REMEDIAL CONSERVATION:
PRINCIPLES

Guldbeck, P., *The Care of Historical
Collections – A Conservation Handbook for
the Non-specialist* (American Association
for State and Local History, 1972).

Kuhn, H., *Conservation and Restoration of Works of Art and Antiquities*, vol. 1 (London, 1986). ISBN 0 408 10851 7.

55 REMEDIAL CONSERVATION: PRACTICE

Thompson, J. M. A. (ed.), *Manual of Curatorship* (London, 1984). ISBN 0 408 01411 3.

56 DISASTER PLANNING/INSURANCE

Agbabian, M. S., Masri, S. F. and Nigbor, R. L., *Evaluation of Seismic Mitigation Measures* (Getty Conservation Institute, 1990).

Association of Art Museum Directors, *Planning for Emergencies – A Guide for Museums* (Association of Art Museum Directors, 1987).

57 COLLECTIONS SECURITY: PHYSICAL AND ELECTRONIC

Burke, R. and Adloye, S., *Basic Museum Security* (ICOM, 1986). ISBN 0 85022 209 5.

Fennelly, L. J., *Museum, Archive and Library Security* (London, 1983). ISBN 0 409 95058 0.

Hoare, N., *Security for Museums* (Committee of Area Museum Councils/ Museums Association UK, 1990).

Menkes, D. (ed.), *Museum Security* (ICOM, 1977).

58 COLLECTIONS SECURITY: SYSTEMS AND PROCEDURES

Burke, R. and Adloye, S., *Basic Museum Security* (ICOM, 1986). ISBN 0 85022 209 5.

Fennelly, L. J., *Museum, Archive and Library Security* (London, 1983). ISBN 0 409 95058 0.

Hoare, N., *Security for Museums* (Committee of Area Museum Councils/ Museums Association UK, 1990).

59 MUSEUM BUILDINGS: FORM AND FUNCTION

Hooper-Greenhill, E., *Museums and the Shaping of Knowledge* (London, 1992). ISBN 0 415 06145 8.

Lord, B. and Lord, G., *The Manual of Museum Planning* (Norwich, 1991). ISBN 0 11 290483 1.

60 PLANNING NEW MUSEUM BUILDINGS

Lord, B. and Lord, G., *The Manual of Museum Planning* (Norwich, 1991). ISBN 0 11 290483 1.

61 WORKING WITH ARCHITECTS

Lord, B. and Lord, G., *The Manual of Museum Planning* (Norwich, 1991). ISBN 0 11 290483 1.

62 PREPARING BRIEFS FOR ARCHITECTS

Lord, B. and Lord, G., *The Manual of Museum Planning* (Norwich, 1991). ISBN 0 11 290483 1.

Matthews, G., *Museums and Art Galleries: A Design and Development Guide* (London, 1991). ISBN 0 7506 1227 4.

63 MUSEUM BUILDINGS SECURITY: MANAGEMENT AND MAINTENANCE

Ambrose, T. and Runyard, S. (eds), *Forward Planning: A Handbook of Business, Corporate and Development Planning for Museums and Galleries* (London, 1991). ISBN 0 415 06182 1.

Fennelly, L. J., *Museum, Archive and Library Security* (London, 1983). ISBN 0 409 95058 0.

ICOM and the International Committee on Museum Security, *Museum Security and Protection* (London, 1992). ISBN 0 415 05457 5.

Standing Committee on Museum, Library and Archival Security, *Suggested Guidelines*

Unit 85 Further reading

in Museum Security (American Society for Industrial Security, 1990).

64 ACCESS AND ACCESSIBILITY

Fondation de France and ICOM, *Museums Without Barriers: A New Deal for Disabled People* (London, 1991). ISBN 0 415 05454 0.

65 ATMOSPHERE, PACE AND FLOW

Belcher, M., *Exhibitions in Museums* (Leicester, 1991). ISBN 0 7185 1299 5.

Royal Ontario Museum, *Communicating with the Museum Visitor: Guidelines for Planning* (Toronto, 1976).

66 ORIENTATION

Belcher, M., *Exhibitions in Museums* (Leicester, 1991). ISBN 0 7185 1299 5.

67 LEGAL STATUS AND MANAGEMENT STRUCTURES

Ambrose, T., *New Museums – A Start-up Guide* (Norwich, 1987). ISBN 0 11 493120 8.

Audit Commission, *The Road to Wigan Pier? Managing Local Authority Museums and Art Galleries* (Norwich, 1991). ISBN 0 11 886 047 X.

Cossons, N., *Management of Change* (London, 1985).

Museums and Galleries Commission, *Local Authorities and Museums* (Norwich, 1991). ISBN 0 11 290512 9.

Ullberg, A. and Ullberg, P., *Museum Trusteeship* (American Association of Museums, 1981). ISBN 0 931201 06 3.

68 MANAGEMENT PLANNING AND POLICY DEVELOPMENT

Ambrose, T. and Runyard, S. (eds), *Forward Planning* (London, 1991). ISBN 0 415 06482 1.

Axelrod, N., *The Chief Executive's Role in*

Developing the Non-profit Board (National Center for Non-Profit Boards, 1988). ISBN 0 925299 01 4.

Hebditch, M., *Museum Management and Administration* (London, 1987).

69 MAKING A FORWARD PLAN

Ambrose, T. and Runyard, S. (eds), *Forward Planning* (London, 1991). ISBN 0 415 06482 1.

George, G. and Sherrell-Leo, C., *Starting Right: a Basic Guide to Museum Planning* (American Association for State and Local History, 1987). ISBN 0 910050 78 3.

Museum Assessment Programs, *Shaping the Museum: the MAP Institutional Planning Guide* (American Association of Museums, 1990).

70 PERFORMANCE MEASUREMENT FOR MUSEUMS

Ambrose, T. and Runyard, S. (eds), *Forward Planning* (London, 1991). ISBN 0 415 06482 1.

Ames, P., 'Measuring Museums' Merits', in Kavanagh, G. (ed.), *The Museums Profession: Internal and External Relations* (Leicester, 1991). ISBN 0 7185 1387 8.

Museums & Galleries Commission, *Guidelines for Museum Registration* (Museums & Galleries Commission, 1987).

Museums Association Guidelines on Performance Measurement (Museums Association, 1991). ISBN 0 902102 69 9.

71 FINANCIAL MANAGEMENT

Ambrose, T. and Runyard, S. (eds), *Forward Planning* (London, 1991). ISBN 0 415 06482 1.

Dalsiner, J. P., *Understanding Non-profit Financial Statements: A Primer for Non-profit Boards* (National Center for Non-Profit Boards, 1991). ISBN 0 925299 10 3.

Education, Science and Arts Committee,

Should Museums Charge? (Norwich, 1988). ISBN 0 10 209490 X.

72   FUNDRAISING

Allen, M., *Sponsoring the Arts, New Business Strategies for the 1990s* (London, 1990). ISBN 0 85058 383 7.

Ambrose, T. (ed.), *Money, Money, Money and Museums* (Norwich, 1991). ISBN 0 11 494110 6.

Blume, H., *Fundraising – A Comprehensive Handbook* (London, 1977). ISBN 0 7100 8549 4.

Howe, F., *The Board Members Guide to Fund-raising: What every Trustee Needs to Know about Raising Money* (Jersey Bass, 1991). ISBN 1 55542 322 1.

Sleight, S., *Sponsorship. What It Is and How to Use It* (Berkhamstead, 1989). ISBN 0 07 707084 4.

Ware, M., *Fundraising for Museums* (Association of Independent Museums, 1988). ISBN 0 907331 04 1.

73   INTERNAL COMMUNICATIONS AND PROCEDURES

Ambrose, T. and Runyard, S. (eds), *Forward Planning* (London, 1991). ISBN 0 415 06482 1.

Gawlinski, G. and Graegsle, L., *Planning Together: The Art of Effective Teamwork* (London, 1989). ISBN 0 7199 1202 4.

Orna, E., *Practical Information Policies. How to Manage Information Flow in Organisations* (Aldershot, 1990). ISBN 0 566 03632 0.

74   STAFF STRUCTURES

Ambrose, T. and Runyard, S. (eds), *Forward Planning* (London, 1991). ISBN 0 415 06482 1.

75   VOLUNTEERS IN MUSEUMS

Mattingley, J., *Volunteers in Museums and Galleries* (Berkhamstead, 1984). ISBN 0 904647 35 8.

Millar, S., *Volunteers in Museum and Heritage Organisations* (Norwich, 1991). ISBN 0 11 290491 2.

Ontario Ministry of Citizenship and Culture, *Working with Volunteer Boards* (Ontario, 1984). ISBN 0 7743 9663 6.

Wilson, M., *The Effective Management of Volunteer Programs* (Volunteer Management Associates, 1976). ISBN 0 9693362 0 6.

76   RECRUITING MUSEUM STAFF

Shackleton, V., *How to Pick People for Jobs* (London, 1989). ISBN 0 00 63 7386 0.

77   CONDITIONS OF SERVICE

Miller, R., *Personnel Policies for Museums: a Handbook for Management* (American Association of Museums, 1980).

78   PERFORMANCE STANDARDS FOR THE INDIVIDUAL

Miller, R., *Personnel Policies for Museums: A Handbook for Management* (American Association of Museums, 1980).

79   JOB APPRAISAL AND PERFORMANCE MEASUREMENT

Miller, R., *Personnel Policies for Museums: A Handbook for Management* (American Association of Museums, 1980).

80   STAFF TRAINING

Harrison, R., *Training and Development* (London, 1988). ISBN 0 85292 392 9.

Unit 85   Further reading

Matelic, C. and Brick, E. M., *Cooperstown Conference on Professional Training* (American Association for State and Local History, 1990). ISBN 0 942063 08 2.

Museums & Galleries Commission, *Museum Professional Training and Career Structure* (Norwich, 1987). ISBN 0 11 290455 6.

81   HEALTH AND SAFETY

Howie, F. (ed.), *Safety in Museums and Galleries* (London, 1987). ISBN 0 408 02362 7.

82   ADMINISTRATIVE PROCEDURES

Thompson, J. M. A. (ed.), *Manual of Curatorship* (London, 1984). ISBN 0 408 01411 3.

Appendix

ICOM CODE OF PROFESSIONAL ETHICS

I Preamble

The ICOM Code of Professional Ethics was adopted unanimously by the 15th General Assembly of ICOM meeting in Buenos Aires, Argentina on 4 November 1986.

It provides a general statement of professional ethics, respect for which is regarded as a minimum requirement to practise as a member of the museum profession. In many cases it will be possible to develop and strengthen the *Code* to meet particular national or specialised requirements and ICOM wishes to encourage this. A copy of such developments of the *Code* should be sent to the Secretary General of ICOM, Maison de l'Unesco, 1 rue Miollis, 75732 Paris Cedex 15, France.

For the purposes of Articles 2 para. 2, 9 para. 1(d), 14 para. 17(b), 15 para. 7(c), 17 para. 12(e) and 18 para. 7(d) of the ICOM *Statutes*, this *Code* is deemed to be the statement of professional ethics referred to therein.

1 *Definitions*

1.1 THE INTERNATIONAL COUNCIL OF MUSEUMS (ICOM)

ICOM is defined in Article 1 para. 1 of its *Statutes* as 'the international non-governmental organisation of museums and professional museum workers established to advance the interests of museology and other disciplines concerned with museum management and operations.'

The objectives of ICOM, as defined in Article 3 para. 1 of its *Statutes*, are:

(a) To encourage and support the establishment, development and professional management of museums of all kinds;
(b) To advance knowledge and understanding of the nature, functions and role of museums in the service of society and of its development;
(c) To organise co-operation and mutual assistance between museums and between professional museum workers in the different countries;
(d) To represent, support and advance the interests of professional museum workers of all kinds;
(e) To advance and disseminate knowledge in museology and other disciplines concerned with museum management and operations.

Appendix

1.2 MUSEUM

A museum is defined in Article 2 para. 1 of the *Statutes* of the International Council of Museums as

> a non-profit making, permanent institution in the service of society and of its development, and open to the public which acquires, conserves, researches, communicates and exhibits, for purposes of study, education and enjoyment, material evidence of people and their environment.
>
> (a) The above definition of a museum shall be applied without limitation arising from the nature of the governing body, the territorial character, the functional structure or the orientation of the collections of the institution concerned.
>
> (b) In addition to institutions designated as 'museums' the following qualify as 'museums' for the purposes of this definition:
>
> (i) natural, archaeological and ethnographic monuments and sites of a museum nature that acquire, conserve and communicate material evidence of people and their environment;
>
> (ii) institutions holding collections of and displaying live specimens of plants and animals, such as botanical and zoological gardens, aquaria and vivaria;
>
> (iii) science centres and planetaria;
>
> (iv) conservation institutes and exhibition galleries permanently maintained by libraries and archive centres;
>
> (v) nature reserves;
>
> (vi) such other institutions as the Executive Council, after seeking the advice of the Advisory Committee, considers as having some or all of the characteristics of a museum, or as supporting museums and professional museum workers through museological research, education or training.

1.3 THE MUSEUM PROFESSION

ICOM defines the members of the museum profession, under Article 2 para. 2 of its *Statutes*, as follows:

> Professional museum workers include all the personnel of museums or institutions qualifying as museums in accordance with the definition in Article 2 para. 1 (*as detailed under para. 1.2 above*), having received specialised training, or possessing an equivalent practical experience, in any field relevant to the management and operations of a museum, and privately or self-employed persons practising in one of the museological professions and who respect the *ICOM Code of Professional Ethics*.

1.4 THE GOVERNING BODY

The government and control of museums in terms of policy, finance and administration etc., varies greatly from one country to another, and often from one museum to another within a country according to the legal and other national or local provisions of the particular country or institution.

In the case of many national museums the Director, Curator or other professional head of the museum may be appointed by, and directly responsible to, a Minister or a Government Department, whilst most local government museums are similarly governed and controlled by the appropriate local authority. In many other cases the government and control of the museum is vested in some form of independent body, such as a board of trustees, a society, a non-profit company, or even an individual.

For the purposes of this *Code* the term 'Governing Body' has been used throughout to signify the superior authority concerned with the policy, finance and administration of the museum. This may be an individual Minister or official, a Ministry, a local authority, a Board of Trustees, a Society, the Director of the museum or any other individual or body. Directors, Curators or other professional heads of the museum are responsible for the proper care and management of the museum.

II Institutional ethics

2 *Basic principles for museum governance*

2.1 MINIMUM STANDARDS FOR MUSEUMS

The governing body or other controlling authority of a museum has an ethical duty to maintain, and if possible, to enhance, all aspects of the museum, its collections and its services. Above all, it is the responsibility of each governing body to ensure that all of the collections in their care are adequately housed, conserved and documented.

The minimum standards in terms of finance, premises, staffing and services will vary according to the size and responsibilities of each museum. In some countries such minimum standards may be defined by law or other government regulation and in others guidance on and assessment of minimum standards is available in the form of 'Museum Accreditation' or similar schemes. Where such guidance is not available locally, it can usually be obtained from appropriate national and international organisations and experts, either directly or through the National Committee or appropriate International Committee of ICOM.

2.2 CONSTITUTION

Each museum should have a written constitution or other document setting out clearly its legal status and permanent, non-profit nature, drawn up in accordance with appropriate national laws in relation to museums, the cultural heritage, and non-profit institutions. The governing body or other controlling authority of a museum should prepare and publicise a clear statement of the aims, objectives and policies of the museum, and of the role and composition of the governing body itself.

2.3 FINANCE

The governing body holds the ultimate financial responsibility for the museum and for the protecting and nurturing of its various assets: the collections and related documentation, the premises, facilities and equipment, the financial assets, and the staff. It is obliged to develop and define the purposes and related policies of the institution, and to ensure that all of the museum's assets are properly and effectivley used for museum purposes. Sufficient funds must be available on a regular basis, either from public or private sources, to enable the governing body to carry out and develop the work of the museum. Proper accounting procedures must be adopted and maintained in accordance with the relevant national laws and professional accountancy standards.

2.4 PREMISES

The board has specially strong obligations to provide accommodation giving a suitable environment for the physical security and preservation of the collections. Premises must be adequate for the museum to fulfil within its stated policy its basic functions of collection, research, storage, conservation, education and display, including staff accommodation, and should comply with all appropriate national legislation in relation to public and staff safety. Proper standards of protection should be provided against such hazards as theft, fire, flood, vandalism and deterioration, throughout the year, day and night. The special needs of disabled people should be provided for, as far as practicable, in planning and managing both buildings and facilities.

2.5 PERSONNEL

The governing body has a special obligation to ensure that the museum has staff sufficient in both number and kind to ensure that the museum is able to meet its responsibilities. The size of the staff, and its nature (whether paid or unpaid, permanent or temporary), will depend on the size of the museum, its collections and its responsibilities. However, proper arrangements should be made for the museum to meet its obligations in relation to the care of the collections, public access and services, research, and security.

The governing body has particularly important obligations in relation to the appointment of the director of the museum, and whenever the possibility of terminating the employment of the director arises, to ensure that any such action is taken only in accordance with appropriate procedures under the legal or other constitutional arrangements and policies of the museum, and that any such staff changes are made in a professional and ethical manner, and in accordance with what is judged to be the best interests of the museum, rather than any personal or external factor or prejudice. It should also ensure that the same principles are applied in relation to any appointment, promotion, dismissal or demotion of the personnel of the museum by the director or any other senior member of staff with staffing responsibilities.

The governing body should recognise the diverse nature of the museum profession, and the wide range of specialisations that it now encompasses, including conservator/restorers, scientists, museum education service personnel, registrars and computer specialists, security service managers, etc. It should ensure that the museum both makes appropriate use of such specialists where required and that such specialised personnel are properly recognised as full members of the professional staff in all respects.

Members of the museum profession require appropriate academic, technical and professional training in order to fulfil their important role in relation to the operation of the museum and the care for the heritage, and the governing body should recognise the need for, and value of, a properly qualified and trained staff, and offer adequate opportunities for further training and re-training in order to maintain an adequate and effective workforce.

A governing body should never require a member of the museum staff to act in a way that could reasonably be judged to conflict with the provisions of this *Code of Ethics*, or any national law or national code of professional ethics.

The Director or other chief professional officer of a museum should be directly responsible to, and have direct access to, the governing body in which trusteeship of the collections is vested.

2.6 EDUCATIONAL AND COMMUNITY ROLE OF THE MUSEUM

By definition a museum is an institution in the service of society and of its development, and is generally open to the public (even though this may be a restricted public in the case of certain very specialised museums, such as certain academic or medical museums, for example).

The museum should take every opportunity to develop its role as an educational resource used by all sections of the population or specialised group that the museum is intended to serve. Where appropriate in relation to the museum's programme and responsibilities, specialist staff with training and skills in museum education are likely to be required for this purpose.

The museum has an important duty to attract new and wider audiences within all levels of the community, locality or group that the museum aims to serve, and should offer both the general community and specific individuals and groups within it opportunities to become actively involved in the museum and to support its aims and policies.

Appendix

2.7 PUBLIC ACCESS

The general public (or specialised group served, in the case of museums with a limited public role), should hace access to the displays during reasonable hours and for regular periods. The museum should also offer the public reasonable access to members of staff by appointment or other arrangement, and full access to information about the collections, subject to any necessary restrictions for reasons of confidentiality or security as discussed in para. 7.3 below.

2.8 DISPLAYS, EXHIBITIONS AND SPECIAL ACTIVITIES

Subject to the primary duty of the museum to preserve unimpaired for the future the significant material that comprises the museum collections, it is the responsibility of the museum to use the collections for the creation and dissemination of new knowledge, through research, educational work, permanent displays, temporary exhibitions and other special activities. These should be in accordance with the stated policy and educational purpose of the museum, and should not compromise either the quality or the proper care of the collections. The museum should seek to ensure that information in displays and exhibitions is honest and objective and does not perpetuate myths or stereotypes.

2.9 COMMERCIAL SUPPORT AND SPONSORSHIP

Where it is the policy of the museum to seek and accept financial or other support from commercial or industrial organisations, or from other outside sources, great care is needed to define clearly the agreed relationship between the museum and the sponsor. Commercial support and sponsorship may involve ethical problems and the museum must ensure that the standards and objectives of the museum are not compromised by such a relationship.

2.10 MUSEUM SHOPS AND COMMERCIAL ACTIVITIES

Museum shops and any other commercial activities of the museum, and any publicity relating to these, should be in accordance with a clear policy, should be relevant to the collections and the basic educational purpose of the museum, and must not compromise the quality of those collections. In the case of the manufacture and sale of replicas, reproduction or other commercial items adapted from an object in a museum's collection, all aspects of the commercial venture must be carried out in a manner that will not discredit either the integrity of the museum or the intrinsic value of the original object. Great care must be taken to identify permanently such objects for what they are, and to ensure accuracy and high quality in their manufacture. All items offered for sale should represent good value for money and should comply with all relevant national legislation.

2.11 LEGAL OBLIGATION

It is an important responsibility of each governing body to ensure that the museum complies fully with all legal obligations, whether in relation to national, regional or local law, international law or treaty obligations, and to any legally binding trusts or conditions relating to any aspect of the museum collections or facilities.

3   Acquisitions to museum collections

3.1 COLLECTING POLICIES

Each museum authority should adopt and publish a written statement of its collecting policy. This policy should be reviewed from time to time, and at least once every five years. Objects acquired should be relevant to the purpose and activities of the museum, and be accompanied by evidence of a valid legal title. Any conditions or limitations relating to an acquisition should be clearly described in an instrument of conveyance or other written documentation. Museums should not, except in very exceptional circumstances, acquire material that the museum is unlikely to be able to catalogue, conserve, store or exhibit, as appropriate, in a proper manner. Acquisitions outside the current stated policy of the museum should only be made in very exceptional circumstances, and then only after proper consideration by the governing body of the museum itself, having regard to the interests of the objects under consideration, the national or other cultural heritage and the special interests of other museums.

3.2 ACQUISITION OF ILLICIT MATERIAL

The illicit trade in objects destined for public and private collections encourages the destruction of historic sites, local ethnic cultures, theft at both national and international levels, places at risk endangered species of flora and fauna, and contravenes the spirit of national and international patrimony. Museums should recognise the relationship between the market-place and the initial and often destructive taking of an object for the commercial market, and must recognise that it is highly unethical for a museum to support in any way, whether directly or indirectly, that illicit market.

A museum should not acquire, whether by purchase, gift, bequest or exchange, any object unless the governing body and responsible officer are satisfied that the museum can acquire a valid title to the specimen or object in question and that in particular it has not been acquired in, or exported from, its country of origin and/or any intermediate country in which it may have been legally owned (including the museum's own country), in violation of that country's laws.

So far as biological and geological material is concerned, a museum should not acquire by any direct or indirect means any specimen that has been collected, sold or otherwise transferred in contravention of any national or international wildlife protection or natural history conservation law or treaty of the museum's own country or any other country except with the express consent of an appropriate outside legal or governmental authority.

Appendix

So far as excavated material is concerned, in addition to the safeguards set out above, the museum should not acquire by purchase objects in any case where the governing body or responsible officer has reasonable cause to believe that their recovery involved the recent unscientific or intentional destruction or damage of ancient monuments or archaeological sites, or involved a failure to disclose the finds to the owner or occupier of the land, or to the proper legal or governmental authorities.

If appropriate and feasible, the same tests as are outlined in the above four paragraphs should be applied in determining whether or not to accept loans for exhibition or other purposes.

3.3 FIELD STUDY AND COLLECTING

Museums should assume a position of leadership in the effort to halt the continuing degradation of the world's natural history, archaeological, ethnographic, historic and artistic resources. Each museum should develop policies that allow it to conduct its activities within appropriate national and international laws and treaty obligations, and with a reasonable certainty that its approach is consistent with the spirit and intent of both national and international efforts to protect and enhance the cultural heritage.

Field exploration, collecting and excavation by museum workers present ethical problems that are both complex and critical. All planning for field studies and field collecting must be preceded by investigation, disclosure and consultation with both the proper authorities and any interested museums or academic institutions in the country or area of the proposed study sufficient to ascertain if the proposed activity is both legal and justifiable on academic and scientific grounds. Any field programme must be executed in such a way that all participants act legally and responsibly in acquiring specimens and data, and that they discourage by all practical means unethical, illegal and destructive practices.

3.4 CO-OPERATION BETWEEN MUSEUMS IN COLLECTING POLICIES

Each museum should recognise the need for co-operation and consultation between all museums with similar or overlapping interests and collecting policies, and should seek to consult with such other institutions both on specific acquisitions where a conflict of interest is thought possible and, more generally, on defining areas of specialisation. Museums should respect the boundaries of the recognised collecting areas of other museums and should avoid acquiring material with special local connections or of special local interest from the collecting area of another area of another museum without due notification of intent.

3.5 CONDITIONAL ACQUISITIONS AND OTHER SPECIAL FACTORS

Gifts, bequests and loans should only be accepted if they conform to the stated collecting and exhibition policies of the museum. Offers that are subject to special conditions may have to be rejected if the conditions proposed are judged to be contrary to the long-term interests of the museum and its public.

3.6 LOANS TO MUSEUMS

Both individual loans of objects and the mounting or borrowing of loan exhibitions can have an important role in enhancing the interest and quality of a museum and its services. However, the ethical principles outlined in paras 3.1 to 3.5 above must apply to the consideration of proposed loans and loan exhibitions as to the acceptance or rejection of items offered to the permanent collections: loans should not be accepted nor exhibitions mounted if they do not have a valid educational, scientific or academic purpose.

3.7 CONFLICTS OF INTEREST

The collecting policy or regulations of the museums should include provisions to ensure that no person involved in the policy or management of the museum, such as a trustee or other member of a governing body, or a member of the museum staff, may compete with the museum for objects or may take advantage of privileged information received because of his or her position, and that should a conflict of interest develop between the needs of the individual and the museum, those of the museum will prevail. Special care is also required in considering any offer of an item either for sale or as a tax-benefit gift, from members of governing bodies, members of staff, or the families or close associates of these.

4 Disposal of collections

4.1 GENERAL PRESUMPTION OF PERMANENCE OF COLLECTIONS

By definition one of the key functions of almost every kind of museum is to acquire objects and keep them for posterity. Consequently there must always be a strong presumption against the disposal of specimens to which a museum has assumed formal title. Any form of disposal, whether by donation, exchange, sale or destruction requires the exercise of a high order of curatorial judgement and should be approved by the governing body only after full expert and legal advice has been taken.

Special considerations may apply in the case of certain kinds of specialised institutions such as 'living' or 'working' museums, and some teaching and other educational museums, together with museums and other institutions displaying living specimens, such as botanical and zoological gardens and aquaria, which may find it necessary to regard at least part of their collections as 'fungible' (i.e. replaceable and renewable). However, even here there is a clear ethical obligation to ensure that the activities of the institution are not detrimental to the long-term survival of examples of the material studied, displayed or used.

4.2 LEGAL OR OTHER POWERS OF DISPOSAL

The laws relating to the protection and permanence of museum collections, and to the power of museums to dispose of items from their collection vary greatly from country to country, and often from one museum to another within the same country. In some cases no disposals of any kind are permitted, except in the case of items that have been seriously damaged by natural or accidental deterioration. Elsewhere, there may be no explicit restriction on disposals under general law.

Where the museum has legal powers permitting disposals, or has acquired objects subject to conditions of disposal, the legal or other requirements and procedures must be fully complied with. Even where legal powers of disposal exist, a museum may not be completely free to dispose of items acquired: where financial assistance has been obtained from an outside source (e.g. public or private grants, donations from a Friends of the Museum organisation, or private benefactor), disposal would normally require the consent of all parties who had contributed to the original purchase.

Where the original acquisition was subject to mandatory restrictions these must be observed unless it can be clearly shown that adherence to such restrictions is impossible or substantially detrimental to the institution. Even in these circumstances the museum can only be relieved from such restrictions through appropriate legal procedures.

4.3 DE-ACCESSIONING POLICIES AND PROCEDURES

Where a museum has the necessary legal powers to dispose of an object the decision to sell or otherwise dispose of material from the collections should only be taken after due consideration, and such material should be offered first, by exchange, gift or private treaty sale, to other museums before sale by public auction or other means is considered. A decision to dispose of a specimen or work of art, whether by exchange, sale or destruction (in the case of an item too badly damaged or deteriorated to be restorable) should be the responsibility of the governing body of the museum, not of the curator of the collection concerned acting alone. Full records should be kept of all such decisions and the objects involved, and proper arrangements made for the preservation and/or transfer, as appropriate, of the documentation relating to the object concerned, including photographic records where practicable.

Neither members of staff, nor members of the governing bodies, or members of their families or close associates, should ever be permitted to purchase objects that have been de-accessioned from a collection. Similarly, no such person should be permitted to appropriate in any other way items from the museum collections, even temporarily, to any personal collection or for any kind of personal use.

4.4 RETURN AND RESTITUTION OF CULTURAL PROPERTY

If a museum should come into possession of an object that can be demonstrated to have been exported or otherwise transferred in violation of the principles of the Unesco *Convention on the Means of Prohibiting and Preventing the Illicit Import, Export and Transfer of Ownership of Cultural Property* (1970) and the country of origin seeks its return and demonstrates that it is part of the country's cultural heritage, the museum should, if legally free to do so, take responsible steps to co-operate in the return of the object to the country of origin.

In the case of requests for the return of cultural property to the country of origin, museums should be prepared to initiate dialogues with an open-minded attitude on the basis of scientific and professional principles (in preference to action at a governmental or political level). The possibility of developing bi-lateral or multilateral co-operation schemes to assist museums in countries which are considered to have lost a significant part of their cultural heritage in the development of adequate museums and museum resources should be explored.

Museums should also respect fully the terms of the *Convention for the Protection of Cultural Property in the Event of Armed Conflict* (The Hague Convention, 1954), and in support of this *Convention*, should in particular abstain from purchasing or otherwise appropriating or acquiring cultural objects from any occupied country, as these will in most cases have been illegally exported or illicitly removed.

4.5 INCOME FROM DISPOSAL OF COLLECTIONS

Any moneys received by a governing body from the disposal of specimens or works of art should be applied solely for the purchase of additions to the museum collections.

III Professional conduct

5 *General principles*

5.1 ETHICAL OBLIGATIONS OF MEMBERS OF THE MUSEUM PROFESSION

Employment by a museum, whether publicly or privately supported, is a public trust involving great responsibility. In all activities museum employees must act with integrity and in accordance with the most stringent ethical principles as well as the highest standards of objectivity.

Appendix

An essential element of membership of a profession is the implication of both rights and obligations. Although the conduct of a professional in any area is ordinarily regulated by the basic rules of moral behaviour which govern human relationships, every occupation involves standards, as well as particular duties, responsibilities and opportunities that from time to time create the need for a statement of guiding principles. The museum professional should understand two guiding principles: first, that museums are the object of a public trust whose value to the community is in direct proportion to the quality of service rendered; and, secondly, that intellectual ability and professional knowledge are not, in themselves, sufficient, but must be inspired by a high standard of ethical conduct.

The Director and other professional staff owe their primary professional and academic allegiance to their museum and should at all times act in accordance with the approved policies of the museum. The Director or other principal museum officer should be aware of, and bring to the notice of the governing body of the museum whenever appropriate, the terms of the *ICOM Code of Professional Ethics* and of any relevant national or regional Codes or policy statements on Museum Ethics, and should urge the governing body to comply with these. Members of the museum profession should also comply fully with the *ICOM Code* and any other Codes or statements on Museum Ethics whenever exercising the functions of the governing body under delegated powers.

5.2 PERSONAL CONDUCT

Loyalty to colleagues and to the employing museum is an important professional responsibility, but the ultimate loyalty must be to fundamental ethical principles and to the profession as a whole.

Applicants for any professional post should divulge frankly and in confidence all information relevant to the consideration of their applications, and if appointed should recognise that museum work is normally regarded as a full-time vocation. Even where the terms of employment do not prohibit outside employment or business interests, the Director and other senior staff should not undertake other paid employment or accept outside commissions without the express consent of the governing body of the museum. In tendering resignations from their posts, members of the professional staff, and above all the Director, should consider carefully the needs of the museum at the time. A professional person, having recently accepted a new appointment, should consider seriously their professional commitment to their present post before applying for a new post elsewhere.

5.3 PRIVATE INTERESTS

While every member of any profession is entitled to a measure of personal independence, consistent with professional and staff responsibilities, in the eyes of the public no private business or professional interest of a member of the museum profession can be wholly separated from that of the professional's institution or other official affiliation, despite disclaimers that may be offered. Any museum-related activity by the individual may reflect on the institution or be attributed to it. The professional must be concerned not only with the true personal motivations and interests, but also with the way in which such actions might be construed by the outside observer. Museum employees and others in a close relationship with them must not accept gifts, favours, loans or other dispensations or things of value that may be offered to them in connection with their duties for the museum (see also para. 8.4 below).

6   Personal responsibility to the collections

6.1 ACQUISITIONS TO MUSEUM COLLECTIONS

The Director and professional staff should take all possible steps to ensure that a written collecting policy is adopted by the governing body of the museum, and is thereafter reviewed and revised as appropriate at regular intervals. This policy, as formally adopted and revised by the governing body, should form the basis of all professional decisions and recommendations in relation to acquisitions.

Negotiations concerning the acquisition of museum items from members of the general public must be conducted with scrupulous fairness to the seller or donor. No object should be deliberately of misleadingly identified or valued, to the benefit of the museum and to the detriment of the donor, owner or previous owners, in order to acquire it for the museum collections nor should be taken nor retained on loan with the deliberate intention of improperly procuring it for the collections.

6.2 CARE OF COLLECTIONS

It is an important professional responsibility to ensure that all items accepted temporarily or permanently by the museum are properly and fully documented to facilitate provenance, identification, condition and treatment. All objects accepted by the museum should be properly conserved, protected, and maintained.

Careful attention should be paid to the means of ensuring the best possible security as a protection against theft in display, working or storage areas, against accidental damage when handling objects, and against damage or theft in transit. Where it is the national or local policy to use commercial insurance arrangements, the staff should ensure that the insurance cover is adequate, especially for objects in transit and loan items, or other objects, which are not owned by the museum but which are its current responsibility.

Members of the museum profession should not delegate important curatorial, conservation, or other professional responsibilities to persons who lack the appropriate knowledge and skill, or who are inadequately supervised, in the case of trainees or approved volunteers, where such persons are allowed to assist in the care of the collections. There is also a clear duty to consult professional colleagues within or outside the museum if at any time the expertise available in a particular museum or department is insufficient to ensure the welfare of items in the collections under its care.

6.3 CONSERVATION AND RESTORATION OF COLLECTIONS

One of the essential ethical obligations of each member of the museum profession is to ensure the proper care and conservation of both existing and newly-acquired collections and individual items for which the member of the profession and the employing institutions are responsible, and to ensure that as far as is reasonable the collections are passed on to future generations in as good and safe a condition as practicable having regard to current knowledge and resources.

In attempting to achieve this high ideal, special attention should be paid to the growing body of knowledge about preventative conservation methods and techniques, including the provision of suitable environmental protection against the known natural or artificial causes of deterioration of museum specimens and works of art.

There are often difficult decisions to be made in relation to the degree of replacement or restoration of lost or damaged parts of a specimen or work of art that may be ethically acceptable in particular circumstances. Such decisions call for proper co-operation between all with a specialised responsibility for the object, including both the curator and the conservator or restorer, and should not be decided unilaterally by one or the other acting alone.

The ethical issues involved in conservation and restoration work of many kinds are a major study in themselves, and those with special responsibilities in this area, whether as director, curator, conservator or restorer, have an important responsibility to ensure that they are familiar with these ethical issues, and with appropriate professional opinion, as expressed in some detailed ethical statements and codes produced by the conservator/restorer professional bodies. (See 'The Conservator-Restorer: A Definition of the Profession': *ICOM News*, Vol. 39, No. 1, 1986, pp. 5–6.)

6.4 DOCUMENTATION OF COLLECTIONS

The proper recording and documentation of both new acquisitions and existing collections in accordance with appropriate standards and the internal rules and conventions of the museum is a most important professional responsibility. It is particularly important that such documentation should include details of the source of each object and the conditions of acceptance of it by the museum. In addition specimen data should be kept in a secure environment and be supported by adequate systems providing easy retrieval of the data by both the staff and by other *bona fide* users.

6.5 DE-ACCESSIONING AND DISPOSALS FROM THE COLLECTIONS

No item from the collections of a museum should be disposed of except in accordance with the ethical principles summarised in the Institutional Ethics section of this *Code*, paras 4.1 to 4.4 above, and the detailed rules and procedures applying in the museum in question.

6.6 WELFARE OF LIVE ANIMALS

Where museums and related institutions maintain for exhibition or research purposes live populations of animals, the health and well-being of any such creatures must be a foremost ethical consideration. It is essential that a veterinary surgeon be available for advice and for regular inspection of the animals and their living conditions. The museum should prepare a safety code for the protection of staff and visitors which has been approved by an expert in the veterinary field, and all staff must follow it in detail.

6.7 HUMAN REMAINS AND MATERIAL OF RITUAL SIGNIFICANCE

Where a museum maintains and/or is developing collections of human remains and sacred objects these should be securely housed and carefully maintained as archival collections in scholarly institutions, and should always be available to qualified researchers and educators, but not to the morbidly curious. Research on such objects and their housing and care must be accomplished in a manner acceptable not only to fellow professionals but to those of various beliefs, including in particular members of the community, ethnic or religious groups concerned. Although it is occasionally necessary to use human remains and other sensitive material in interpretative exhibits, this must be done with tact and with respect for the feelings for human dignity held by all peoples.

6.8 PRIVATE COLLECTIONS

The acquiring, collecting and owning of objects of a kind collected by a museum by a member of the museum profession for a personal collection may not in itself be unethical, and may be regarded as a valuable way of enhancing professional knowledge and judgement. However, serious dangers are implicit when members of the profession collect for themselves privately objects similar to those which they and others collect for their museums. In particular, no member of the museum profession should compete with their institution either in the acquisition of objects or in any personal collecting activity. Extreme care must be taken to ensure that no conflict of interest arises.

In some countries and many individual museums, members of the museum profession are not permitted to have private collections of any kind, and such rules must be respected. Even where there are no such restrictions, on appointment, a member of the museum profession with a private collection should provide the governing body with a description of it, and a statement of the collecting policy being pursued, and any consequent agreement between the curator and the governing body concerning the private collection must be scrupulously kept. (See also para. 8.4 below.)

7 Personal responsibility to the public

7.1 UPHOLDING PROFESSIONAL STANDARDS

In the interests of the public as well as the profession, members of the museum profession should observe accepted standards and laws, uphold the dignity and honour of their profession and accept its self-imposed disciplines. They should do their part to safeguard the public against illegal or unethical professional conduct, and should use appropriate opportunities to inform and educate the public in the aims, purposes and aspirations of the profession in order to develop a better public understanding of the purposes and responsibilities of museums and of the profession.

7.2 RELATIONS WITH THE GENERAL PUBLIC

Members of the museum profession should deal with the public efficiently and courteously at all times, and should in particular deal promptly with all correspondence and enquiries. Subject to the requirements of confidentiality in a particular case, they should share their expertise in all professional fields in dealing with enquiries, subject to due acknowledgement, from both the general public and specialist enquirers, allowing *bona fide* researchers properly controlled but, so far as possible, full access to any material or documentation in their care, even when this is the subject of personal research or special field of interest.

7.3 CONFIDENTIALITY

Members of the museum profession must protect all confidential information relating to the source of material owned by or loaned to the museum, as well as information concerning the security arrangements of the museum, or the security arrangements of private collections or any place visited in the course of official duties. Confidentiality must also be respected in relation to any item brought to the museum for identification and, without specific authority from the owner, information on such an item should not be passed to another museum, to a dealer, or to any other person (subject to any legal obligation to assist the police or other proper authorities in investigating possible stolen or illicitly acquired or transferred property).

There is a special responsibility to respect the personal confidences contained in oral history or other personal material. Investigators using recording devices such as cameras or tape recorders or the technique of oral interviewing should take special care to protect their data, and persons investigated, photographed or interviewed should have the right to remain anonymous if they so choose. This right should be respected where it has been specifically promised. Where there is no clear understanding to the contrary, the primary responsibility of the investigator is to ensure that no information is revealed that might harm the informant or his or her community. Subjects under study should understand the capacities of cameras, tape recorders and other machines used, and should be free to accept or reject their use.

8 Personal responsibility to colleagues and the profession

8.1 PROFESSIONAL RELATIONSHIPS

Relationships between members of the museum profession should always be courteous, both in public and in private. Differences of opinion should not be expressed in a personalised fashion. Notwithstanding this general rule, members of the profession may properly object to proposals or practices which may have a damaging effect on a museum or museums, or the profession.

8.2 PROFESSIONAL CO-OPERATION

Members of the museum profession have an obligation, subject to due acknowledgement, to share their knowledge and experience with their colleagues and with scholars and students in relevant fields. They should show their appreciation and respect to those from whom they have learned and should present without thought of personal gain such advancements in techniques and experience which may be of benefit to others.

The training of personnel in the specialised activities involved in museum work is of great importance in the development of the profession and all should accept responsibility, where appropriate, in the training of colleagues. Members of the profession who in their official appointment have under their direction junior staff, trainees, students and assistants undertaking formal or informal professional training, should give these the benefit of their experience and knowledge, and should also treat them with the consideration and respect customary among members of the profession.

Members of the profession form working relationships in the course of their duties with numerous other people, both professional and otherwise, within and outside the museum in which they are employed. They are expected to conduct these relationships with courtesy and fair-mindedness and to render their professional services to others efficiently and at a high standard.

Appendix

No member of the museum profession should participate in any dealing (buying or selling for profit), in objects similar or related to the objects collected by the employing museum. Dealing by museum employees at any level of responsibility in objects that are collected by any other museum can also present serious problems even if there is no risk of direct conflict with the employing museum, and should be permitted only if, after full disclosure and review by the governing body of the employing museum or designated senior officer, explicit permission is granted, with or without conditions.

Article 7 para. 5 of the ICOM *Statutes* provides that membership of ICOM shall not be available, under any circumstances, to any person or institution that is dealing (buying or selling for profit) in cultural property.

8.4 OTHER POTENTIAL CONFLICTS OF INTEREST

Generally, members of the museum profession should refrain from all acts or activities which may be construed as a conflict of interest. Museum professionals by virtue of their knowledge, experience, and contacts are frequently offered opportunities, such as advisory and consultancy services, teaching, writing and broadcasting opportunities, or requests for valuations, in a personal capacity. Even where the national law and the individual's conditions of employment permit such activities, these may appear in the eyes of colleagues, the employing authority, or the general public, to create a conflict of interest. In such situations all legal and employment contract conditions must be scrupulously followed, and in the event of any potential conflict arising or being suggested, the matter should be reported immediately to an appropriate superior officer or the museum governing body, and steps must be taken to eliminate the potential conflict of interest.

Even where the conditions of employment permit any kind of outside activity, and there appears to be no risk of any conflict of interest, great care should be taken to ensure that such outside interests do not interfere in any way with the proper discharge of official duties and responsibilities.

8.5 AUTHENTICATION, VALUATION AND ILLICIT MATERIAL

Members of the museum profession are encouraged to share their professional knowledge and expertise with both professional colleagues and the general public (see para. 7.2 above).

However, written certificates of authenticity or valuation (appraisals) should not be given, and opinions on the monetary value of objects should only be given on official request from other museums or competent legal, governmental or other responsible public authorities.

Members of the museum profession should not identify or otherwise authenticate objects where they have reason to believe or suspect that these have been illegally or illicitly acquired, transferred, imported or exported.

They should recognise that it is highly unethical for museums or the museum profession to support either directly or indirectly the illicit trade in cultural or natural objects (see para. 3.2 above), and under no circumstances should they act in a way that could be regarded as benefiting such illegal trade in any way, directly or indirectly. Where there is reason to believe or suspect illicit or illegal transfer, import or export, the competent authorities should be notified.

8.6 UNPROFESSIONAL CONDUCT

Every member of the museum profession should be conversant with both any national or local laws, and any conditions of employment, concerning corrupt practices, and should at all times avoid situations which could rightly or wrongly be construed as corrupt or improper conduct of any kind. In particular no museum official should accept any gift, hospitality, or any form of reward from any dealer, auctioneer or other person as an improper inducement in respect of the purchase or disposal of museum items.

Also, in order to avoid any suspicion of corruption, a museum professional should not recommend any particular dealer, auctioneer or other person to a member of the public, nor should the official accept any 'special price' or discount for personal purchases from any dealer with whom either the professional or employing museum has a professional relationship.

Note on illustrations

We gratefully acknowledge permission to reproduce photographs on the Section titles of this book:

Illustrations on Section titles I, II, IV (the Institut du Monde Arabe, Paris) and VI (the café at the Musée d'Orsay, Paris). Photographs taken by Marcus Tate (6 Benbow House, Benbow Street, London SE8 3HE).

Section III, from the Museum of the Big Bend, Alpine, Texas. Photograph by B. Richerson.

Section V, from the Smithsonian Institution, Washington.

Index

access and accessibility 27, 34, 216–20, 299–300; for disabled users 31–3, 219–20
accessioning 150–2
accident books 273
acquisition: of collections 125–6, 127, 132–7, 307; of illicit material 301–2
activities and events 43, 49–56, 300
actors, use of 78
adhesives 175
administrative procedures 273–5
admission charges 26, 34, 57, 219
air-conditioning 169, 172
air pollution 171–2; see also chemical damage
animals, live 309
animatronics 76, 278
annual reports 237
architects 208–9; preparation of briefs for 209–11
atmosphere 220–1
audio recordings 76, 147–50
audio-visual presentation techniques 75–7
authentication 312–13

bequests 126, 302–3
briefing: of architects 209–11; team 250, 274
broadcasting media 119, 120–1
budgets: capital 243–4; operating 242–3, 244–5
buildings: design of 31–2, 34, 35; form and function 202–5; management and maintenance of 214–16; planning new 205–11; security of 212–14; storage 176–7

capital budgets 243–4
carers 54, 278
case-dressing 104
cataloguing 152–3
catering facilities see food and drink
ceramic collections, storage of 180
chemical damage 173–6; see also air pollution
children 52, 218; guide-booklets

for 37; holiday activities for 43; see also education services
children's clubs 43
cleaning lighting 8
cloakrooms 34–5
Cloze test 92
collecting policies 127–9, 301, 302, 307
collecting programmes 140–1
collections: acquisition of 125–6, 127, 132–7, 307; private 309–10; role in research of 156–8; security of 193–8, 307; types of 124–7; see also conservation; documentation; storage
colour temperature and rendering of light 81
commercial activities 300; see also publications; shops
commercial sponsorship 246–8, 300
communications: internal 248–51; with visitors see communications policy; interpretation
communications policy 70
competition 17
competitors, research into 23
computer systems 76, 226
computerisation of documentation 155
confidentiality 310–11
conflicts of interest 303, 312
conservation 308; preventive 161, 162–4, 280, 308; remedial 158, 159, 161, 162, 185–9, 280; see also environmental monitoring and control
conservation planning 158–60
conservators 160–2, 187
constitution 232, 297
contemplative displays 86
contracts for exhibition production 103
cooperation: between museums 302; with other organisations 122; professional 311–12
corporate benefits of museums 11
correspondence 113
corruption 313
costs 26–7; publication 115; see

also expenditure
critical appraisal of exhibitions 109
'critical path' for exhibition design and production 105
cultural benefits of museums 9
cultural restitution 131, 305
cultural values; transmission of 16

de-accessioning policies and procedures 304–5, 309
dealing 312
dehumidifiers 169, 278
demonstration 78
deposit forms 150
design briefs 95–100, 101, 102
design of museums 31–2, 34, 35
designers 99
desk research 21, 278
didactic displays 86
dioramas 74, 278
disabled people 30–3, 53, 219–20
disaster management and planning 32, 189–93
disaster reaction teams 189–90
discipline and analysis of collections 126
discovery displays 86
display cases see showcases
display panels 72–3, 89
displays 300; lighting for 71, 79–81; physical orientation of 35; planning of 84–7; research for 87–8; security of 194; sequence, pacing and flow of 35–6, 221–2; types of 86–7, see also exhibitions; presentation techniques; texts
disposal policies 128, 129–32, 303–5, 309
documentation 308–9; see also documentation systems; field documentation; record centres; recording information with objects
documentation systems 150–5
donations 125–6, 132–3, 152, 302–3
dry-transfer lettering 73
duplicate items 130

economic benefits of

museums 10
education centres 57
education materials 39
education policies 45–8
education rooms 40
education services 37–49, 299;
    see also informal education
education specialists 37–8
electronic media: storage of
    182; see also audio
    recordings; computer systems;
    video
electronic security 194–5
emergency lighting 80
enquiries: research 113–14;
    telephone 113
enquiry desks 111–12
entry forms 150
environmental monitoring and
    control 164–73, 177; see also
    conservation; humidity and
    temperature
environmental records 143
ethical obligations of members
    of museum profession 305–7
ethics of disposal of items
    131–2
ethnographic collections, storage
    of 180
evaluation of exhibitions
    106–11
events and activities 43, 49–56,
    300
exchange of items or collections
    126, 130
exhibitions 300; design and
    production of 100–6;
    evaluation of 106–11;
    temporary 54–6; touring 54;
    see also displays; presentation
    techniques; texts
exit documentation 153–4
expenditure: capital 243–4;
    operating 242–3, 244–5; see
    also costs
external organisations: hire
    facilities for 64–7; working
    with 121–2, 157

fabrics, harmful 174–5
facilities: for hire 64–7; for
    visitors 56–63; see also
    cloakrooms; food and drink;
    seating; shops; toilets
fakes 129
families 52, 218–19
fatigue, museum 223
feasibility studies: for
    exhibitions 101; for new
    museum buildings 205–7

field documentation 141–2; see
    also audio recording ; film;
    photography; video
field study and collecting 126,
    142, 302
film 144–5, 146
finance and financial
    management 242–5, 298; see
    also costs; fundraising;
    income
first aid 272–3
flow 35–6, 222
fluorescent lighting 80, 166
food and drink 36, 57, 61–3,
    218
'formative' evaluation 106,
    107–8, 278
forward plans 235–9, 248–9,
    278
framed pictures, security of
    193–4
Friedman 109
Friends' groups 123–4, 278
'front end' evaluation 106, 107,
    278
Fry test 91
fundraising 245–8

geological collections, storage of
    182–3
gifts see donations
glass collections, storage of 182
governing bodies 230–1, 248–9,
    278, 296–7
graphics 71–3; see also lettering;
    signs and signposting
Griggs 109
grouped displays 86
guide-booklets for children 37
guides and guided tours 77, 225

handling and packing 183–5
health and safety 268–72, 298
heat damage 166–7
heating 32
heritage centres 7, 279
hire facilities 64–7
holiday activities for children 43
human remains 309
humidifiers 169, 279
humidity and temperature
    167–70, 177, 179, 180
hygrometers 167, 168, 279, 280

ICOM (International Council of
    Museums) 295
identification services 112–13
identity numbers 151
illicit material 301–2, 312–13
income: from disposal of

collections 305; see also
    fundraising; operating
    budgets
indexing 153
induction loops 32
informal education 51–3
information services 57,
    111–14; see also publications
information sources 281–3
insect/pest attack 172–3
insurance 273
intellectual orientation 35,
    225–6
intellectual rationale of
    collections 125
interactive presentation
    techniques 75–7, 226
International Council of
    Museums (ICOM) 295
interpretation 67–71, 85
interviewing visitors 108

job advertisements 257
job appraisal 264–5
job descriptions 256–7

labels, object 89–95
language of object labels 90
leaflets 113, 224
learning: leisure 51–3; from
    objects 44
lectures 78
legal powers of disposal 131,
    304
legal status and obligations 230,
    300
leisure learning 51–3
lettering 73, 94
libraries 281, 282
licensing: for production of sales
    items 60; for provision of
    food and drink 62
light levels 164–6
lighting 32, 79–81, 83, 164–7
'Living History' 49, 78
loan services to schools 41–2
loans to museums 126, 134,
    151–2, 302–3
location of museums 27, 219

maintenance of buildings
    214–16
management 230–75
management planning 232; see
    also forward plans
management structures 230–1
managers, museum 5, 230, 231,
    249–50, 279
market, concept of 17, 18, 25,
    279

Index

market analysis 23–5, 279
market intelligence 18, 279
market research 18–25, 279
market segmentation 19–21, 279
market surveys 22, 279
marketing 26–30, 217, 279; of publications 116–17
marketing materials 113
material categories 127
materials testing 173–5
media and public relations 118–21
membership programmes 123–4, 278
metallic objects, storage of 179–80
mission statements 233, 234
mobile services 42
models 74, 76
movement control 153
museum fatigue 223
museum managers 5, 230, 231, 249–50, 279

natural history collections, storage of 181
news media 119, 120–1

object labels 89–95
offer cards 135
opening hours 34, 57, 218
operating budgets 242–3, 244–5
oral history 147–50, 311
organisations see external organisations
orientation: intellectual 35, 225–6; physical 35, 224–5
orientation galleries 35, 226
outreach 56, 280; see also events and activities; mobile services; school loan services; touring exhibitions

pacing 35–6, 221–2
packing and handling 183–5
paint vapours 175
paintings: security of 193–4; storage of 180–1
panels, display 72–3, 89
participation of users 16–17; see also interactive presentation techniques
patrons 27–8; see also commercial sponsorship
people-movers 74, 280
'Pepper's Ghost' 76, 280
performance measurement 239–42, 264–5, 280
performance standards for staff

261–3
personnel see staff
pest/insect attack 172–3
photographs 72; storage of 182
photography 142, 144–6; by visitors 36
physical orientation of displays 35, 224–5
plans 35, 224
plastics 175
policy development 232–4
political benefits of museums 11
pollution see air pollution
posters 113
pre-school children 52
presentation techniques: audio-visual/interactive 75–7; graphics 71–3; three-dimensional 73–4; using people 77–8
press releases 119, 120–1
preventive conservation 161, 162–4, 280, 308
pricing policies 26–7
private collections 309–10
private interests 306–7
professional conduct 305–13
professional relationships 311
promotion 27–30
psychological orientation 35
public relations 27, 28, 118–21, 280
publications 36–7, 114–18; see also leaflets
publicity media 28–9
purchase of items 126, 133–4

radio releases 120–1
're-enactment' (Living History) 49, 78
reception desks 111–12
reconstruction displays 86
record centres 142–4
recording information with objects 136–7
recording thermohygrographs 168–9, 280
recruitment: of paid staff 256–9; of volunteers 253
refreshments see food and drink
remedial conservation 158, 159, 161, 162, 185–9, 280
reports of events and activities 53
research: for displays and exhibitions 87–8, 101; market 18–25; role of collections in 156–8
research enquiries 113–14
resin vapours 174

restitution of cultural property 131, 305
restoration 186–7, 308
retail outlets see shops
role of museums 9–11
room settings 73
rubber 175

sacred objects 309
safety reviews 269, 270–2
sale of museum objects 130
sales areas see shops
school loan services 41–2
school visits 39–41
schools: contacts with 38; talks in 42
screens for display panels 71–2
seating 32, 36, 56
security: of buildings 212–14; of collections 193–8, 307
security staff 195–6, 218
shops, museum 36, 57, 58–61, 300
showcases 82–4; lighting in 80, 83; security of 193; see also case-dressing
sign painting 72
signs and signposting 31, 32, 35, 224
silkscreening 72
slide-tape programmes 75
social benefits of museums 9
special events and activities 43, 49–56, 300
special needs 30–3, 36, 53, 57
sponsorship, commercial 246–8, 300
staff 35, 60–1, 298–9; conditions of service 259, 261; performance standards and measurement 239–42, 261–5, 280; professional conduct of 305–13; recruitment of 256–9; role in communications procedures 251; security 195–6, 218; selection of 258–8; training of 254, 266–7, 299; see also museum managers; volunteers
staff briefings 250, 274
staff handbooks 260
staff structures 251–2
standards: minimum 297; of performance 261–3
storage: large and heavy objects 176–8; small and light objects 178–83; visible 86
study facilities 57
study galleries 226
'summative' evaluation 106, 108–9

supporters' groups 122–4
SWOT analysis 237

tableaux 73–4, 280
'talking heads' 76, 280
talks 77–8
tape recordings 76, 147–50
tape-slide programmes 75
team briefing 250, 274
telephone enquiries 113
television releases 120–1
temperature and humidity
    167–70, 177, 179, 180
temporary exhibitions 54–6
textile collections, storage of
    181–2
texts, writing of 88–95
theatrical presentation
    techniques 78

themes, display 85
theming of food and drink areas
    62
thermohygrographs 168–9, 280
three-dimensional presentation
    techniques 73–4
tickets 34
toilets 32, 36, 57
touring exhibitions 54
training: of paid staff 266–7,
    299; of volunteers 254
transport, provision of 34,
    219
Tressel 109
tungsten light 79–80, 166
types of museum 6–9

ultra-violet light 166
unprofessional conduct 313

user groups, identification of
    19–20, 52–3
users: disabled 30–3, 53;
    participation of see
    participation

valuation 312–13
video 75, 144–5, 146–7
visible storage 86
visit experiences 34–7
volunteers 57, 252–6
volunteers' groups 122–3, 280

wood vapours 174
work plans for exhibition design
    and production 105
writing text 88–95

young people 52–3